Can We Talk?

THE RISE OF RUDE, NASTY, STUBBORN POLITICS

Editors

Daniel M. Shea
Allegheny College

Morris P. Fiorina
Stanford University

PEARSON

New York Boston San Francisco
London Toronto Sydney Tokyo Singapore Madrid
Mexico City Munich Paris Cape Town Hong Kong Montreal

Executive Editor: Reid Hester
Executive Marketing Manager: Wendy
  Gordon
Editorial Assistant: Emily Sauerhoff
Project Coordination, Text Design, and
  Electronic Page Makeup: Vijayakumar
Sekar, Jouve India Private Limited

Creative Director: Jayne Conte
Designer: Mary Siener
Cover Art: © Derek Audette/Alamy
Manufacturing/Production: Pat Brown
Printer/Binder: R.R. Donnelley
Cover Printer: R.R. Donnelley

Credits and acknowledgments borrowed from other sources and reproduced, with permission, in this textbook appear on the appropriate page within text.

Library of Congress Cataloging-in-Publication Data on file

10 9 8 7 6 5 4 3 2 1—15 14 13 12

www.pearsonhighered.com

ISBN 10: 0-205-88518-7
ISBN 13: 978-0-205-88518-3

TABLE OF CONTENTS

PREFACE

For those of us who regularly observe politics, it's easy to point to recent events that seem to be harbingers of important long-term shifts. For example, in 2008, we saw the first truly viable female presidential candidate and the first-ever woman on the GOP ticket. In the 2000 presidential contest, some $528 million was collected by the two major candidates, but by 2008, that figure had jumped to $1.75 billion. Surely the Supreme Court's ruling in the *Citizens United* case will continue to reshape the financing of elections. Candidates and their handlers have discovered social networks, Twitter, video-sharing sites, and myriad other net-root tools that will change the way voters get information and the way operatives reach out. And, of course, we have witnessed the election of the first African-American president, the first female Speaker of the House, and the first openly gay House committee chair. In many important ways, our political system seems more dynamic, open, and democratic.

But the shifting nature of politics seems to extend beyond the types of candidates winning important offices and the tools and resources used to aid candidates. For many, the fundamental difference these days is the way we *do* politics in America. We have moved, some would suggest, to rude, nasty, stubborn politics.

Commenting on what he perceives to be the growing vitriol in politics, *New York Times* columnist Thomas Friedman suggests, "The American political system was, as the saying goes, 'designed by geniuses so it could be run by idiots.' But a cocktail of political and technological trends have converged in the last decade that are making it possible for the idiots of all political stripes to overwhelm and paralyze the genius of our system." Friedman refers to the growing popularity of antagonistic websites and blogs, bombastic radio and television talk shows, and video-sharing sites, such as YouTube, where acts of incivility are given a massive audience. It also seems likely that the drive for ratings in the 24-hour news cycle is part of the problem.

David Gergen, a political commentator and former adviser to several presidents, suggests that malicious remarks spring from and perpetuate hyperpartisanship: "Because there is so much hunger for red meat in the bases of each party, and people are looking for someone to throw them a piece, you get a short-term benefit from going after the other side with certain colorful viciousness."

Other commentators suggest that changes in our society and the economy have created disequilibrium, leading some to strike out at perceived injustices. Peggy Noonan, a seasoned operative and columnist for the *Wall Street Journal,* offered, "A modern, high-tech, highly politicized democracy is a busy beehive, and sometimes the bees are angry. . . . People are angry at their economic vulnerability. They are angry at the deterioration of our culture, angry at our nation's deteriorating position in the world, at our debts and deficits. . . . Their anger is stoked by cynical politicians and radio ranters and people who come home at night, have a few drinks, and spew out their rage on the comment thread."

The bitterness surrounding the final health care reform vote of 2010 stunned even the most seasoned observers. Protesters yelled racial slurs at

African-American members of Congress. Another outburst on the floor made headlines, and radio and television commentators were unrepentant in their use of incendiary language. With death threats against legislators, bricks thrown through legislative office windows, and a coffin left at the door of a member of Congress, it seemed Brookings Institution scholar Darrell West hit the mark when he suggested we have entered an "arms race of incendiary rhetoric, and it's quickly reaching the point of mutually assured destruction."

While some would suggest the root of this change has been conservative outrage over the election of Barack Obama, others are quick to recall that a few years earlier a prominent member of the U.S. Senate called George W. Bush a "liar" and another suggested, "I sometimes feel that Alfred E. Neuman is in charge in Washington" (a reference to the iconic doofus of *Mad* magazine fame). President Bush was hung in effigy on numerous occasions. Sarah Palin and many other GOP officials have confronted much coarse behavior from those on the left. The violence at the 2009 summer town hall meetings involved opponents *and* supporters of health care reform.

High-profile events, like a congressman yelling, "You lie!" at the president during a State of the Union address, or the assessment of media commentators like Friedman and Noonan, do not necessarily imply systemic change. Indeed, it would not be the first time that gut interpretations of events were later proved wrong. Two decades ago, in the wake of tough campaign ads during the 1988 presidential election, many forecasted all sorts of evils from negative spots: lower voter turnout, increased cynicism, less informed voters. We now understand that the so-called "unintended consequences" of these ads are complex and, in many ways, far less harmful than we might have assumed two decades ago. Believe it or not, there may even be some important benefits to hard-hitting campaign commercials.

So, are things really less civil than in the past? If so, how might we define and distinguish uncivil politics from, say, passionate activism? What is more discouraging, an angry electorate or an apathetic electorate? If our politics has become less civil, what are the precise causes and implications? Are all citizens more engaged, more polarized than in the past, or is it just a particular group of citizens? Are regular Americans even paying attention? Is there historical precedence that can shed light on where we are and where we might be headed?

The goal of this volume is to draw upon the insights of some of the best scholars and journalists in American politics. Rather than simply accept that rude, nasty politics is here to stay, and that our system will suffer because of it, we thought it prudent to take a step back and sort through complex issues in a more detailed, sophisticated way.

We owe a heartfelt thanks to the contributors of this volume. Not only did they heed our call for thoughtful, high-quality assessments, but they did so in ways that are accessible for general interest readers. As you will find, the issues of civility and compromise in American politics are multi-faceted and dynamic— and quick assessments and easy solutions are elusive. Some chapters will likely lead to a bit of discouragement, but may be seen in a sanguine light. At the very least, these chapters offer novel, important insights.

If nothing else, it is our hope that the pages to follow will spur conversations, new questions, and a wide range of fresh scholarship.

1

Can We Talk? The Rise of Rude, Nasty, Stubborn Politics

Daniel M. Shea and Morris P. Fiorina

On the morning of January 8, 2011, U.S. Congresswoman Gabrielle "Gabby" Giffords, a Democrat from Arizona, was holding a town meeting at a Tucson area Safeway when a crazed young man opened fire, shooting Giffords and 18 others. Giffords was shot in the head, but survived the attack. Six others died.

Recriminations began almost immediately. Liberal blogger Markos Moulitsas tweeted, "Mission Accomplished, Sarah Palin," a reference to a map with cross-hairs superimposed on congressional districts—including Giffords'—that were targeted by Palin's PAC during the 2010 congressional election campaign.[1] Liberal *New York Times* economics columnist Paul Krugman speculated that the shooter's actions were stimulated by "eliminationist rhetoric" from the political right.[2] University of California, Berkeley, Chancellor Robert Birgeneau sent the following e-mail campus-wide: "A climate in which demonization of others goes unchallenged and hateful speech is tolerated can lead to such a tragedy. I believe it is not a coincidence that this calamity has occurred in a state which has legislated discrimination against undocumented persons. This same mean-spirited xenophobia played a major role in the defeat of the Dream Act by our legislators in Washington."[3]

Conservative commentators reacted with outrage, noting that the shooter was obviously deranged and had no comprehensible political inclinations (his bookshelf included the *Communist Manifesto* and Hitler's *Mein Kampf*, among other works). More neutral observers pointed out that the use of violent imagery is a staple of politics, citing such references as the "campaign"; the "war room"; the "ad wars" and "air wars"; incumbents to be "targeted," "knocked-off," or "taken-out"; hostile electoral territory to be "captured"; and a campaign's "last stand."[4] Indeed, in 2004, the Democratic Leadership Council had published a map with bull's-eyes superimposed on the states narrowly won by President George Bush.[5]

A few days after the Tucson shooting, Sarah Palin responded to the charge that her cross-hairs map had incited the tragedy. She claimed on her Facebook page that her detractors were guilty of "blood libel."[6] This set off a second firestorm as some commentators noted that the phrase "blood libel" had historically been a reference to the assertion that Jews used the blood of Christian children in their religious rituals. So Palin was guilty of historical ignorance, at best, or anti-Semitism, at worst. In response, other commentators pointed out that in recent years the term had been applied by both liberals and conservatives to false accusations against blacks, gays, Muslims, Vietnam veterans, 9/11 victims, the casualties at Pearl Harbor, and even Al Gore.[7]

In a memorial speech on January 13, President Obama calmed the waters. He noted that something in human nature makes us try to find rational explanations for irrational behavior. In an important passage, he cautioned, "But what we can't do is use this tragedy as one more occasion to turn on one another. As we discuss these issues, let each of us do so with a good dose of humility. Rather than pointing fingers or assigning blame, let us use this occasion to expand our moral imaginations, to listen to each other more carefully, to sharpen our instincts for empathy, and remind ourselves of all the ways our hopes and dreams are bound together."[8] Polls reported that those who watched the speech had an overwhelmingly positive reaction.[9]

American politicians toned down the nasty rhetoric almost immediately. Perhaps they were sobered by the shooting of a colleague, or maybe they became sensitive to the possibility that voters might respond negatively to further contentious discussion after such a tragedy. Instead of sitting on opposite sides during President Obama's State of the Union Address at the end of January 2011, Republican and Democratic members of Congress intermixed, with some noted conservatives pairing off with noted liberals.[10] For a few weeks at least, the volume of partisan rhetoric in Washington diminished and American politics seemed a bit calmer.

TROUBLED WATERS

Today, we understand that Jared Loughner, the alleged shooter, is a mentally unstable young man. In light of subsequent revelations, it is clear that his violent acts in Tucson did not spring from logically coherent political motivations, nor were they the direct result of the words or deeds of any politician or commentator. Yet, when average Americans first learned of the shooting, many assumed it was politically motivated, surmising that Loughner had become enraged by an issue or a cause. Some believed he was a "radical conservative" whose rage against the system compelled him to shoot a Democratic member of Congress. Others probably recalled the tragedy in Oklahoma City in April 1995, when Timothy McVeigh, deeply troubled by what he perceived as the growing control of the federal government, bombed the Alfred P. Murrah Federal Building, claiming 168 lives.

Even a few days after the Tucson shooting, as more evidence regarding the depths of Loughner's mental instability became widely known, a poll conducted by CBS News found that nearly 45 percent of all Americans *still* thought the shooting was at least in part politically motivated. Some 51 percent of Democrats thought Loughner's political views were "probably a factor" in the shooting, with 42 percent of Republicans suggesting the same. This was true for 37 percent of the independents, too.[11]

Probably it is human nature to conjure up simplistic explanations for tragic events. Snap judgments are common not only among average citizens, but also among members of the media—the very group charged with interpreting the meaning of these events. But why would so many people leap to the conclusion that the acts of a killer should be linked to the broader political climate? One day after the shooting, the Pima County sheriff, whose jurisdiction includes Tucson, seemed to speak for many Americans: "I think it's time as a country we need to do a little soul-searching because I think that the vitriolic rhetoric that we hear day in and day out from the people in the radio business, and some people in the TV business, and what we see on TV and how our youngsters are being raised. It may be free speech but it does not come without consequences."[12] Simply stated, connecting the Tucson shooting to the tone of politics seemed logical because of what we have witnessed in recent years.

Every presidential campaign is tough, and heated rhetoric always has been routine. But in some ways the 2008 election was distinctive. In her book *Rude Democracy*,[13] Susan Herbst suggests that Sarah Palin added a unique element. Americans of all political persuasions were fascinated by the governor from Alaska for several reasons—she was mostly unknown, she was the first female on a Republican presidential ticket, and she was quite attractive. She was the most "googled" person in the world in 2008 (Barack Obama was a distant sixth place).[14] Yet the fascination was also due to her unique rhetorical style. According to Herbst, Palin was able to merge myriad elements in the same speech: "She has been rabid, mean-spirited, catty, empathetic, warm, humane, and engaging, all at the same time."[15]

Beyond her rhetorical style, a great deal of attention was paid to the size and demeanor of the crowds at Palin's rallies. Numerous reports suggested that her followers were enraged and "calling for blood."[16] It was widely reported that at one rally a supporter yelled, "Kill him!" and another shouted, "Off with his head," in reference to Barack Obama. Other news accounts noted that Palin rally attendees shouted "terrorist" and "treason," and many wore t-shirts saying "No communists!" and "Palin's Pit Bulls."[17]

Palin was (is) clearly a passionate orator, and her style has elicited many emotions and passions. Nevertheless, it is debatable whether her style was rougher or more mean-spirited than that of other candidates, or whether the crowds at her events were more or less civil than those at the events of other candidates in 2008. Herbst suggests much of the perception of incivility surrounding Palin was due to an inordinate level of media coverage. Robust demonstrations are common at campaign events for Republican and Democratic candidates. Whether the perception was real or not, however, Americans were given a heavy dose of "nasty" politics in the fall of 2008 because Sarah Palin was on the GOP ticket.

In many respects, however, those on the left of the ideological spectrum were equally vicious during the 2008 campaign. Most would agree that neither Barack Obama nor Hillary Clinton, his principal opponent during the nomination phase of the race, used uncharacteristically harsh rhetoric, but the gloves came off on liberal blogs—particularly when it came to Sarah Palin. One conservative blogger noted the following about posts related to Palin:

> They make up tales about Palin's childhood health care, whether she had a boob job, make jokes about her giving hand jobs, claim she "rolled her eyes" when told someone was a teacher, examine the color of her bracelet to claim she dishonored war dead, falsely claim she advocated war with Iran, distort polling about her, attack her intelligence, berate her for recommending followers read a Thomas Sowell column, move next door to her to snoop on her, go after a blogger who defends her on MSNBC, claim her success is because men are aroused by her . . . [18]

For a brief period, around the time that Barack Obama was sworn into office, political rhetoric seemed to cool a bit—or at least the media coverage of these events had abated. But by the spring and summer of 2009, politics again took a nasty turn, centered mostly on the president's signature policy initiative: health care reform. Democratic congressional leaders reasoned that if average voters knew more about the advantages of the Democratic proposal, public opinion would turn in their favor. Democrats believed they had lost the battle over health care reform in 1994 because they had lost the war over public misperceptions. This time, they would get the word out by hosting a series of "town hall meetings" across the country. They would take the issue directly to the American people and hold detailed, rational conversations.

Many of these meetings were organized, thoughtful, and civil. Others were not. A significant number degenerated into angry protests. In early August, for instance, a health care town hall meeting was held in Tampa, Florida. It was sponsored by Democratic Congresswoman Kathy Castor and Florida State Representative Betty Reed. Upwards of 1,500 people packed the meeting room and spilled over into the street. As Castor began to speak, scuffles broke out as people tried to get into the meeting room. Her introductory remarks were drowned out by chants of "Read the bill, read the bill!" and "Tyranny!" An event organizer came to the microphone to admonish the crowd: "If pushing and shoving continues, we will have to clear the room. The police will make the decision if it is still safe." At one point, a freelance videographer was pushed to the ground. Another man was treated for minor injuries after a scuffle left his shirt partially torn from his body. "That's the most violent anyone has been towards me," noted the man. "It was surprising, to say the least."[19]

Then-Democratic Senator Arlen Specter of Pennsylvania confronted truly hostile crowds at a number of his events. In Philadelphia, Specter was accompanied by Health and Human Services Secretary Kathleen Sebelius to a town hall meeting. Over and over, both were shouted down by angry protesters. A week later, some 300 people packed a community college auditorium in Lebanon, Pennsylvania. Barely able to address the crowd due to persistent interruptions and shouts, Senator Specter became increasingly frustrated. At one point, an irate constituent jumped to the isle, waving a set of papers in Specter's face. Security guards quickly jumped in, holding the ranting man back. In a rage, the man told Specter, "One day, God is going to stand before you and he's going to judge you and the rest of your damn cronies up on the hill, and then you will get your just dessert."[20]

Stories of angry conservative protesters were common. A man opposing health care reform hung freshman legislators in effigy, placing an awkwardly worded placard nearby that read, "Congress Traitors the American." After seeing his colleagues endure these difficult town hall meetings, one member of Congress cancelled his own meeting, only to later receive a death threat for doing so. The district office of a Georgia congressman was defaced with a swastika.

Editors of the *Telegraph Herald*, of Dubuque, Iowa, summed up the summer's meetings this way:

> Opponents of the current health care proposal have resorted to hanging in effigy one Democratic member of Congress in Maryland while drowning out discussion with chants of "Just say no!" Members of Congress from Texas to Wisconsin have been shouted down by angry constituents in town hall meetings. A North Carolina congressman even had a death threat called in to his office. The district office of a Georgia congressman was defaced with a swastika, and the lawmaker, who happens to be African-American, has been the recipient of racist hate mail. [. . .] Iowa's own Chuck Grassley, whose work we usually support and admire, fed into the scare tactics. Grassley told a town hall audience that he is opposed to any plan that "determines when you're going to pull the plug on Grandma." He was referring to a proposal for optional consultations regarding living wills and other end-of-life issues. To repeat, that counseling would be optional, and living wills are a common consideration for many people, a far cry from Grassley's euthanasia reference.[21]

Heated constituent events are not unprecedented. Americans pride themselves in speaking out when they believe government is heading in the wrong direction. Legislators also realize that facing an angry constituent is part of their job. After being verbally assaulted by that angry man in Lebanon, Arlen Specter, who had been in the Senate for nearly 30 years, advised the crowd, "We've just had a demonstration of democracy." Rancor has been especially acute during tough times and when government has faced momentous issues, such as the economic crisis in the summer of 2009. One can only imagine what some of the meetings were like during the civil rights era and the Vietnam War. To many, the significant difference today is that everything is captured on film and then instantaneously posted on YouTube and/or broadcast on mainstream media outlets. Rude, nasty politics is dragged into our homes and into our daily lives, with or without our consent.

Thus, all of America was watching during these tumultuous months of political incivility. In the wake of those acrimonious town hall meetings, *New York Times* columnist Thomas Friedman pondered whether we can "seriously discuss serious issues any longer and make decisions on the basis of the national interest."[22] A few months later, a Republican congressman shouted, "You lie!" during a presidential address to Congress, an unprecedented display.

The vitriol surrounding the *final* health care reform vote, nearly a year later, in April of 2010, stunned even the most seasoned observers. Protesters yelled racial slurs at African-American members of Congress, and one legislator was allegedly spat on as he entered the Capitol Building to vote. Outbursts on the floor of the House made headlines, and radio and television commentators were unrepentant in their use of incendiary language. With death threats made against legislators, bricks thrown through legislative office windows, and a coffin left at the door of a congressperson, it seemed that seasoned conservative commentator Peggy Noonan was right when she asserted in the *Wall Street Journal,* "It's a mistake not to see something new, something raw and bitter and dangerous, in the particular moment we're in."[23]

One might be tempted to conclude that nearly all the nasty politics of the past few years was rooted in conservative anger, particularly over losing control of the White House. Indeed, one study found that a large majority of the news stories that linked harsh rhetoric to Loughner's acts in Tucson focused on the alleged role of conservatives in the past few years.[24] But the political right has no monopoly on vicious rhetoric and other forms of incivility. George W. Bush was the target of a great deal of vitriol during his eight years in the White House. A prominent member of the U.S. Senate called him a "liar," and another suggested, "I sometimes feel that Alfred E. Neuman is in charge in Washington" (a reference to the iconic dufus of *Mad* magazine fame). Bush was hung in effigy on numerous occasions, skewered on liberal blogs, and often depicted as Hitler on posters and signs.

In 2009, MSNBC host Keith Olbermann said that conservative columnist Michelle Malkin was "a big mashed-up bag of meat with lipstick on it." Chris Matthews, of *Hardball,* fantasized about the death of Rush Limbaugh, saying, "Somebody's going to jam a CO_2 pellet into his head and he's going to explode like a giant blimp." On his national radio show, Ed Schultz said of former Vice President Dick Cheney, "He is an enemy of the country, in my opinion, Dick Cheney is, he is an enemy of the country. . . . Lord, take him to the Promised Land, will you?" About a year later, Schultz screamed, "Dick Cheney's heart's a political football. We ought to rip it out and kick it around and stuff it back in him!" Another radio host, Mike Malloy, said of Rush Limbaugh, "I'm waiting for the day when I pick it up, pick up a newspaper or click on the Internet and find out he's choked to death on his own throat fat or a great big wad of saliva or something, you know, whatever. Go away, Rush, you make me sick!" And, of course, as noted above, the liberal blogosphere has savagely attacked many conservatives, most notably Sarah Palin.

Recent surveys have confirmed a perceived decline in civility in the past few years. A CBS News poll, conducted a few weeks before Congresswoman Giffords was shot, found that 50 percent of Americans believe our politics has become less civil over the last 10 years, with just 15 percent saying things have become more civil.[25] Another study, conducted by the Center for Political Participation at Allegheny College in the fall of 2010, found that 58 percent of registered voters believed politics had become less civil since Barack Obama became president. A full 46 percent said the 2010 election was the "most negative they had ever seen." An additional 26 percent said that it was "more negative than in the past," but they had seen worse. Only 4 percent said that campaigns were more positive than in the past.[26]

In sum, the initial reaction to the tragic events in Tucson sprang from what many perceived to be a radically different tone in contemporary American politics. Whether truly unique or simply a manifestation of greater media attention, many citizens had come to see politics as nasty, negative, and uncivil. Darrell West's contention that we have moved into an "arms race of incendiary rhetoric and it's quickly reaching the point of mutually assured destruction,"[27] likely captured the outlook of many Americans.

NASTY POLITICS OR NOTHING NEW?

Some skeptics dismiss much of the hand-wringing about the coarse nature of contemporary politics. Harsh political conflict is nothing new, they argue. Indeed, compared to earlier episodes in American history, the conduct of politics today seems relatively tame. Others argue that our focus on the tone of political discourse is a distraction, given the hefty policy challenges we confront. Shortly before the Tucson shooting, a prominent opinion writer remarked, "The notion that civility and nominal bipartisanship would accomplish any of the heavy lifting required to rebuild America is childish magical thinking, and, worse, a mindless distraction from the real work before the nation."[28] Still others argue that efforts to curtail "uncivil" discourse are, at base, an attempt to stifle conservative criticism of Barack Obama and the Democratic agenda.

It is certainly true that American history is replete with instances of intense politics. In the early days of the Republic, newspapers were viciously partisan and pulled no punches in their characterizations of the opposition. Arguments over the proper role of the federal government and a host of important policy disputes in the late 1790s led to some rather nasty, vitriolic language. In a letter written to a friend, Alexander Hamilton offered an opinion of his nemesis, John Adams: "[He is] petty, mean, egotistic, erratic, eccentric, jealous natured, and hot-tempered . . . there are great and intrinsic defects in his character." Adams returned the view of Hamilton, also in a letter: "[He is] an intriguant [meaning schemer], the greatest intriguant in the world—a man devoid of every moral principle—a bastard." Both these letters were made public and widely circulated. One of the largest papers of the day, the *Connecticut Currant,* claimed that if Thomas Jefferson were to win the 1800 presidential election, "murder, robbery, rape, adultery and incest will be openly taught and practiced . . . The soil will be soaked with blood."[29] To be sure, our formative national years were marked by malicious political rhetoric.

Another round of heated politics occurred in the wake of the alleged Corrupt Deal of 1824, when it was widely believed that House Speaker Henry Clay rigged the Electoral College vote to give John Quincy Adams the presidency—instead of Andrew Jackson, who won more Electoral College and popular votes. By 1830, suggests political historian Joel Silbey, "politics was woven into the fabric of the society at all levels,"[30] leading to a great deal of intensity in political discourse. When novelist Charles Dickens traveled throughout the United States in the 1840s, he observed:

> Quiet people avoid the question of the Presidency, for there will be a new election in three years and a half, and party feelings run very high: the great constitutional feature of this institution being, that (as soon as) the acrimony of the last election is over, the acrimony of the next begins; which is an unspeakable comfort to all strong politicians and true lovers of their country; that is to say, to ninety-nine men and boys out of every ninety-nine and a quarter.[31]

In the 1850s, when the country was descending into Civil War, armed political violence was common. Battles between pro- and anti-slavery forces in Kansas cost the lives of 56 Americans and injured many more. President Abraham Lincoln was viewed by his opponents as an "awful woeful ass," a "dictator," a "coarse vulgar joker," and a "grotesque baboon."[32] In the 1870s and 1880s, native Protestant Americans prepared to resist armed insurrection by Catholic immigrants. The presidential election of 1884 was particularly nasty. Grover Cleveland, the Democrat, was a "lecherous beast," an "obese nincompoop," and a "drunken sot."[33] He was charged with having an affair with a young widow, who had borne a child out of wedlock a few years earlier. Soon his opponents made up a nasty chant: "Ma, ma, where is pa? Gone to the White House, ha! ha! ha!" Cleveland supporters responded by spreading rumors that his opponent was corrupt. They had their own chant, "Blaine, Blaine, James G. Blaine, the monumental liar from the state of Maine."[34]

In the decades bracketing the turn of the twentieth century, members of labor unions fought pitched battles with private police forces and public agencies that were under the control of business interests. After World War I, the United States experienced a "Red Scare," during which civil liberties were trampled and innocent people were imprisoned and even executed. The Ku Klux Klan revived and this time organized nationwide to fight the so-called Catholic and Jewish menace, as well as African-Americans. After World War II, U.S. Senator Joseph McCarthy launched a witch-hunt for Communists in government, and things became both hyper-tense and nasty.

Then came the Vietnam War, along with the political and social upheaval known collectively as the 1960s. Violent protest, property destruction, bombings, and several shootings testify to the intensity of this period. The '60s ushered in 30-second television attack ads and the incessant drive to amass greater campaign resources (fundraising letters are notoriously nasty). Writing in the *Christian Science Monitor* in 2004, columnist William Schambra noted, "In fact, politics for our parents' 'greatest generation' was just as boisterous, nasty, and over the top as it is today—indeed, as it always has been, for Americans."[35] One detailed account of the era, *America's Uncivil Wars: The Sixties Era from Elvis to the Fall of Richard Nixon*, argues that deep-seated disagreements about emerging social and cultural mores, massive protests against the Vietnam War, and race riots in many American cities combined to divide Americans more deeply than they had been since the Civil War.[36]

An important question, then, is whether today's politics exceeds in intensity this litany of conflicts from the past. Politics might seem nasty today, but Barack Obama's opponents will likely not claim that during his administration we will see "rape, adultery and incest openly taught and practiced." Democrats may not like House Speaker John Boehner, but it is doubtful he will be called a "drunken sot" or a "coarse vulgar joker." Maybe things are really not so bad.

But another way of thinking about this issue is through a perceptual lens. That is, regardless of how politics was conducted in the past, are things bad from the perspective of citizens today? Do Americans believe things are headed in the wrong direction? A series of studies conducted by the Center for Political Participation at Allegheny College in the spring and fall of 2010, as well many other studies by other organizations in the past few years, find that a hefty majority of Americans *believe* our politics is rude and nasty . . . and getting worse. Average citizens believe respectful politics is important for our democracy and that without it we are headed for trouble. In this light, one could argue that comparative assessments, based on past political eras, are of modest value. That is, if we *think* things have gotten worse, perhaps they have, at least relative to prevailing standards.

A CHANGING POLITICAL CONTEXT

The question of whether the current period of nasty politics is exceptional will be debated in several of the chapters to follow—as well as by pundits and scholars elsewhere—for years to come. America has always had, and benefited from, a robust exchange of political ideas. Some would even argue that the real danger in a democracy is not overheated rhetoric, but rather a passive, disengaged electorate. When things are too tranquil, leaders become complacent and the status quo is rarely questioned. We want civil politics, but we should reject "sleepy" politics.

The twenty-first century has brought with it a number of important changes—shifts and alterations—that may bear directly on politics in the future. Most of the following chapters highlight key adjustments in the way we conduct politics in America. It may prove useful to touch upon some of these contextual changes here.

One reason the tone of contemporary politics may seem particularly sharp is that we are coming out of a period of subdued political engagement. Voter turnout in the years following World War II hovered around 60 percent, but by the 1996 election, it had dipped to 50 percent. In the 1950s, roughly 35 percent of Americans were "very much interested" in political campaigns; by the 1990s, this figure had dropped to 20 percent. The electorate had also grown detached from political parties and partisan labels in the later decades of the twentieth century—perhaps more so than at any point in our nation's history. We saw record levels of split-ticket voting in the 1970s and 1980s, along with a high number of independent voters. In the 1950s, about 2 percent of Americans made up their minds *on* Election Day; by the 1980s, that figure had more than tripled.[37]

And then things changed some more. Turnout for the 2008 election rose to near post–World War II highs, with interest among young Americans especially strong. A Gallup poll conducted in late January 2008 found 71 percent of respondents were giving "quite a lot" of thought to the presidential election—what they suggested was a "record level of interest."[38] That is a jump of 13 percent from February 2004, and a jump of 33 percent from January 2000. According to American National Election Study data, there was a 22 percent increase in the number of Americans who care which party wins the presidency from the 1980s to the 2000s. There was a 16-percent increase in the number who were politically active beyond voting, and a 19-percent increase in the number who care which party controls Congress.[39] One scholar claims that "We have seen that the level of political engagement in the American electorate [in 2004 and 2008] set a modern record."[40] While still rather modest in some respects, our willingness to read news stories and talk with friends and family about politics suggests a more attentive, engaged electorate than in previous decades.

Thus, we may be evaluating contemporary politics through the perspective of the more passive recent years. Our assessment of the tone of politics is necessarily subjective, dependent on our comparative framework.

If we see the 1990s as the "normal" period, then the current climate may seem overheated. But if we use the 1960s, for example, as our benchmark, then things today might not seem so exceptional. Again, using ANES data, the percentage of Americans who attended political meetings in 2008 was nearly double the percentage found in the 1990s, for example, but precisely the same as during the period of the 1964 and 1968 elections. Indeed, many, but certainly not all, of the politicians and commentators who lived through other periods of partisan acrimony say, in essence, "What's all the fuss about declining levels of civility? We've seen this before." It is also possible that a renewed interest in politics has led to an excessive zeal because the stakes are so high. In other words, the very reasons that pushed Americans back to the political trenches also make us equally passionate in defending our positions.

A related issue has been the extent of a so-called ideological polarization of the electorate. A number of scholars, and certainly a host of media commentators, believe a core aspect of our nasty politics has been this partisan polarization—the movement of large blocs of voters into either the Democratic/liberal camp or the Republican/conservative camp. Conversely, the "moderate middle" has shrunk. Alan Abramowitz, in his book *The Disappearing Center*, suggests party polarization has been broad and particularly sharp among the most active members of the public.[41] Moreover, this large group of partisan activists draws even more citizens into the political fray, thereby invigorating the electorate. Abramowitz argues that our renewed interest in politics, discussed above, is partly due to partisan polarization: "Growing partisan-ideological polarization has had important consequences for almost every aspect of the electoral process in the United States."[42] Much of the change, which Abramowitz believes has been occurring since the 1970s, has been the shift of conservatives into the Republican ranks; there are few conservative Democrats left. The consequences of this change will be profound, not the least of which will be an inability to find compromise in policy solutions: "[A]ny serious attempt at compromise by party leaders would almost certainly produce a backlash among their most politically active and informed supporters."[43]

Yet, others offer another explanation for this ideological polarization. In his book, *Disconnect: The Breakdown of Representation in American Politics*, Morris Fiorina, one of the editors of this volume, argues that while the number of Americans in the ideological middle has remained more or less the same, those at the ideological wings (what he calls the "political class") have become more distinct, organized, and vocal than in the past. He writes, "What many observers mean by polarization is what we call party sorting—the development of a tighter fit between party affiliations on the one hand and ideology and issue position on the other."[44] No more numerous than in previous generations, those in the political class are simply more homogeneous and more animated than their predecessors. And it is certainly not the case that we have become a "deeply divided" nation, as Fiorina shows in an earlier book, *Culture War? The Myth of a Polarized America*.[45]

From either perspective, the impact of these changes on the tone of politics may be significant. While Abramowitz does not note an explicit connection to political rhetoric, a logical conclusion of his perspective is that broad-based polarization creates greater intensity among a greater number of Americans, leading to a harsher tone in politics. Fiorina is more explicit: "Partisans on each side attack their counterparts on the other as ignorant, stupid, corrupt and unpatriotic. Reasonable compromises are sell-outs and those who arrange them are defectors and traitors."[46]

Clearly, an important element of the current tone of politics is the role of the media. The advent of overt partisan programming on radio and television has been both rapid and weighty. There have always been liberal- and conservative-leaning print periodicals, and certain newspapers have always been thought to tilt one way or the other. Yet electronic media outlets moved in a novel direction, starting in the late 1980s. Three forces were fundamental. The first was a growing conservative intellectual movement, springing in large measure from the perceived success of President Ronald Reagan and so-called Reaganomics. Conservative intellectuals believed that the true success of Reagan's economic policies was not being acknowledged by the "mainstream media," an institution thought by these conservatives to be infected by a liberal bias. Second, the 1980s saw the rise of the Christian Right political movement, centered on a number of cross-cutting cultural issues (particularly abortion). They too believed that the media was not reflecting "core American values." Finally, in 1987, the Federal Communication Commission (FCC) abolished the Fairness Doctrine, which had stipulated that opposing sides of heated political issues be given coverage on radio and television stations. This paved the way for conservative talk-radio personalities, such as Rush Limbaugh, and for a more overt political theme on many Christian television programs, such as the *700 Club*.

Due in large measure to the success of niche audience marketing (where smaller numbers of dedicated listeners/readers/viewers lead to significant profits), during the past decade we have seen an explosion of partisan media outlets and personalities. Many of these, but certainly not all, have been geared to conservatives. Limbaugh led the way on radio, but many others have followed, including Michael Savage, Sean Hannity, Laura Ingraham, and Neil Boortz. There are a few left-leaning talk-radio programs, but their market share is minuscule in comparison. While a bit less overt and widespread, the crossover to television has also occurred, with Fox News leading the way on the right, and MSNBC on the left. In the drive to keep viewers attuned, many of the hosts on these stations, heighten the importance of every issue, use ever-harsher rhetoric, and vilify the opposition. One thing is certain: The number of news programs featuring hard core partisans has mushroomed. "In the cut-throat competition for ratings, the more extreme cable TV shout shows emulate the style of professional wrestling and shed about as much light on politics."[47] The authors of an important new book on the causes and implications of the partisan press, Kathleen Hall Jamison and Joseph N. Cappella, suggest several implications: Some of the dangers of the partisan media are that it incites moral outrage by engaging emotions, it feeds the assumption that the opposition is the enemy, and it replaces argument with ridicule.[48]

Beyond traditional news outlets, politics on the Internet has taken a different tone in recent years. Blogs, especially those that allow anonymous posts, seem particularly vitriolic. According to one study, political discourse on blogs has become "excessively harsh," crossing the line between political discussion and name-calling, contempt, and derision of the opposition.[49]

A related mix of new and old media may play a role in shifting the perceived tone of politics. Many newspapers are published online, of course, and this provides readers with the opportunity to post anonymous comments on articles and opinion pieces. Often these posts are harsh, nasty, and uncivil, and they would not have been published in previous eras. We also should point to the advent of video sharing and social networking sites. Whereas in the past, rude displays were generally witnessed by only a handful of those at an event, today's rude exchanges are captured on cell phones, quickly posted on YouTube or Facebook, and spread "virally" across the nation. Again, the tone of politics might be no rougher than in past eras, but we simply are exposed to more of it.

Some have suggested that an important factor has been a social and economic disequilibria. That is, Americans have seen a number of significant changes in recent years, many of which seem disturbing to citizens. The most important change, of course, is our prolonged economic slump. The "Great Recession" is one of the worst in our history, leading to unemployment hovering around 10 percent, underemployment near 20 percent, decreasing home values, and lackluster economic growth. This has led to a decline in tax revenue, pushing nearly every state and community to scramble for funds and to cut services. Perhaps related to this is the fact that the shift from the manufacturing base to a service-sector foundation has altered the very nature of "employment" in America. Gone are the factory jobs that helped create the large, vibrant middle class in America. Demographic changes are significant, too. America is an increasingly diverse nation. In his op-ed titled "The Rage is Not About Health Care," *New York Times* columnist Frank Rich attributes much of the current vitriol to racial changes. He writes, "Demographics are avatars of a change bigger than any bill contemplated by Obama or Congress. The week before the health care vote, *The Times* reported that births to Asian, black and Hispanic women accounted for 48 percent of all births in America, in the 12 months ending in July 2008."[50] In brief, when one takes a look at the most heated periods in our politics, we also quite often see dramatic social and economic changes. This period may be no different.

Finally, we might speculate about the relationship between cultural changes and the rise of ugly political discourse. There are a host of issues that might be raised under this broad heading, not the least of which has been the changing nature of personal communications. The number of "contacts" we make in a given day has grown exponentially. In the past, we connected face to face, by telephone, or through snail mail. Today, we touch base with family, friends, and colleagues at a staggering pace via texts, e-mails, tweets, and social networking sites. But these connections are quick and impersonal. One could reasonably argue that being nasty on Facebook or Twitter is much easier than saying the same thing to someone's face or over the telephone. Might the impersonal nature of our communications elevate the possibility of a widespread nasty political rhetoric? One might also point to the prominence of reality television programming, with a great majority of shows that seem to pit participants against each other and almost compel rude exchanges. Rather than being shunned by the producers of these programs, it seems as though on-screen arguments are pitched as the high point of the episodes. Mixed with all the special and tender moments of the popular *American Idol* show are callous comments by the judges.

To summarize, the topics, claims, and charges discussed above—and elsewhere in our cultural conversation—will be addressed in the pages to follow. Our aim in this introductory chapter has been to identify some of the forces that may be adversely affecting how we conduct politics in America today. Our goal, both as editors and as citizens of our democracy, is to understand these myriad forces, to consider their implications, and, if necessary, to suggest steps to move the tone of our politics in a more positive direction.

Endnotes

1. TBOGG, "Sarah Palin's Hit List," January 8, 2011. Accessed at: http://tbogg.firedoglake.com/2011/01/08/sarah-palins-hit-list/.
2. Paul Krugman, "Assassination Attempt In Arizona," *New York Times,* January 8, 2011. Accessed at: http://krugman.blogs.nytimes.com/2011/01/08/assassination-attempt-in-arizona/.
3. UC Berkeley News Center, "Chancellor Issues Statement on Arizona Shootings," January 20, 2011. Accessed at: http://newscenter.berkeley.edu/2011/01/10/arizona/.
4. Howard Kurtz, "Should We Blame Sarah Palin for Gabrielle Giffords' Shooting?" *The Daily Beast,* January 8, 2011. Accessed at: http://www.thedailybeast.com/blogs-and-stories/2011-01-08/gabrielle-giffords-shooting-dont-blame-sarah-palin/?cid=hp:beastoriginalsC1.
5. Will Marshall, "Heartland Strategy," DLC, December 13, 2004. Accessed at: http://www.dlc.org/ndol_ci.cfm?contentid=253055&kaid=127&subid=171.
6. John Whitesides, "Palin's 'Blood Libel' Charge Ignites Firestorm," Reuters, January 12, 2011. Accessed at: http://www.reuters.com/article/2011/01/12/us-usa-shooting-palin-idUSTRE70B3W320110112.
7. Jim Geraghty, "No Man Dares Cross the Cravaack," National Review Online, February 25, 2011. Accessed at: http://www.nationalreview.com/campaign-spot.
8. CBS News, "Text of President Obama's Tucson Memorial Speech," January 12, 2011. Accessed at: http://www.cbsnews.com/8301-503544_162-20028366-503544.html.

9. Paul Steinhauser, "Poll: Obama's Speech Scored with Viewers," CNN Politics, February 24, 2009. Accessed at: http://politicalticker.blogs.cnn.com/2009/02/24/poll-obamas-speech-scored-with-viewers/.

10. Ibid.

11. CBSNews.Com, "Poll: 45% Say Politics Motivated Jared Loughner," January 11, 2011.

12. Sarah Hopkins, "Could "Vitriolic Rhetoric" Have Contributed to Arizona Massacre?" WGRZ.Com, January 10, 2010. Accessed at: http://www.wgrz.com/news/local/story.aspx?storyid=104184.

13. Susan Herbst, *Rude Democracy: Civility and Incivility in American Politics* (Philadelphia: Temple University Press, 2010).

14. Ibid., p. 27.

15. Ibid., p. 32.

16. Huffington Post, "Palin Rally: Kill Him Yelled Again," October 14, 2008. Accessed at: http://www.huffingtonpost.com/2008/10/14/palin-rally-kill-him-yell_n_134597.html.

17. Herbst, *Rude Democracy,* 2010, p. 45.

18. Free Republic Forum, "The Obsession with Liberals' Obsession with Palin," November 28, 2010. Accessed at: http://www.freerepublic.com/focus/f-gop/2634073/posts.

19. FoxNews.Com, "Health Care Town Hall Turns Violent in Tampa and St. Louis," August 7, 2009. Accessed at: http://www.foxnews.com/politics/2009/08/07/health-care-town-halls-turn-violent-tampa-st-louis/#.

20. Phillip Rucker, "Specter Faces Raucous Crowd at Town Hall Meeting," *Washington Post*, August 11, 2009. Accessed at: http://www.washingtonpost.com/wp-dyn/content/article/2009/08/11/AR2009081101880.html.

21. Editorial Board. "Reform Requires a Dose of Civility." *Telegraph Herald*, Dubuque, IA, August 23, 2009. Accessed at: http://www.thonline.com/article.cfm?id=254190.

22. Thomas Friedman, "Where did 'We' Go?" *New York Times*, September 29, 2009. Accessed at: http://www.nytimes.com/2009/09/30/opinion/30friedman.html.

23. Peggy Noonan, "The Heat Is On: We May Get Burned," *Wall Street Journal*, March 25, 2010. Accessed at: http://www.peggynoonan.com/article.php?article=516.

24. Media Research Center, "MRC Study: By 8 to 1 Margin, Media Target Conservative Speech After Tucson Shooting," MRC Website, January 18, 2011. Accessed at: http://www.mrc.org/realitycheck/realitycheck/2011/20110118034318.aspx.

25. http://www.pollingreport.com/politics.htm.

26. Daniel M. Shea, et al., "Allegheny College Surveys on Civil Discourse," Center for Political Participation Website. Accessed at: http://sites.allegheny.edu/civility/.

27. As cited in Daniel Libit, "The Pros and Cons of Hissy Fits," *Politico*, September 30, 2009.

28. Frank Rich, "The Civility Racket," *New York Times,* December 18, 2010.

29. Richard K. Scher, *The Modern Political Campaign: Mudslinging, Bombast, and the Vitality of American Politics* (New York: M.E. Sharp, 1997), pp. 30–31.

30. Joel H. Silbey, "Beyond Realignment and Realignment Theory," in Byron E. Shafer, ed., *The End of Realignment: Interpreting American Electoral Ears* (Madison, WI: University of Wisconsin Press, 1991), p. 11.

31. Charles Dickens, *American Notes* (London and Hall, 1842), 149, as cited in Howard Reiter, *Parties and Elections in Corporate America,* 2nd Edition (New York: Longman, 1993), p. 6.

32. William Schambra, "Nasty Politics? Puhleez! Get a Historic Grip," *Christian Science Monitor,* October 24, 2004.

33. Ibid.

34. Scher, *The Modern Political Campaign*, p. 44.

35. Schambra, "Nasty Politics?" October 24, 2004.

36. Mark Hamilton Lytle, *America's Uncivil Wars: The Sixties Era from Elvis to the Fall of Richard Nixon* (New York: Oxford University Press, 2006).

37. American National Election Study, "Timing of Presidential Vote Choice." Accessed at: http://www.electionstudies.org/nesguide/toptable/tab9a_3.htm.

38. Gallup Polling Center, "Americans Display Record Levels of Interest in the Election," Gallup.com, February 1, 2008. Accessed at: http://www.gallup.com/poll/104155/americans-display-record-level-interest-election.aspx.

39. As cited by Alan Abramowitz, *The Disappearing Center: Engaged Citizens, Polarization and American Democracy* (New Haven, CT: Yale University Press, 2010), p. 19.

40. Ibid., p. 112.

41. Ibid.

42. Ibid., p. 84.

43. Ibid., p. 170.

44. Morris P. Fiorina, with Samuel J. Abrams, *Disconnect The Breakdown of Representation in American Politics* (Norman, OK: University of Oklahoma Press, 2009), p. 61.

45. Morris P. Fiorina, with Samuel J. Abrams and Jeremy C. Pope, *Culture War? The Myth of a Polarized America* (Upper Saddle River, NJ: Pearson, 2006).

46. Fiorina, *Disconnect,* p. 38.

47. Ibid., pp. 37–38.

48. Kathleen Hall Jamison, and Joseph N. Cappella, *Echo Chamber: Rush Limbaugh and the Conservative Media Establishment* (Oxford England: Oxford University Press, 2008), p. 245.

49. D. J.Brooks, and J. G. Geer, "Beyond Negativity: The Effects of Incivility on the Electorate." *American Journal of Political Science,* 2007, *51,* 1–16.

50. Frank Rich, "The Rage is Not About Health Care," *New York Times*, March 28, 2010.

2

The Powerful—
if Elusive—Nature
of Civility[1]

Susan Herbst

*Give me thy hand: I am sorry I beat thee; but, while
thou livest, keep a good tongue in thy head.*

STEPHANO,

In Shakespeare's *The Tempest*, Act III

*Many senators said the current vitriol [over
health care legislation] . . . was unlike anything
they had seen. "It has gotten so much more
partisan," said Senator John D. Rockefeller IV,
Democrat of West Virginia.*
"This was so wicked. This was so venal."

DAVID HERSZENHORN,

"In Health Vote, A New Vitriol," *New York Times*

One of the issues that bedevil scholars is whether politics has really become nastier than in the past. Even a cursory look at the nature of campaigns in American history suggests things always have been rough, and in some respects what we now see would be considered tame in other eras. In this chapter, scholar and University of Connecticut President Susan Herbst offers an excerpt of her book, *Rude Democracy*. Instead of seeing incivility as an unfortunate byproduct of polarized political activity, Herbst suggests we might best understand it as a resource used by politicians. At times it makes good strategic sense to be tough, perhaps even mean, but at other times it does not. Incivility, then, becomes one of many tools in the arsenal of politicians in their fight to win elections and to enact policy preferences.

High-minded rhetoric about "civility" courses throughout issue debates across the nation. We find hopes for civility expressed in speeches by the mighty all the way down to the posts of lone, unknown bloggers. But the gap between our language about civility and the real nature of American political discourse and practice is at least as wide as it has ever been. [My] book explores that gap—what it looks like, how it persists, and whether it matters for a contemporary democracy like our own.

Our particular historical moment is fraught with the concerns of our day: an economic downturn, energy independence, health care reform, the conduct of major military efforts in Afghanistan and Iraq, and a fierce ideological divide between political parties that seems to grow worse each month. It is also a moment created—most of all, perhaps—by the extraordinary presidential campaigns of 2008 and an equally extraordinary election outcome. Presidential elections and their aftermaths, despite their uniqueness, have proven to be among the best analytic tools we have for studying our political culture, and they are superb windows into the nature of civility. So my focus is on civility writ large in American politics, but viewed through the distinctive lens of the 2008 campaigns and election.

Because the debates about health care reform have continued to evolve, I have been able to extend my analysis well into the winter of 2010, even though this national discussion remained far from settled. Some town hall meetings, called to debate health care reform in the summer of 2009, challenged many ideals about civility. And the now infamous shout "You lie!"—uttered by South Carolina's Representative Joe Wilson during President Barack Obama's address to a joint session of Congress in September 2009—marked some sort of American milestone. But in many ways the passionate absence of bipartisanship and the accolades Wilson gathered from his party reflect an anger that had developed during the 2008 presidential election campaign. Fallout from that election and new manifestations of party conflict have much to do with civility.[2]

It was unexpected, but our most recent presidential contest turned out to be particularly helpful in studying the contemporary practice of both civility and incivility. It boasted a variety of fascinating aspects—the tenor of the campaigns, the tone and content of media coverage, and the nature of interpersonal dialogues all around us. While voter turnout figures may have been a disappointment to scholars hoping for astronomical numbers, there is no question that—although impossible to measure precisely—emotions ran much higher than those from prior recent presidential elections. We might speculate on why the emotional pitch was so high. An economic downturn of epic proportions? The first African American presidential candidate? The proliferation of engaging Web sites and bloggers? Fierce, lengthy primary battles? No matter the causes, it was a riveting year of campaigns, and we are forever changed by the people and events of 2008.

It seems clear in retrospect that 2008 mattered to Americans in profound ways. In a context where an already-intense campaign was ratcheted up by a severe recession and two wars in progress, civility was bound to emerge as a central issue. Was the campaign civil, or should we say, civil enough for America? Did those who participated in it—from candidates to journalists to citizens—treat each other with the respect deemed appropriate in our (self-proclaimed) world's greatest democracy? And, most interesting, should we even worry about civility, a "pie-in-the-sky" concept with an old-fashioned, nineteenth century ring to it?

When I told people I was writing a book on civility, they thought of opening doors for women, naughty children misbehaving in public, and suppressing the desire to give others "the finger" in traffic. These niceties or hoped-for niceties are related to civility, no doubt. But my interest is in the fundamental tone and practice of democracy, in the wake of an unusual presidential campaign and at the start of the twenty-first century.

While a single presidential election offers but one window into the debates over civility, my empirical investigations seem to point to far larger, longitudinal conundrums of political culture. Some Americans, citizens and leaders, are distraught about what they see as a decline in civility. Others find the worriers both naïve and cowardly: The line between passionate engagement and civility seems chronically fuzzy and arbitrary. Both views can be persuasive, and it does us no good to choose sides. Norms of civility certainly exist, but civility is also very much in the eye of the beholder. Where you sit—as a journalist, an ideologue, a candidate, or a citizen—matters immensely. Perspectives vary, and while this is all somewhat messy, it suits a democracy that must wrestle with both policy and the tone of policy debate.

The questions I want to raise about civility are challenging to answer, and the vague meaning of "civility" has much to do with that challenge. But as I argue in my book, debates over its definition, its rise, or its fall are a distraction. What we should attend to are the *strategic uses* of civility and incivility. Civility is best thought of as an asset or tool, a mechanism, or even a technology of sorts. This approach opens up a wide and productive range of empirical phenomena to study *and* captures the context-dependent, historical nature of civility. If we think of civility as a strategic asset, we can pull away from the "more or less" debates and study newer forms of political discourse and behavior with far more sophistication and success.

I assume a strong free-speech framework. There is no question . . . that much uncivil talk in our present-day political communication is racist, sexist, or just plain rude. No one, except a mindless provocateur, would want these sorts of hateful speech acts to be commonplace. And, of course, speech that threatens violence—as we saw in the aftermath of the March health care bill passage in 2010—is unacceptable. But in my work, I have come to admit that lines are fuzzy and that *imputation* of motives from rhetoric is a dangerous game. Congressman Joe Wilson's 2009 shout at President Obama provoked considerable debate about underlying racial motives: Would he have yelled at a white president? Why the shout during Obama's discussion of illegal immigrants? I'm afraid that answers to such questions are elusive, empirically at least, regardless of our gut feeling. So while I do indeed find certain remarks clearly inappropriate, I will hold judgment on what I think is and is not constructive debate. I leave these matters to editorial writers and thinkers who seek particular policy or social change.

Another assumption I make here is that "facts"—notions that we can prove through widely accepted standards of evidence—are important in democratic debate, but they may have only a marginal relationship to the struggle over civility. Of course, facts matter, and there is tremendous interest in them, hence the appearance of "fact-checking" Web sites that put our political officials under scrutiny. This is absolutely essential work in any polity, without question. But there are significant gray areas, both during political campaigns and between them, so again, I tread carefully. When leaders are actively, intentionally deceiving us, and we can prove—perhaps at a much later date—that they knew they lied, where do we place this phenomenon in relation to civility?

My belief is that truly interesting and important cases of intentional public lying are somewhat rare, and that creative stretching of the truths one holds dear is probably far more common. In any case, awful lies are typically revealed after the debate in question has passed, and they should be judged with vigor whenever they appear. The challenge of determining who is using facts well and who is not is a moving target, and I applaud the effort, even if it is a rough fit to thinking about civility.[3]

STRATEGIC CIVILITY

It is most useful to think of civility as a tool in the rhetorical and behavioral arsenals of politics.[4] Sometimes people are unknowingly civil or uncivil, of course. These actions may be natural aspects of our typical participation in politics. Indeed, some individuals seem to emanate civility or incivility as part of their approach, so much so that it seems central to their very fabric of being. While partisanship abounds in the higher reaches of American politics, it is fair to say, for example, that a variety of U.S. senators, past and present, have been consistently civil in their behavior. This is one reason why they are commonly selected for sensitive and controversial tasks. (For example, Senator George Mitchell was chosen to investigate illegal uses of performance-enhancing drugs in baseball, and then was chosen as Middle East envoy.) And on the uncivil end of the continuum, we have actors like the late Lee Atwater, a political consultant who broke new ground in the pursuit of brutal and highly personal campaign mudslinging.

Apart from these cases of chronic, uniform, or innate civility or incivility, which are unusual, we should think of civility as a strategic tool or weapon in politics. It is a tool that is used intentionally, for better or worse. Someone might use incivility to great effect in a negative advertising campaign. Or, alternately, take the "high road" in advertising, hoping to gain accolades for the use of civility and even generosity of feeling toward an opponent. As noted previously, many have viewed civility as a state of a society (more or less civil) and a constellation of social norms associated with that state. I differ in this book, treating it is a tool. Table 2.1 sets out characteristics implied by the two different perspectives on civility.

Most theorists, historians, and writers have viewed civility as a set of social and cultural norms. These observers find different levels of civility in different eras. Some see civility on the rise, and others see it in decline, scholars Stephen Carter and Robert Putnam being among the strongest proponents of the latter view. But if we think of civility as something employed for tactical purposes, we are able to pull away from these debates, which are not always as productive as they might be in an age of Web communication. This is not to say that these scholars have not contributed to the study of civility; they have done so mightily, with erudition and panache. But the time has come to shift the debate and analysis of civility. With the arrival of the Internet, we have a seemingly endless number of communicators, forever inventing new sites, channels, and techniques for persuasion, conversation, and assault.

If, as in Table 2.1, we view civility as most authors have—as a set of norms and practices—we are left with a generally static approach. Of course, the norms and ideas about civility change, but typically such changes take decades and often generations to occur. However, we now live in an intensely communicative age where no one waits on the passage of decades: These days, communicators are utilizing, playing with,

TABLE 2.1 Two Approaches to Civility	
Civility as a Set of Norms	**Civility as a Strategic Tool**
Static, within eras	Temporary and changeable
Conflated with culture	Easily discerned and singled out
Tethered to a context	Fluid in use across contexts
Without a particular communicator	With a clear communicating agent
Not conducive to Internet communication styles	Conducive to Internet communication styles
Difficult to manipulate intimacy by communicators	Easy to manipulate intimacy by communicators

and transforming civility and incivility daily, shaping American political discourse as a result.

Sometimes the experimentation of bloggers and average citizens challenges broader cultural norms in profound ways, as we saw during the 2008 presidential election. One particularly interesting example was the role of YouTube: A variety of contributors to the site posted video footage (taken surreptitiously) of people removing Obama or McCain yard signs.[5] This is a superb illustration of the complex uses of incivility, one that would be difficult to parse and understand if we did not think about civility and incivility as weapons. People steal or deface signs in order to further their own candidate in a local community. Then, enterprising people catch thieves on video, thereby exposing the practice but raising the implicit prospect that stealing yard signs has become *normative*—an acceptable ground game of politics.

Again, the older view of civility as a norm (the first column) cannot help us with these new, more complicated activities, made possible by the Internet, viewed by tens of millions. YouTube, as well as many other sites, enables people to make arguments through video, audio, blogging, and chatting. If we see civility as a strategic tool, it becomes a rich, relevant topic again, one that could not be more fitting to an Internet age, with so many varied participants worldwide. The old ways of thinking about civility—as a static part of culture, not easily manipulated or quickly altered, that is widely shared—seem downright inappropriate. These days, civility can be exploited or not, with tremendous speed and ease. Communicators can "grab" it for their purposes, and the venues for the uses of civility and incivility seem limitless. Far beyond stealing or destroying signs, fascinating as that is, are the "photoshopping" of images (e.g., candidate faces attached to other bodies), the continual distortion and reediting of candidate videos, citizen battles via Wikipedia page revisions, the chronic decontextualization of quotations, speeches, and ideas, and a variety of other communicative actions, easy enough for middle school children to carry out.

One question that arises when we treat civility and incivility as strategic tools is whether they are good or bad, helpful or hurtful for democracy. An easy answer is the one we so often see in the scholarly politics literature: Incivility is destructive and blocks proper democratic debate. I find this a banal and unsophisticated answer, one that ignores the reality of politics, communication culture, and the social environment of the twenty-first century. In my book, I do not dodge this question, but there is no definitive answer to it either, and we would be dishonest to grandstand on it. It depends entirely on issue and situational context, and is closely tied to ideology and passion. Someone who believes that an embryo is a human being, for example, thinks it good for democracy and morality to use incivility—perhaps peacefully displaying images of horribly destroyed fetuses—as a strategic weapon. To these actors, such discourse enhances the debate and injects vital reality to it. And there are examples from the political left, just as powerful. In fact, Herbert Marcuse, a leading Marxist public intellectual of the

1960s, advocated forms of incivility—harsh interference with the speech of others, for example—if they furthered the values of social movements and justice.[6] In any case, it is not productive to go round and round on these matters . . . I will argue that tying ourselves up in knots about what is right or wrong, civil or uncivil, is far less useful than educating Americans about how to debate and develop the thick skin that strong democratic debate demands. *The real question is whether we want both depth of debate and the work that comes with it.*

Nonetheless, my thesis may be hard to swallow for some, because we have for so long seen the issues as black and white—civility is good, incivility is bad. Would not acceptance of incivility as a valid rhetorical tool like so many others lead to even more tactical, nasty, and ultimately destructive public discourse? Far from it, as I argue throughout [my] book. If we see civility and incivility as strategic assets, we humanize the players on our political scene, in our town councils, and in our work-places. Civil people can say uncivil things and uncivil people can be civil. Second, thinking about the *uses* of civility and incivility boosts our self-consciousness about the nature of political talk, reflection that is absolutely essential for a healthy nation. Finally, if we can view uncivil talk as just that, there can be change: If civility and incivility are "states" and not "traits," as the early psychologists used to say, how we talk to each other is changeable—daily.

SO WHICH IS IT? ARE WE MORE CIVIL OR LESS CIVIL?

Without question, the dominant strain in the literatures on both manners and political civility has been a struggle over the *trend*: Is civility on the decline? Journalists, scholars, and statesmen have asked the question repeat-edly in different venues and for varying purposes. This discussion takes on many forms. During presidential campaigns, for example, we ask whether the nasty mudslinging is a new phenomenon. Inevitably, a historian points out that things were worse in the eighteenth or nineteenth century, and that assertion is either believed or not.

Most scholars and writers—apart from cultural historians like Elias and Kasson, who have seen manners as contextually bound—have bemoaned a decline of civility in American politics and social life. This ruefulness is a shame, since so many historians have documented phenomena to disprove this view, such as the horrendous dirty presidential campaigning of the past. (Thomas Jefferson and John Adams attacked each other viciously; Lyndon Johnson's "Daisy" ad against Barry Goldwater was quite over the top.) But I suppose the popular logic goes something like this, even if it does not match history: We have gone "downhill," but we can regain that civility, an American ideal we somehow lost over time.

In any case, the alleged decline of civility, of manners, and the public sphere in the United States more generally, has captured the imagination of the academy and Americans well beyond college campuses. One writer who has made the strong argument for a decline is Stephen Carter, law professor and novelist. Carter believes that the American civility decline began dramatically in the 1960s.[7] He argues that, before the 1960s, there was a "golden age" in the United States where people generally held the same dreams for the American experience. It is not so much that life before the 1960s was better, he posits. But there was a shared creed about America, and it was diminished by the Vietnam War and the student movement. John Kennedy, Martin Luther King, and Robert Kennedy were assassinated, and division—not solidarity—prevailed. Carter bemoans the destruction of a common morality and set of values, and notes

> As the sixties swept into the seventies, leaving behind the wreckage of the illusion, there was nothing available to put in its place: no shared meanings, no shared commitments, none of the social glue that makes a people a people. . . . Having abandoned the illusion of commonality, we have adopted an even more dangerous illusion: that social norms are not important and thus we can do as we like.[8]

The most compelling empirically based arguments about our decline have come from the sociologist Robert Putnam. While his "bowling alone" hypothesis spurred a rancorous debate and significant criticism from many quarters, the contributions he has made to current discourse are extraordinarily valuable and worth our time here. Putnam is concerned broadly with social life in America, but his arguments about how we treat each other in daily life are certainly relevant to a study on political civility.[9]

While Putnam takes on a variety of topics in the general arena of social life and culture, he is interested in civility as it is manifest in altruistic behavior. Hence he studies volunteerism, philanthropy, and other forms of individual contributions to neighborhood and community. He also studies polite behavior toward faceless "others." One of the premier examples from his enormously popular *Bowling Alone* is the decline in number of drivers who obey stop signs, an intriguing indicator of how people act, not toward others directly, but toward fellow citizens *in theory*. He notes that, according to studies of New York intersections with stop signs: "In 1979, 37 percent of all motorists made a full stop, 34 percent a rolling stop, and 29 percent no stop at all. By 1996, 97 percent made no stop at all at the very same intersections."[10]

Attacks on Putnam—his propositions and data—are abundant and vehement in many scholarly circles. But so is the chronic appeal of his decline argument, hence the attention he has received. I do not hope to settle long-running debates over the "bowling alone" thesis here, but it seems clear from the historical literature pioneered by Elias that arguments about decline are a bit dangerous when it comes to political civility. We have many well-documented cases of incivility, from well over two centuries of American electoral politics (poor Martin Van Buren, already vice president, was accused of wearing a woman's corset!), not to mention outstanding cases of incivility by sitting statesmen, such as Senator Joseph McCarthy's performances and the hearings of the House Un-American Activities Committee in the 1950s.

These moments in American history underscore to us just how disrespectful, worrisome, and downright mean political discourse has been in our past. To argue that we do much better today is a difficult proposition to uphold. But it is not clear that we do worse either. What is easier to argue is that the uncivil tendencies in American culture are more apparent and abundant thanks to pervasive media. One might have been able to ignore gruesome partisan bickering in the early nineteenth century simply by neglecting the newspaper or avoiding the local tavern. But the "in your face" quality of contemporary media makes this avoidance impossible: We wait in airport gates, car washes, and doctors' offices with the blare of CNN keeping us company, even if we would prefer a different soundtrack as we go about our business.

So I will not argue here that civility has declined—clearly the most popular argument these days—or is on the rise. Neither assertion seems supportable, and both are far too broad to be stated definitively. What we can do, however, is document the tendencies and tools related to civility and incivility, and try to make sense of what they mean for American political culture.

CONCLUSION

In closing, I raise the earlier question one last time: Is there a danger in my approach—treating civility and incivility as tactics or strategies? Can this perspective demean American politics, making civility seem less valuable and important? I do not believe so. Seeing civility as a tool can enable citizens and leaders to approach their activities with more self-consciousness and more care. When we think about what we do and realize our own agency, there is an opportunity for greater integrity of action and attention to real democratic ideals.

While civility in politics is a concept with many faces and my case studies [in my book] probe only a few aspects of it, they are helpful in understanding the challenges we face as Americans. Are we prone to incivility in our discourse? What does it actually look like, and how much does it matter? How do different actors on the political stage approach civility, be they journalists, our elected officials, or the college students who will one day set the tone for American citizenship and leadership? . . .

I shall not close with a definitive meaning of civility, since its meaning will always be tied to the changing nature of social relations. What was civil and acceptable in the nineteenth century is often uncivil today, and the same may well be true in the future. Taking on a grand concept like civility may seem outrageously ambitious, but in the end I hope to develop and value it in a way that fits our immensely complicated moment in political culture.

Endnotes

1. This chapter is an excerpt of Herbst's book, *Rude Democracy: Civility and Incivility in American Politics* (Temple University Press, 2010).
2. One of the most useful fact-checking sites is Politifact.com, which won the 2009 Pulitzer Prize: available at http://www.politico.com/blogs/bensmith/0909/Wilson_campaign_Fundraising_breaks_1_million_passes_Miller.html (accessed March 25, 2010).
3. The only useful occurrence of the phrase "strategic civility" I could locate is from an attorney's essay on using etiquette in the practice of law-in treatment of the judge, opposing counsel, and others. While perhaps helpful to attorneys, this brief essay is primarily about the importance and effectiveness of being polite. See Eugene Meehan, "Civility as a Strategy in Litigation: Using It as a Tactical Tool." Available at http://www.supremecourtlaw.ca/default_e.asp?=77 (accessed March 25, 2010).
4. For an incident of Obama signage being stolen, see http://wwwyoutube.com/wathc?v=ZERbqcPyfZE&feature=related (accessed March 25, 2010). There are many videos on YouTube of both Obama and McCain yard sign theft.
5. See the excellent book edited by Samantha Besson, Jose Luis Marti, and Verena Seiler, *Deliberative Democracy and Its Discontents* (Surrey, U.K.: Ashgate Publishing, 2006).
6. One of the best scholarly books on the feeling citizens seek (and sometimes get) from media is Roderick Hart's *Seducing America: How Television Charms the Modern Voter* (Thousand Oaks, CA: Sage, 1998).
7. Stephen Carter, *Civility: Manners, Morals and the Etiquette of Democracy* (New York: Basic, 1998). Carter's work has stimulated a variety of excellent critiques, including Randall Kennedy, "The Case against Civility," *American Prospect* (November 1, 1998), available at http:www.prospect.org/cs/articles?article=the_case_against_civility (accessed March 25, 2010).
8. Carter, *Civility*, 53.
9. See Robert Putnam, *Bowling Alone: The Collapse and Revival of American Community* (New York: Simon and Schuster, 2001). The number of books, articles, and popular essays inspired by Putnam's work is enormous, evidenced in part by a whopping nearly 11,000 citations captured by Google Scholar alone (accessed January 16, 2009). One excellent book on the subject is Nan Lin's *Social Capital: A Theory of Social Structure and Action* (Cambridge: Cambridge University Press, 2002). There is a lively dialogue in Robert Putnam, "Robert Putnam Responds," *American Prospect* 25 (March-April 1996): 26–28, available at http://www.prospect.org/cs/articles?article=unsolved_mysteries_the_tocqueville_files_311996_rp (accessed March 25, 2010).
10. Putnam, *Bowling Alone*, 143.

3

What is Civil Engaged Argument, and Why Does Aspiring to it Matter?

Kathleen Hall Jamieson and Bruce W. Hardy

As the chapters in this volume illustrate, discussions of civility in politics are complicated by the fact that different people hold somewhat different notions of what constitutes civility. In this chapter Jamieson and Hardy carefully define civility and associated concepts, and argue that the rise of partisan media threatens civil, engaged argument. They provide a case study of the kind of political exchange that many political observers believe has become increasingly rare.

To begin the task of answering the question posed by the title of this essay, we will sketch what we mean by the concepts of civility, argument, and engagement, note the ways in which the rise of partisan media menaces civil engaged argument, and close with analysis of an exchange between prominent Democrat and Republican leaders that illustrates the importance of common definitions and sources of trusted evidence.

COMITY OR CIVILITY

Communities are sets of relationships writ large. Be they town councils, state legislatures, or the U.S. House or Senate, when groups deliberate, they often do so in a rule-governed environment. For some, the regulatory framework consists simply of Robert's Rules of Order, a regimen known to everyone who has ever participated in a student government. For the U.S. House of Representatives, the rules are somewhat more complex and include rituals and precepts designed to ensure civility or comity.

In the U.S. Congress, comity is based on the norm of reciprocal courtesy and presupposes that the differences between members and parties are philosophical and not personal, that parties to a debate are entitled to the presumption that their views are legitimate even if not correct, and that those on all sides are persons of good will and integrity motivated by conviction.[1]

By adopting rules of deliberation at the beginning of a new U.S. Congress, the membership voluntarily limits the range of rhetoric acceptable on the floor. When a member wonders why he cannot call another member a liar or a hypocrite even if the evidence justifies the label, the answer is not simply that the rules of the House forbid it but also that the membership has voluntarily agreed by vote that these are the constraints under which the House will operate during that Congress. Among other things, House rules caution members who have the floor not to call their fellows liars even if they are not telling the truth, not to impugn their integrity even if their actions invite it, and not to call another member a hypocrite even if s/he is being hypocritical. These guides to appropriate conduct are designed to create a climate conducive to deliberation. And central to the ability to deliberate is a rhetoric of mutual respect.

The founders recognized the importance of civility to deliberation. In the debates at the Constitutional Convention, liberality "as well as prudence induced the delegates to treat each other's opinions with tenderness," recalled John Jay, "to argue without asperity, and to endeavor to convince the judgment without hurting the feelings of each other. Although many weeks were passed in these discussions, some points remained on which a unison of opinions could not be effected. Here again that same happy disposition to unite and conciliate induced them to meet each other; and enable them, by mutual concessions, finally to complete and agree to the plan they have recommended."[2]

In the debate over representation, argument grew heated as delegates favoring a weaker national government pressed the advocates of a strong federal system for assurances that groups of states would not combine to abuse the rights of smaller states. John Lansing, Jr., of New York, spoke on behalf of perfectly equal representation among the states, regardless of size. James Madison, architect of the Virginia proposal, lost patience and replied heatedly. "Can any of the lesser States be endangered by an adequate representation?" he asked. "Where is the probability of a combination? What are the inducements? Where is the similarity of customs, manners or religion? If there possibly can be a diversity of interest it is the case of the three large states. Their situation is remote, their trade different. The staple of Massachusetts is fish, and the carrying trade; of Pennsylvania, wheat and flour; of Virginia, tobacco. Can states thus situated in trade ever form a combination?"[3]

Delegates were accustomed to attacks on positions. So, for example, Hamilton pointed to problems with the reasoning—rather than deficiencies of the person doing the reasoning—when he noted, "He deduces from these principles the necessity that states entering into a confederacy must retain the equality of votes. This position cannot be correct."[4] The advocate is insulated from direct attack by Alexander Hamilton's emphasis on the claim.

However, James Madison violated the principles of comity by specifying slovenly habits of mind and attributing them to the thinkers rather than focusing on the argument: "Those gentlemen who oppose the Virginia plan do not sufficiently analyze the subject," he said. "Their remarks, in general, are vague and inconclusive."[5] Sensitive to the effects of insult, Benjamin Franklin rose to propose reflection and the need to seek divine grace.[6] A later commentator observed that "this timely and gracious advice of the aged diplomat produced its desired effect, and the debate resumed the highly impersonal tone of its early stages."[7]

The lessons learned in such clashes were shared in memoirs and autobiographies. Franklin recalled:

> When another asserted something that I thought an error I deny'd myself the pleasure of contradicting him abruptly, and of showing immediately some absurdity in his proposition; and in answering I began by observing that in certain cases of circumstances his opinion would be right, but in the present case there appear'd or seem'd to me some difference, etc. I soon found the advantage of this change in my manner; the conversations I engag'd in went on more pleasantly. The modest way in which I propos'd my opinions procur'd them a readier reception and less contradiction; I had less mortification when I was found to be in the wrong and I more easily prevail'd with the others to give up their mistakes and join with me when I happened to be in the right.[8]

In the case of the founders, the urgency of the matter at hand ensured that those involved in the deliberation would focus their claims and counterclaims on the specific resolutions being debated. Making the case for one side of an issue over the alternatives is best accomplished in engaged argument.

THE CONCEPTS OF ARGUMENT AND ENGAGEMENT

In its simplest incarnation, an argument offers a statement and proof in the form of relevant supportive evidence. When the evidence is sufficient to justify the conclusion, the statement has been "warranted." The rules of argument include the notions that assertions should be backed by relevant evidence that constitutes proof, the fairness and accuracy of evidence should be subject to scrutiny, the testimony of those who are self-interested should be suspect, evidence must not be ripped from its context, relevant evidence must be disclosed and not suppressed, like items should be compared to like items, and a plan should be tested by asking whether it meets the need and whether its advantages outweigh its disadvantages. These tacit understandings of the norms involved in social interchange include the idea that alternative sides have the right to be heard and accurately paraphrased by those of opposed bent. Shouting an opponent down violates this understanding, as does reducing an opposing argument to a straw figure.

Postmodernism aside, at a primal level, deliberation presupposes the existence of common definitions, agreement upon factual terrain on which the exchange rests, and embrace of the norms that permit us to distinguish legitimate discourse from the kinds reserved for playground bullies and ranting talk show hosts. Without this common ground, engaged argument is impossible. Beyond the pale are engagement-fracturing moves that employ what the rules of the U.S. House of Representatives call "personalities" (or ad hominem). And central to this notion of argument is the precept that, like ad hominem and guilt by association, ridicule ends engagement.

Engagement is the process that enables audiences to ascertain which argument is more cogent. At the root of the concept of engagement are notions that theorists of debate cast as "clash" and "extension." The former pits position against position in a manner that invites comparison. The latter carries the argument forward through response to response. Implicit in the notion of engagement is the supposition that those who are attacked should have the right to reply.

So fundamental are some of our notions of fair engagement that they have been enshrined in the U.S. Constitution and in the U.S. courts' rules of evidence. For example, the so-called confrontation clause of the 6th Amendment guarantees that a person brought into criminal court has the right "to be confronted with the witnesses against him [and] to have compulsory process for obtaining witnesses in his favor." And in the courts, relevant evidence is that which "tends to prove or disprove" a proposition "properly provable in the case."[9] However, not all relevant evidence is admissible. For example, Rule 403 "authorizes exclusion of it when its 'probative value' is substantially outweighed by the danger of unfair prejudice, confusion of the issues, or misleading the jury, or by considerations of undue delay, waste of time, or needless presentation of cumulative evidence."[10]

In cases in which these norms are honored, areas of agreement and disagreement are clarified, the collective understanding of the issue at hand is advanced, the commitment of participants to the legitimacy of the system is reinforced, and judgment is based on reasoned argument and not prejudice, force, or fear. When it characterizes campaigns for president, as it did in 1960 and 1980, this conception of discourse enables citizens to ratify their own futures by participating in a discussion of the challenges facing the country and the ways and means of addressing them. Out of the open discussion of the ends and means of national policy, a campaign can forge a consensus. From such a clash of alternatives will emerge a stronger final plan and a better president—one to whom even those who voted for the loser are more likely than they otherwise would be to pledge allegiance. Importantly, the sort of discourse environment nurtured by these norms makes it more likely that a Democratic Speaker of the House such as Tip O'Neill and a Republican President such as Ronald Reagan could fashion a plan to "save" Social Security in 1983 by raising the retirement age, increasing the payroll tax, having federal workers begin to contribute to the system, and delaying a cost of living adjustment.

THE THREAT PARTISAN MEDIA POSE TO CIVIL ENGAGED ARGUMENT

The presence of explicitly ideological media greatly expands the range of audience choices and in the process opens the possibility that conservatives' views will be reinforced by exposure to right-leaning media outlets and liberals or progressives will be enveloped in media that underscore rather than challenge the arguments and evidence amenable to them. These venues create a natural platform for opposing ideological sides to selectively argue their cases by featuring the "facts" that benefit their side and suppressing those that do not.

One result is "the tendency of channel audiences to be composed of devotees and non-viewers,"[11] a phenomenon evident in the 2004 presidential election, when Fox viewers and Rush Limbaugh listeners were more likely than other conservatives to reside in a world in which their view of challenged facts coincided with those of their party.[12] So, too, were CNN viewers and NPR listeners when it came to Democratic claims.[13] Evidence that watching partisan opinion talk shows polarizes attitudes was also uncovered by a study that found Fox viewers less likely than CNN audiences to watch accounts critical of the Bush administration and more likely than non-watchers to underestimate the number of Americans killed in the Iraq War.[14]

The implication of such enclaving was evident in our Annenberg finding that Fox news viewers were significantly more likely than other non-Fox watching conservatives to report that "George W. Bush told the truth about John Kerry's record" and significantly less likely to say that "John Kerry told the truth about George W. Bush's record." When we asked respondents about the veracity of specific claims such as "George W. Bush's tax cuts reduced taxes for everyone who pays taxes" or "John Kerry's health plan would have provided health insurance to all Americans," both of which are false, partisans who were Fox News reliant embraced the view consistent with their own ideology more often than non-Fox News-reliant conservatives. That study also found that when assertions by their preferred candidate were involved, partisan cable outlets often failed to correct duplicitous statements.[15]

By 2008, MSNBC had moved aggressively into the partisan media business. Consistent with our earlier Annenberg work, during that election season, listening to Limbaugh or viewing Fox News' *The O'Reilly Factor* or Hannity and Colmes were positively related to taking a pro-Republican stance on contested claims. Watching MSNBC's *Countdown with Keith Olbermann* and *The Rachel Maddow Show* produced the same result for Democratic views. In this study, partisan media exposure explained significant variance in the adoption of partisan claims, regardless of their truthfulness.

The rise of partisan media of the right and left carries both benefits to democracy and causes for concern.[16] On the positive side, ideologically tinged outlets increase their audience's ability to understand the complexities of politics by consistently framing arguments from one point of view. At the same time, by building a supportive base of evidence for the beliefs advanced from one ideological perspective, they help their audiences distinguish between "liberal (or progressive)" and "conservative" positions. They also arm their audiences with key points of advocacy and attack and school them in effective means of sustaining those arguments. And they minimize the likelihood of defection from their ideology by creating a community of listeners and viewers who share a worldview and political preference.

On the downside, partisan media insulate their audiences from alternative media sources by branding them untrustworthy, and at the same time they protect their audiences from influence from opposing views by balkanizing and polarizing their perceptions of those with whom they disagree. Partisan media also contest only those facts hospitable to their opponents, invite moral outrage by engaging emotion, replace argument with ridicule and ad hominem, and often invite their audiences to see the political world as a Manichean place unburdened by complexity, ambiguity, or common ground. It is this second set of tendencies that menaces civil engaged deliberation in politics. Note that all of these negative tendencies that we see in partisan cable shows characterize at least some political advertising on each side of the ideological divide as well.

HOW JOHN McCAIN AND JOHN KERRY FOUND THE GROUNDS ON WHICH TO AGREE AND DISAGREE IN THE HEALTH CARE REFORM DEBATE OF 2009 IN THE U.S. SENATE

An exchange between 2004 Democratic presidential nominee John Kerry and 2008 Republican nominee John McCain that occurred during the December 5, 2009, health care reform debate in the U.S. Senate illustrates the two major distinctions on which this chapter focuses: the divide that separates respectful civil discourse from the disdainful, uncivil sort and the difference between disengaged argument and substantive civil argumentative engagement, clash, and extension mediated by common evidence. It also illustrates the tendency of opposing sides in political argument to speak past each other because of their reliance on "partisan or contested fact." As we have argued earlier, rather than increase civil argumentative engagement, partisan media and political advertising destroy common ground by creating enclaves of "partisan fact and definition." As our Kerry–McCain case study will illustrate, these tendencies can bleed into the legislative realm in ways that threaten civil engagement and clarifying argument.

The backdrop of the exchange between the two senators is more than half a century of Democratic attack on Republicans for their presumed plans to "cut," "destroy," or "eliminate" social programs. These exchanges more often than not center on contested definitions and facts. What the Republicans cast as "reductions in the rate of growth," Democrats label as "cuts." What the G.W. Bush Social Security plan characterized as "personal retirement savings accounts," the Democrats saw as "privatization." And each envisioned very different consequences should the other's point of view prevail.

Indeed, in 1996, the presumed "Dole-Gingrich threat" to Medicare was a staple of President Bill Clinton's attack ads; in 2000, Democratic nominee Al Gore campaigned on the threat that Republican nominee Governor George W. Bush wanted to take a trillion dollars out of Social Security and on his own pledge to protect Social Security and Medicare; and in 2004, Democratic presidential nominee John Kerry's ads alleged, falsely in Republicans' view, that incumbent Republican President George W. Bush's Social Security Plan would cut benefits 30 to 45 percent. Unsurprisingly, in 2009, when the Obama health care reform plan "slowed the rate of growth" in Medicare to achieve $500 billion in savings over ten years, the Republicans turned the tables, using the same "cut" language routinely employed against them in decades past.

Our story begins with the Democratic senator from Massachusetts implying that on the sensitive and occasionally electorally decisive issue of Medicare, the Republicans, in general, and, by implication, the Republican senator from Arizona, are engaging in histrionic distortive scare tactics, falsely pretending to protect senior citizens and, in the case of 2008 Republican nominee John McCain, employing lines of argument inconsistent with his own past rhetoric. It doesn't require heroic effort to hear Kerry's attack as an allegation of hypocrisy and a questioning of the integrity of those advancing such ideas.

Although the form of meta-communication Kerry is employing can be grounded in substantive differences—he is, after all, arguing that the Republicans are attacking the Democrats for a position their own 2008 presidential nominee espoused—such allegations can easily be heard as a personal attack on the integrity of both Republicans and the specific members of the party who had been speaking in the previous half hour. In short, whether accurate or not, by the definition we offered earlier, Kerry's remarks are comity shattering. And, if past is prophet, such an attack will elicit a counterattack in kind rather than substantive engagement. Our plotline is launched when Senator Kerry says:

> We have heard an incredible amount of scare tactics, Senator after Senator standing there, jumping up, pounding out one sort of misstatement or one distortion or another. The bottom line is, they have stood there for the last hour or so, claiming they are standing there to protect seniors. It is ironic, when one Senator, the Senator from Arizona [John McCain], who said yesterday and sort of repeated it today—this is what he said yesterday:
> "I will eagerly look forward to hearing from the authors of this legislation as to how they can possibly add $1.2 trillion in cuts without impacting existing Medicare programs negatively and eventually lead to rationing of health care. . . ."[17]

However, notes the senator from Massachusetts, in 2008, presidential Republican contender John McCain held a contradictory position by underwriting his health plan with reductions of $1.3 trillion to Medicare and Medicaid:

> John McCain would pay for his health plan with major reductions to Medicare and Medicaid," a top aide said, "in a move that independent analysts estimate could result in cuts of $1.3 trillion in 10 years to the government programs."

"Consistency" Kerry adds, fueling the flames, "obviously, has never constrained anybody in politics."[18]

Instead of simply asking McCain to explain how the Democratic "cuts" he was attacking differed from "the reductions in rate of growth" he proposed in 2008, Kerry has tagged the difference he sees between the two McCain positions as "ironic" and also seemed to identify his Senate colleague as among those who "for the last hour or so" have employed "scare tactics," been "jumping up and pounding out one sort of mis-statement or one distortion or another" and "claiming [but obviously, from Kerry's perspective, not actually intending] to protect seniors." In short, according to the Democrat from Massachusetts, the Republicans have been engaging in hypocritical attack.

Importantly, Kerry is quoting others to demonstrate the inconsistency. He is not warranting the claim from his own personal authority. And noteworthy from McCain's standpoint, the second of the two quotes does indeed use the word "reductions," albeit attributed by a news source to an anonymous McCain aide in 2008 and not to the Arizona senator himself.

Later in the same debate, the 2004 Democratic Party presidential nominee returns to this theme but without the meta-communicative characterizations:

> I want to go back to the comments of the Republican nominee for President last year. This is a quote. John McCain, from an article in the *Wall Street Journal:* "John McCain would pay for his health care plan with major reductions to Medicare and Medicaid, a top aide said, in a move that independent analysts estimate could result in cuts of $1.3 trillion."

If the 2004 and 2008 nominees of their respective political parties are to engage, they must acknowledge that they are using different language to characterize the reductions/savings/cuts to Medicare and Medicaid depending on the political party making the proposal. And they need to clarify their assumptions. From the statements of Senator McCain that Kerry cites, it is unclear whether the two agree on the extent of the "reductions" entailed by the Arizonan's 2008 proposals. Nor from this exchange is it apparent where McCain in 2008 and the Democrats in 2009 would find the "savings (reductions/cuts)." Also unclear is the purpose to which the "savings/reductions/cuts" would be put. Moreover, each side seems to believe that the other's "reductions/savings cuts" would injure older Americans, whereas their own would not.

One way to find common ground from which to engage would be by agreeing on common definitions and an arbiter of evidence that both trust. In many legislative debates, that source is either the Congressional Budget Office or the Government Accountability Office, non-partisan federal agencies that provide data for Congress. In this debate the senators focused instead on FactCheck.org, the independent watchdog website run by the Annenberg Public Policy Center of the University of Pennsylvania. This source entered the debate after Kerry's first attack on McCain's putative inconsistency when Republican Senator Richard Burr asked Kerry, "Have you seen Factcheck.org [on the McCain statements in 2008]?"

After Kerry's staff had located the article, he stated:

> Now I have seen the article. I wanted to know what the Senator from North Carolina was referring to, so I went and got Factcheck.org. Factcheck.org went through the Obama campaign ads and their ads and fact checked what was being said. The McCain adviser is a fellow named Holtz-Eakin. In a conference call with reporters after the ad was released, what he said was, "No service is being reduced. Every beneficiary will in the future receive exactly the benefits that they have been promised from the beginning."

Focusing on that section of the FactCheck.org posting, Kerry concludes:

> That is the same thing as we are doing. No benefit is being cut. But he didn't say he was not going to reduce the overall amount of money. What he said subsequently, and I am quoting from factcheck.org—here it is as late as October 17, about 2 weeks before the election—Mr. Holtz-Eakin said in a telephone conference call with reporters, representing the campaign for the Republican party: "Any shortfall in McCain's health care plan will be covered without cutting benefits by such measures as Medicare fraud and abuse reduction, employing a new generation of treatment models for expensive chronic diseases, speeding adoption of low-cost generic drugs, and expanding the use of information technology in medicine . . . "

Kerry has now acknowledged that McCain believed in 2008 that a large amount could be "cut/reduced/saved" in Medicare/Medicaid without cutting benefits. Does McCain grant that the same might be true of the Obama administration's "reductions/savings/cuts"? After intervening debate, Senator McCain takes the floor with two pieces of evidence in hand. Specifically, "my campaign position paper on a specific plan of action lowering health care costs" and "a statement from FactCheck.org, of October 20, 2008, that says: 'Obama's False Medicare Claim,' which were the attacks on me which were not based on fact." He asks that the two documents be entered in the record. Doing so requires unanimous consent.

Both Kerry and McCain are now relying on FactCheck.org. "I quote from FactCheck.org," said McCain of the source that Kerry has legitimized with his own recital of evidence. The Arizonan then notes that Kerry has stated that he did propose cuts, reductions, and savings. McCain extends the argument to note that the same move remains available to Obama and the Democrats. While clarifying the point of disagreement, the Arizona senator does not dispute that both his and Obama's health care plans would have cut, reduced, and saved substantial dollar amounts from Medicare and Medicaid. Rather, he disagrees with the intended use the Democrats would make of those funds. "Nowhere in my wildest imagination did I ever believe we were going to cut benefits in order to create a $2.5 trillion new entitlement program when the system is already going broke." In making this claim, McCain has shifted ground. Indeed, Kerry is correct that McCain had expressed doubts that the Democrats could find substantial savings cuts and reductions in Medicare.

To this point the charges and countercharges have escalated. Each implies that the other is ignoring facts and being distortive if not deceptive. Each has offered claims and evidence, hence argument, but the two have not engaged on the same terms. Importantly, however, both have cited FactCheck.org. Additionally, McCain has asked that this now uncontested source of credible evidence become part of the record. In doing so he has seeded the basis for engagement if the two will take the next step, called "extension" in the argument literature. It is in this context that Kerry tries to gain the floor:

> Mr. KERRY. Madam President, I am not going to object to putting something important in, but I would like my colleague to stay for a moment because this is very important.

To dampen tensions, senators customarily refer to each other as "colleague," a term designed to protect comity but one that seems strange when one has just implied that the other is a deceptive scaremonger. It is nonetheless a characterization Kerry invokes. Whereas in the earlier attack he referred to McCain as the senator from Arizona and the person who ran for president in 2008, McCain is now cast as "my colleague." The invocation is tied to a request that McCain not leave the chamber. As the noise level in the Senate escalates, the Republican floor manager, Senator Charles Grassley (R Iowa), calls for "Regular order" and the presiding officer announces that "The majority's time has expired." Calling on the next Republican scheduled to speak, Senator Grassley "yield[s] the remaining time on our side to Senator Thune."

Under the rules, Kerry has a means of shifting the focus back to his disagreement with McCain:

> MR. KERRY.   I have objected to a statement [he is referring to the FactCheck.org article] being put in [The Record] unless I have a chance to explain it.
>
> THE PRESIDING OFFICER.   Objection is heard.

Senator McCain has indeed stayed on the floor and responds to Senator Kerry's plea by asking unanimous consent that the senator from Massachusetts be allowed three additional minutes and that he be allowed two. The presiding officer asks if there is objection. Hearing none, he recognizes the senator from Massachusetts.

In a dramatic shift from his earlier tone, Kerry then identifies McCain as his "friend" and moves to clarify their substantive disagreement. Gone are third-person labels and accusations of scare tactics and deception. Kerry is going to salve the wounds he has earlier inflicted on McCain by noting that the 2008 Republican Party nominee for president was indeed wronged by the Obama campaign on this issue. That concession and the rhetoric of respect that accompanies it provide the scaffolding on which the two can substantively engage on their points of disagreement:

SENATOR KERRY: I thank my friend from Arizona because this is the way the Senate ought to work. I totally agree with what the Senator said. I want the Senator to know I agree with him. He is correct that the statement in FactCheck.org calls the Obama campaign to account for a misstatement about his proposal. I agree. It did that. It [the McCain campaign] did not recommend a reduction in benefits.

But that is not what I suggested that it did. What I am talking about is, the Senator said—and his staff insisted—he could get the savings for his reductions that would benefit Medicare from waste, fraud, and abuse from new treatment models, from expanding the use of information technology and that there is a complete similarity between what we are doing in order to achieve these savings and what he was doing.

I am trying to point out the similarity, not the difference. I am not here to debate the campaign ad. I think it didn't accurately reflect the Senator's position. But I do believe, if you read the whole article, which is why I will not object to it being put in there, you will see it clearly says he is supportive of savings in Medicare, so you can do it without cutting benefits, which is exactly what we are doing.

I yield the floor and thank my colleague for his courtesy.

Importantly, Kerry has now replaced "reduction" with "savings" in his characterization of the McCain 2008 plan.

Senator McCain then extends the discussion by elaborating on their disagreement. The senators are no longer accusing each other of distortion or hypocrisy. Nor are they selectively attacking each other for proposing cuts in sacred programs. Whether realistically or not, each side is conceding that "cuts/savings/reductions" can be made without reducing benefits. Their disagreement is now focused on how the funds freed by the "savings/reductions/cuts" will be used:

SENATOR MCCAIN: Madam President, I thank the Senator from Massachusetts. This has been a vigorous debate . . . . The fundamental point, I would say to my friend from Massachusetts, is that I never envisioned, nor do I believe the American people ever envisioned, we would be "cutting" benefits or, as the Senator says, "making savings" in order to transfer that to a brand new entitlement program. That is what the debate is about, whether we are going to take a failing system that in 7 years is going bankrupt, according to the Medicare trustees, and then take all this money, no matter how these savings are made—and I believe they are cuts of huge magnitude—and then fund a brand new entitlement program. That is what this real debate is about. I thank my friend from Massachusetts for his courtesy . . . .[19]

The exchange is not ideal. Since McCain's 2008 proposal has not been translated into legislation before the chamber, there is not a ready way for the two to engage on the merits of the way each would make use of the funds. Nor has either assumed responsibility for showing exactly where that large amount of funding was hiding in the current system. But at the exchange's end, they are talking to and not past each other. The level of hostility and tension has been reduced. And McCain and Kerry are modeling mutual regard, respect for evidence, and a form of exchange recognizable as argument and engagement.

How aberrational is this moment? In politics in the United States, some forms of discourse increase civil engaged argument while others tend to foster the opposite. In the Sunday morning interview shows (i.e., NBC's *Meet the Press*, ABC's *This Week*, CBS's *Face the Nation*, CNN's *State of the Union*, and Fox's *Sunday with Chris Wallace*) treat their guests with respect, employ evidence with care, and work to secure engaged argument from the national leaders who appear in this elite venue. Overall, presidential general election debates do the same. As a result, a substantial body of evidence confirms that debate watchers of all educational levels learn issue distinctions and candidate positions.[20] By contrast, despite their many beneficial characteristics, political ads are more likely to selectively use evidence and pretend to respond to the other side while in fact sidestepping its claims. And, at their worst, partisan media supplant argument with ridicule.

Since a substantial body of psychological study suggests humans learn by modeling, instances of civil engaged argument are worthy of public exposure, study, and emulation. However, since conflict is a basic journalistic norm in the United States, examples of it are far more likely to be featured in the news than are models of constructive civil argumentative engagement. And dysfunctional models can spawn offspring of like sort. As David Fahrenthold reports in the *Washington Post,* "This summer, liberal groups have tried to do to Republicans what was done to them two years ago. They have targeted GOP town halls to demand higher taxes on the rich and on corporations, and to push for new jobs in infrastructure and clean energy. Already, there are similar results: Freshman Rep. Lou Barletta (R-Pa.), who blasted his opponent for not holding town halls last year, has suspended his own meetings after disruptions by liberals."[21]

To complicate matters further, in addition to modeling ridicule, cable talk shows and talk radio sometimes showcase talking over or shouting down those who disagree. Witnessing such moments may discourage those in the audience from attempting to thoughtfully engage those of different persuasion whom they encounter in neighborhoods, classrooms, or work places.[22] Tie the effects of such modeling to our disposition to marry, live near, and talk politics only with those with whom we agree, and the chances plummet that we will practice civil engaged argument with those who hold opposing views.

Were Benjamin Franklin alive today, he would be worried about the ability of a country to prosper in a world in which so many forces sabotage its leaders' ability to argue in an engaged fashion about the pressing problems facing it.

Endnotes

1. Kathleen Hall Jamieson, *Civility in the House of Representatives: A Background Report* (Philadelphia: Annenberg Public Policy Center, 1997).
2. John Jay, "An Address to the People of the State of New York on the Subject of the Constitution." *Pamphlets on the Constitution of the United States,* ed. P.L. Ford (1888). This section of the essay is drawn from Jamieson's chapter titled "What Should We Really Expect? How They Talk to Us" in *Everything You Think You Know about Politics and Why You're Wrong* (New York: Basic Books, 2000). Portions of the next section of the essay are drawn from Jamieson's *Dirty Politics: Deception, Distraction and Democracy* (New York: Oxford University Press, 1992).
3. Marion Mills Miller, ed. *Great Debates in American History* (New York: Current Literature, 1913), pp. 219–220.
4. Ibid., p. 335.
5. Ibid., pp. 332–333.
6. Ibid., pp. 333–334.
7. Marion Mills Miller, *American Debate* (New York: G.P. Putnam's and Sons, 1916).
8. Benjamin Franklin, *The Complete Works in Philosophy, Politics, and Morals of the Late Dr. Benjamin Franklin, Vol. 1* (London, n.d.).
9. Jon. R. Waltz, Roger C. Park, and Richard D. Friedman, *Evidence: Cases and Materials* 11th Edition (New York: Foundation Press, 2009), p. 75.
10. Justice David Souter, *Old Chief v. United States.* Supreme Court of the United States, 519 U.S. 172, 117 S.Ct. 644, 136 L.Ed. 2nd (1997), p. 574.
11. James G. Webster, "Beneath the Veneer of Fragmentation: Television Audience Polarization in a Multichannel World," *Journal of Communication,* 2005, June: 366–382.

12. Joseph Capella, and Kathleen Jamieson, *Echo Chamber: Rush Limbaugh and the Conservative Media Establishment* (New York: Oxford University Press, 2008).

13. Ibid.

14. Jonathan S. Morris, "The Fox News Factor," *The Harvard International Journal of Politics*, 2005: 56–79. Whereas the Fox finding was consistent across these two studies, the CNN result differs somewhat from Jamieson and Cappella's that in 2004, CNN's viewers were more likely to accept the liberal view of contested claims.

15. Kathleen Hall Jamieson, and Bruce W. Hardy, "Unmasking Deception: The Capacity, Disposition, and Challenges Facing the Press." *The Politics of News: The News of Politics* 2nd edition, (Washington, D.C.: Congressional Quarterly Press, 2007). pp. 117–138.

16. Capella and Jamieson.

17. Senate, *Congressional Record* (U.S. Government Printing Office, 2009) S12462.

18. Ibid.

19. Senate, *Congressional Record* (U.S. Government Printing Office, 2009) S12491.

20. W. L. Benoit, and G. L. Hansen, "Presidential Debate Watching, Issue Knowledge, Character Evaluation, and Vote Choice." *Human Communication Research, 30*(1), 2004; 121–144.

21. David A. Fahrenthold, "American Town Halls More Contentious Than Ever, In Part by Design." *Washington Post*, 27 August 2011.

22. Paul Avi Waldman, "Deliberation in Practice: Deliberative Theory, News Media, and Political Conversation." University of Pennsylvania, 2000. Proquest Paper AAI9989668.

4

Calls for Civility: An Invitation to Deliberate or a Means of Political Control?

J. Cherie Strachan and Michael R. Wolf

It might seem ironic that many are worried about impassioned politics these days, given ongoing concerns about anemic levels of engagement. If we want an engaged public, a public that really cares about policy alternatives and the conduct of government, doesn't that imply heated debates and some tough rhetoric? As you will read in this chapter, norms of politeness have often stifled concerns and curtailed movements. By "knowing one's place," the political grievances are kept in check. But on the other hand, can society function without attention to respect and civility? This chapter confronts the precarious balance between robust activism and civility.

As the introduction to this work emphasizes, headlines make it clear that average citizens have recently indulged in rude and aggressive political behavior. Yet average citizens are not alone. Over the past several years, members of the political elite, ranging from incendiary media pundits to outraged elected officials, have also engaged in behavior that many consider not only inappropriate but also damaging to democratic governance. The perception that we live during an era of heightened incivility inevitably leads to concerns that Americans no longer have enough in common to pursue a shared agenda and that our long-running democratic experiment will falter. If Americans truly have lost their respect for a legitimate opposition, the ability to admit uncertainty, and the willingness to compromise, this concern is warranted. Current levels of political incivility may be a warning sign that Americans are no longer inclined to peacefully negotiate solutions to collective problems—in which case, the ability to sustain a democracy is indeed at risk.

Yet the very roots of most political issues are grounded in conflict. As James Madison noted in the *Federalist Papers*, if people were angels, government would be unnecessary.[1] Similarly, when citizens agree about an issue, legislation to regulate behavior or fights over the allocation of scarce resources is not needed. When people whole-heartedly agree on a topic, it rarely becomes fodder for political campaigns. Instead, widespread agreement typically constitutes a self-policed cultural standard rather than a controversial political issue. For hundreds of years, for example, no one felt the need to pass a constitutional amendment defining the sexual identity of marriage partners, because social norms meant that only heterosexual couples were marriage partners. The issue only became political as some (but not all) people's notions of appropriate marriage partners began to change—leading both supporters and opponents of gay rights to push for legislative and judicial intervention.

In short, political controversy occurs when issues are gray rather than black and white—when the "right" decision about an issue of concern is debatable, open to interpretation, or simply unclear. Yet, when people's fundamental values and priorities, as well as their personal circumstances and experiences, lead them to dramatically different policy preferences—conflict inevitably occurs. Democratic political institutions were designed to channel this conflict into campaigns, elections, and legislative debates rather than violent confrontations. Perhaps highly contested elections in the United States have been described as "bloodless revolutions" for good reason. When conflict is successfully resolved through political channels, violent civil wars and military coups are avoided. But acknowledging the underpinning role of conflict and disagreement in politics suggests that a certain amount of incivility is inevitable. People who disagree with each other about important and emotional issues are not always very nice to one another. Those who prefer to live in a democracy must come to terms with this reality and develop a higher tolerance for a bit of rude behavior once in a while.

Further, when they are upset by incivility in public settings, Americans should consider why they find such acts so offensive. Norms of appropriate behavior almost always reflect differences in power and authority. Groups of people who lack access to power are often expected to defer politely—and without question—to those who wield authority over them.[2] Hence, when members of these groups purposefully choose to violate these expectations in order to criticize authority figures or to make demands of their own, their behavior is often perceived as rude and sometimes even scandalous. Yet violating expectations about what is and is not acceptable may draw attention to inequalities in a supposedly democratic society. Sometimes people are "rude" in public on purpose—to cause a controversy that will attract publicity and bring attention to their cause. In some cases, then, calls for civility are really a mechanism of political control, intended to re-establish power over a formerly subservient and compliant group. Even now, after the substantial successes of the Civil Rights and Women's Movements, minorities and women are held to a higher standard of polite behavior than white men. So, it is especially important in a democracy that we also ask just who is being called to task for being impolite, and what exactly they are trying to accomplish through their so-called incivility.

WHY BE POLITE?

Thinking through what the current examples of incivility in American politics mean requires a basic understanding of why people ever bother being polite in the first place. Communication scholarship indicates that the purpose of being polite—whether it occurs in private, interpersonal interactions, or in broader political communication—is to enable people who disagree about something to maintain an ongoing and productive relationship. These efforts are accomplished by characterizing potential opponents as likeable and admirable, while at the same time limiting the perception that they have no free will.[3] When people are portrayed as completely unlikeable and without any redeeming qualities, or an effort is made to undermine their autonomy, they are apt to abandon the relationship and to seek other ways to accomplish their agendas. In interpersonal relationships, for example, people dump friends who have insulted or controlled them one too many times.

In politics, rude behavior itself can undermine political opponents' willingness to work together. Interactions characterized by challenges, name-calling, disagreements, and interruptions usually lead to entrenched positions rather than compromise. When opponents feel attacked, especially when those attacks are made in public, they respond by digging in to defend their own position rather than seeking out common ground. An especially nasty fight over one particularly divisive issue can even spill over to other topics that would otherwise have provided common ground. Rude behavior in politics can, in and of itself, result in intended or unintended gridlock.

President Barack Obama, in a May 2010 commencement speech, expressed concern that rude political tactics have had precisely this outcome on the ability to govern the United States. While acknowledging the rough and tumble of politics in a democracy, he cautioned against demonizing political opponents, worrying that efforts to vilify the other side—while always characterizing the rhetoric of ideological fringe—had crept into "the center of our discourse."[4] He went on to argue:

> The problem is that this kind of vilification and over-the-top rhetoric closes the door to the possibility of compromise. It undermines democratic deliberation. It prevents learning—since after all, why should we listen to a "fascist" or a "socialist" or a "right wing nut" or a "left wing nut"? It makes it nearly impossible for people who have legitimate but bridgeable differences to sit down at the same table and hash things out.[5]

In short, Obama's speech underscores scholars' claims that being polite is the essential social lubricant needed to resolve interpersonal disagreements, but it is also necessary for seeking out bipartisan solutions to public policy concerns. Those like Obama, who see deliberation as an integral component of democratic decision-making, place a very high value on civility.[6] After all, the occasions throughout history when one political party has been able to gain complete control over all three branches of government are few and far between, and they are usually short-lived. Americans seem to have internalized the framers' fear of tyranny of the majority, as our voting patterns tend to make majorities difficult to form. Consequently, solving public problems often involves working with the other side. Those who endorse deliberation believe that citizens and elected officials alike should be able to "agree to disagree" on intransigent issues, but still be able to collaborate toward common ends. Maintaining this type of relationship requires basic mutual respect—which is undermined by incivility.

WHY BE RUDE?

Yet rudeness can also be purposeful. At some point, former friends might decide that taking a principled stand is more important than maintaining a relationship. Similarly, being polite is no longer strategically important in politics when one side is rigidly committed to a policy agenda that conflicts with their opponents' political values. Rather than negotiating, politicians may focus on winning a solid majority of legislative seats in an upcoming election—in which case policy can be swept into place without the need for compromise. Or, if overwhelming electoral success is not possible, politicians may prefer to take no action at all—which simply requires blocking opponents' policy proposals rather than negotiating to find common ground. A troublesome cycle can result if elections become the means to policy ends, but policy pursuits become the means for credit claiming during an electoral campaign, with neither side willing to give an inch.

While maintaining a functional relationship so that legislators can undertake the task of shared governance is important, democratic politics also involves letting voters make choices among politicians who advocate distinct policy preferences. The electorate cannot embrace significant social and political change unless politicians not only have sharp disagreements with one another but also clearly communicate those differences to voters. On some highly salient issues, staking out a principled position might be more important to politicians than reaching a compromise, regardless of the consequences to their ability to negotiate over the long term. Perhaps this is why the most dramatic examples of nastiness in politics often occur at pivotal points in American history, when political factions have staked out dramatically different positions on important issues and have forced the electorate to pick a side. Examples of such debates include: whether to ratify the Constitution in the late 1700s, whether to abolish slavery in the 1800s, and whether to regulate laissez-faire capitalism as well as how much to protect civil rights in the 1900s.

At first glance, it seems that over-the-top political tactics make an appearance during every historical era that precedes a realigning election. Party scholars believe these elections serve as critical junctures, where Americans make choices that fundamentally change the future direction of the country.[7] Given the high stakes of these decisions, it is little wonder that the rhetoric of the day became incendiary and that politicians on opposing sides were willing to risk alienating one another.[8] Incivility, in these cases, should be treated as an indicator of the intensity of the public's concerns about these pivotal issues rather than as a judgment of how well-behaved Americans were in a particular era. Yet despite the intensity of these decisions, only one—characterized by the refusal to enact further legislative compromises on the issue of slavery—devolved into a civil war. Yes, Americans' political behavior during these eras has been marked by unseemly tactics. But the fact that the United States has had a stable democracy and has largely avoided violent uprisings, civil wars, and military coups—even while periodically grappling with polarizing, intractable issues—may actually be a sign that our democratic institutions are working.

To push this claim a bit further, negativity plays an important role in educating the public even during more mundane political times. Many political scientists believe that American voters usually engage in retrospective voting—where they look back over the past several years to evaluate an incumbent politician's performance.[9] Most Americans are also cognitive misers, which means that we do not want to spend too much time gathering and processing the information required to make this type of evaluation. Candidates who hope to unseat an incumbent must be willing to point out aggressively how their opponent has failed. Providing this type of information is useful, and some might even argue essential, if we are to effectively hold elected officials accountable for the choices they make as our public servants. Yet asking candidates to provide this critical, albeit important, information without at least occasionally slipping into incivility during the heat of a campaign seems unrealistic.[10]

POLITICAL LEADERS, CITIZENS, AND POWER: WHO IS ALLOWED TO BE RUDE?

Americans have always wrestled with notions of how civil our citizenry should be for a healthy democracy to exist. When the framers were crafting the U.S. Constitution, Thomas Jefferson wondered from Paris whether the new Constitution was a good thing. Part of his hesitation hinged on whether political leaders were overreacting to public distemper and uncivil (not to mention illegal) behavior at the time. In a letter to William Smith, he defended such actions with his now most-quoted line, which states: "The tree of liberty must be refreshed from time to time with the blood of patriots and tyrants. It is its natural manure."[11] Political activists love to borrow this quote to evoke the imagery of patriot champions standing up to a powerful tyrant. Yet a closer reading of the letter reveals a conflicted Jefferson instructive to today's tension over political incivility.

Far from promoting incivility or political violence, Jefferson suggested that the anarchy the framers feared—an armed uprising of Massachusetts farmers labeled Shay's Rebellion—was founded on ignorance and misperception. Jefferson's real remedy was to set these discontented citizens right on the facts—underscoring the notion that political leaders have an important role to play in educating and leading the public. Good leaders, Jefferson argued, should do more than merely respond to and play upon public passions. Clearly, many of today's political leaders prefer to surf the wave of public frustration rather than follow Jefferson's prescription "to set them right as to the facts, pardon and pacify them."[12]

Rather than pacifying the public, many of today's political leaders take advantage of the asymmetry of information and political knowledge to pump up opposition in the public. A media culture drawn to any whiff of conflict rewards such incitement. Recent rumors about President Obama illustrate these types of manipulations, as well as politicians' potential reactions to them. Despite factual evidence to the contrary, critics of Obama continue to question both Obama's religious affiliation and his citizenship. Ever since the 2008 presidential campaign, chain e-mails have circulated false rumors that Obama is a radical Muslim who was born overseas, attended an extreme fundamentalist religious school in Indonesia, and took his Senate oath on a Koran.[13] How far should his Republican opponents go to reject these claims when embracing them will exacerbate core voters' fears, increase their likelihood of turning out to vote, and enhance their willingness to block Obama's policy initiatives? In 2008, John McCain chose to take the high ground, and he corrected an ill-informed supporter at a rally, reassured supporters that they need not be scared of an Obama presidency, and described him as "a citizen that I just happen to have disagreements with on fundamental issues."[14] Yet false claims about Obama persist, especially the "birther" claim that his Hawaiian birth certificate is not authentic.[15] While some prominent Republicans have overtly rejected this claim, others have embraced it, or at least coyly refused to use their visibility and credibility with conservative voters to dismiss it—with the media only too happy to cover any politician willing to advance controversial opinions.

Hence, rumors about Obama not only persist, but flourish. Throughout the early years of his presidency, the number of Americans who believed Barack Obama was a Muslim actually increased, especially among conservative Republicans.[16] More recently, a 2011 poll indicated that about half of Republican primary voters did not believe that Obama was born in the United States.[17] Given both the media's and politicians' inability to correct these inaccurate beliefs, is it any wonder these voters prefer gridlock to compromising with Obama?

Consequently, the danger to democracy may come, as Jefferson recognized, from failure to contain aggressive and uncivil political behavior through reasoned political leadership. On the other hand, Jefferson clearly was unfazed by such political incivility and even violence because he noted that it was so rare, but also because the spirit of resistance brought to life through incivility was important in its own right. It served as a warning to rulers that they could not trample important freedoms. Indeed, if upset citizens remained passive, Jefferson argued that lethargy would be the "forerunner of death to the public liberty."[18] Thus, public distemper—even if driven by ignorance—is an important American political behavior because it motivates citizen participation and serves as an effective way to rein in political leaders. One wonders whether Jefferson would have reacted similarly if he had not been insulated by geographic distance from uprisings threatening the stability of his newly formed country. Further, would he have similar sympathy for contemporary citizen activists' purposeful reliance on both violence and civil disobedience? Examples to ponder include pro-life activists' aggressive efforts to shut down clinics that provide abortions, eco-terrorists' willingness to damage property (like Hummers and sprawling Mc-Mansions) deemed a threat to the environment, gay rights activists' embrace of civil disobedience to call attention to the AIDS crisis, or Occupy Wall Street protesters' camping in public parks to publicize their concern about income inequality. How do contemporary citizens' tactics and issues differ from those undertaken by bands of farmers upset over taxation and debt relief in the 1700s?

In any case, events in his own historical era led Jefferson to worry that the new Constitution might be an overreaction and might go too far in protecting government officials against citizens' resistance. Keeping Jefferson's concerns in mind, those attempting to assess contemporary political tactics should recognize that calls for civility have always been used to suppress political dissent. Good manners are a potent form of social control, as differences in power affect the level of politeness a speaker is expected to use—with those lacking authority expected to be more polite to their superiors.[19] Not surprisingly, democratic theorists have cautioned against overly polite manners, pointing out that they may suppress the intensity of average people's preferences and help to sustain the status quo. John Stewart Mill in particular questioned the role of aristocratic manners in a democracy, arguing that the "despotism of custom" encouraged individuals to moderate their demands and to "desire nothing strongly." In short, commoners were socialized to accept their social station in life without complaint, and many could not fathom questioning their "betters." The few who did were deemed rude and inappropriate—not only by the lords and ladies who were accustomed to such deference, but also by their own peers. In response, Mill advocated rejecting these social niceties, in favor of criticism and conflict playing an essential role in a lively marketplace of ideas.[20]

Yet overcoming deeply engrained notions of appropriate behavior is harder than Mill's commentary might suggest. Even when people develop group consciousness and recognize that they are being oppressed by society's expectations, they typically must convince others both within and beyond their immediate demographic group to agree. One way of doing this is to purposefully violate society's expectations. But those who do so will be perceived as rude, offensive, or scandalous, and they will be penalized in one way or another by those who think that their behavior is inappropriate. In the first wave of the Women's Movement, for example, women began wearing bloomers in an effort to demonstrate that even the clothing they were expected to wear was physically restraining—and prevented them from fully participating in public life outside the home. Their efforts resulted in a major social battle over the propriety of such attire. Similarly, suffragist Susan B. Anthony was arrested and fined for casting a ballot in a national election. The judge was so offended by her act that he refused to allow her to take the witness stand in her own defense, and he declared her guilty without even giving the jury time to deliberate. More recent examples can be found in the Civil Rights Movement, where African Americans were physically attacked for using White-only public facilities, or for having the gall to attempt to register to vote.

Yet all of these examples—once considered not only rude but offensive—eventually became commonplace and acceptable behavior. Americans fought a revolution, in part, to free ourselves from a monarchy that bestowed privileges based on birthright rather than individual merit. Now, no one bats an eye when women wear pants and vote in elections, and few people look back fondly on Jim Crow restrictions in the American South.

Recognizing the way current calls for civility may be linked to contemporary social hierarchies, however, is much more difficult than identifying examples from the past. While women and minorities are no longer legally prevented from voting and participating in politics, norms of appropriate behavior still hold both to different standards than white men. And these expectations may help to explain why both are still less likely than white men to participate in political acts that require discussion and persuasion.[21] Recall, for example, how pundits over the past four years have both praised and criticized Barack Obama for his restrained, analytical, and (some claim) aloof demeanor. Yet this style of political communication was surely more effective for Obama than fiery political rhetoric would have been—because African-American men are judged differently—if not more harshly—when they are openly defiant and angry in public settings.

Similarly, research shows that women are still socialized to be more polite than men. Examples include the fact that women are expected to smile and cooperate more readily than men, to facilitate others' agendas rather than to promote their own, and to refrain from interrupting others or from using intense adjectives and profane language. Of course, not all women modify their behavior to meet these expectations, but those who fail to conform are described as less likeable and, as a result, are less capable of influencing others' decisions.[22] Hence women's political engagement is limited by the way social norms of politeness restrict their expression of strong preferences.

Echoing John Stuart Mill's concerns that British commoners could not fully recognize their own self-interests, some feminist scholars believe that many women internalize society's expectation that they be overly polite. They fear that by embracing this role, women may be prevented from even identifying, let alone voicing, the intensity of their true political concerns.[23] If this is so, then women are functionally denied access to an entire spectrum of political behavior that remains open to men.

This discussion of minorities and women raises one final concern about the potential impact of heightened incivility in the public sphere. If angry voters are the driving force behind elected officials' incivility, they might expect politicians to give angry speeches, to call one another names, or to engage in other over-the-top rude behavior. If these types of candidates are the ones embraced by the electorate, it may become even more difficult than it already is to recruit minority and female candidates to run for elected office.[24] Women and minorities often intuitively know that they are sanctioned for public displays of aggression. Hence they may find it hard to envision themselves as highly visible and inevitably aggressive public figures. The possibility that increasingly rude politics may squelch their political ambitions should at least be considered.

One approach to leveling this linguistic playing field would be to upgrade our expectations for politeness and hold everyone to the same high standards that currently constrain women and minorities. Doing so, however, would run the risk of undercutting political dissent and bolstering support for an otherwise unsatisfactory status quo. Another approach would be to relax our overall expectations for civility, allowing women and minorities the same freedom to aggressively pursue political agendas as white men. Yet if norms of civility are relaxed too much, Americans risk damaging their ability to undertake the most fundamental task of shared governance—deliberation.

BALANCING DELIBERATION AND DISSENT

Ironically, American democracy relies on two deeply rooted traditions to stimulate public debate and resolve public problems. The first and most celebrated tradition is civility, which enables us to work through disagreement and to find consensus. The consensual New England Town Meeting exemplifies the American romance with this tradition. Another, however, is rude disruption to force new issues onto the political agenda or to gain a seat at the table. Overreliance on civility runs the risk of suppressing dissent, especially by those with limited access to power and resources. The classic movie *Mr. Smith Goes to Washington* provides an example of this outcome. Overreliance on disruption, however, runs the risk of shutting down deliberation—and thus problem solving—altogether. Given the choice between these two outcomes, one can see why rude behavior is often seen as the greater threat, and why calls for political civility have such strong appeal. If we are to err, some might say, let it be on the side of civility and stability. After all, isn't an imperfect democracy better than none at all?

Overarching calls for civility—bemoaning why we can't all just get along—may simply be naïve. Americans tend to mistakenly believe that most other people share our basic values, priorities, and lifestyles. As a result we underestimate the level of disagreement that exists in society, and we think that little negotiation or compromise should be required before making binding, collective decisions. Yet some scholars contend that we disagree with one another often, and maybe even more often than we realize.[25] Our political process provides a way to manage the conflicts that occur when our political preferences inevitably clash. The natural by-products of conflict resolution will be a certain amount of criticism, negativity, and perhaps even rudeness. Moreover, calls for a return to civility can, at their worst, be undemocratic. A preference for civility can disguise a vested interest in maintaining the status quo—even (or especially?) if the status quo denies some people equal access to the political process.

So how can we tell the difference? Unfortunately, Americans have not developed a precise way to measure the optimal level of civility in a democratic society. Citizens are left to develop their own criteria, assess the current political climate, and make this judgment for themselves. Some key questions remain as one considers the proper relationship between civility and democratic citizenship:

- Should different types of political actors be held to unique standards of civility? Is it more important, for example, that average citizens be civil to one another when they discuss political issues? Or should public officials' behavior be subject to more scrutiny? Among public officials, should there be uniform expectations for executives, legislators, judges, and bureaucrats? Or do the different functions that they fulfill require some to be more polite than others? What about lobbyists, media pundits, or protesters?
- Are reactions to rude behavior based on preconceived notions of appropriate behavior that only apply to certain demographic groups? Do we allow men, women, and minorities the same linguistic freedom to influence political issues?
- Should Americans have varying expectations for civility in different types of political settings? Is a slip into rude behavior on the floor of the legislature or during a presidential address more or less troubling than mudslinging during a campaign for office?
- What is the nature of the issue being debated? Is taking a principled stand on this issue worth turning potential collaborators into opponents? Would it be better to be polite and allow potential opponents to save face—so that a compromise can be negotiated not only on this particular issue, but in the future as well? Or does the issue really require polarizing the electorate and forcing people to pick a side?
- What is the underlying reason why a particular behavior or comment is seen as rude? Is it because the behavior is likely to undermine Americans' ability to deliberate and resolve issues of public concern? Is

it because Americans are thin skinned and cannot tolerate any hint of disagreement or criticism? Or is it because those engaging in the behavior are no longer willing to be deferential and are instead attempting to exercise their full political rights in a democracy?

Contemplating and answering these types of questions will produce the criteria needed to identify the appropriate level of civility in politics—criteria that should be applied as objectively as possible not only to others' actions but also to our own political contributions. Civility matters—but determining why and how requires balancing a democratic society's need for deliberation with a tolerance for disruption.

Endnotes

1. James Madison, "Federalist #51," In Clinton Rossiter, Ed., *The Federalist Papers* (New York: New American Library, 1961).
2. See Penelope Brown and Stephen E. Levinson, *Politeness: Some Universals in Language Use* (New York: Cambridge University Press, 1987).
3. Ibid.
4. Ann Arbor.com, "Text of President Barack Obama's speech at University of Michigan Commencement," May 1, 2010, Accessed at: http://www.annarbor.com/news/text-of-president-barack-obamas-speech-at-university-of-michigan-commencement/.
5. Ibid.
6. Publications in the area of deliberative democracy are numerous, but see a classic argument about the importance of deliberation in Amy Guttman and Dennis Thompson, *Why Deliberative Democracy?* (Princeton, NJ: Princeton University Press, 2006).
7. Walter Dean Burnham, *Critical Elections and the Mainsprings of American Politics* (New York: W.W. Norton, 1970).
8. For more specific examples, see Glenn Atchuler and Stuart Blumin, *Rude Republic, Americans and their Politics in the Nineteenth Century* (Princeton, NJ: Princeton University Press, 2000); and Joseph Ellis, *Founding Brothers* (New York: Vintage, 2002).
9. Morris Fiorina, *Retrospective Voting in American Elections* (New Haven, CT: Yale University Press, 1986).
10. For a more complete discussion of the way negativity enhances politics, see John Geer, *In Defense of Negativity, Attack Ads in Presidential Campaigns* (Chicago: University of Chicago Press, 2006).
11. Jefferson Thomas, "Tree of Liberty . . ." *Thomas Jefferson Encyclopedia.* Thomas Jefferson Monticello Museum. http://www.monticello.org/site/jefferson/tree-liberty-quotation. Accessed 10/20/2011.
12. Ibid.
13. FactCheck.org, "Sliming Obama," January 11, 2008, Accessed at: http://factcheck.org/2008/01/sliming-obama/.
14. Jonathan Martin, and Amie Parnes, "McCain: Obama not an Arab, Crowd Boos," October 10, 2008, Accessed at: http://www.politico.com/news/stories/1008/14479.html.

15. FactCheck.org, "The Truth about Obama's Birth Certificate," April 27, 2011, Accessed at: http://factcheck.org/2008/08/born-in-the-usa/; and FactCheck.org, "Indeed, Born in the U.S.A., April 27, 2011, Accessed at: http://www.factcheck.org/2011/04/indeed-born-in-the-u-s-a/.

16. The Pew Forum on Religion and Public Life, "Growing Numbers of Americans Say Obama is a Muslim," August 18, 2010, Accessed at: http://pewforum.org/Politics-and-Elections/Growing-Number-of-Americans-Say-Obama-is-a-Muslim.aspx.

17. Andy Barr, "Poll: 51 percent of GOP Primary Voters Think Obama Born Abroad," February 15, 2011, Accessed at: http://www.politico.com/news/stories/0211/49554.html.

18. Jefferson, "Tree of Liberty . . ."

19. Brown and Levinson, *Politeness*. For contemporary insight into the tension between civility and political control, see Kim Severson, "A Last Bastion of Civility, the South, Sees Manners Decline," *The New York Times*, November 1, 2011, Accessed at: http://www.nytimes.com/2011/11/02/us/southern-manners-on-decline-some-say.html.

20. John Stuart Mill (1859), *On Liberty* (New York: Penguin Classics, 1984).

21. Lawrence R. Jacobs, Fay Lomax-Cook, and Michael X. Delli-Carpini, *Talking Together, Public Deliberation and Political Participation in America* (Chicago: University of Chicago Press, 2009).

22. For a thorough review of these findings, see Linda L. Carli, "Gender and Social Influence," *Journal of Social Issues*, Vol. 57(4), 2001; 725–741.

23. This argument was first articulated by Robin T. Lakoff, *Language and Women's Place* (New York: Harper and Row, 1975).

24. Richard L. Fox and Jennifer L. Lawless, "To Run or Not to Run for Office, Explaining Nascent Political Ambition," *American Journal of Political Science*, Vol. 49 (3), 2005; 642–659.

25. Robert Huckfeldt, Paul E. Johnson, and John Sprague, *Political Disagreement: The Survival of Diverse Opinions within Communication Networks* (New York: Cambridge University Press, 2004).

5

The Uncivil and the Incendiary

Todd Gitlin[1]

Todd Gitlin continues the exploration of what we mean by "civility" in politics. He argues that there are a host of important distinctions between incivility, rudeness, and nasty emotions. Efforts to assess changes in political rhetoric are also inextricably linked to shifts in norms of acceptable behavior. As with the Strachan/Wolf chapter, this argues that efforts to curtail particular forms of language and behavior are too often linked with efforts to quell dissent.

Is incivility growing? Is it pernicious? The questions are easily posed—too easily, deceptively so. For the issue of what constitutes incivility is, in fact, disputable, evolving, and specific to our particular era; and one's assessment of the damages of incivility are likewise dependent on whose ox is gored, and how badly.

"Civility," that apparently noncontroversial and timeless virtue, is actually something of a conceptual blur. It is, moreover, a conceptual blur with a history, for it originates, in recent America, as the flip side of a larger phenomenon—the breakdown of the boundary separating private from public expressions of nasty emotion.[2] The preoccupation with civility accompanies the growth of public profanity, obscenity, nudity, and, not least, political turmoil in the 1960s. As historian Rochelle Gurstein has put it, the new sensibility of pornography and profanity was a "deformed offshoot" of the preference for exposure that became normalized—and to a great degree legalized—in the wake of World War II.[3] As a public virtue, civility came to be defined negatively, as a quality of life under assault by black militants, student radicals, Bohemians, hippies, avant-garde artists, and their legal defenders. The harsher and more intense the cultural confrontations and the nastier the vocabulary with which they were conducted, the more fervently was civility promoted as a social virtue. In the 1960s, reticence, to quote Gurstein again, made its "last stand."[4]

But "incivility," or what is commonly called by that name, ropes together a multitude of sins. The very roping together obscures important distinctions.

UNCIVIL MAN BITES CIVIL DOG

Incivility (or what is called by that name) in contemporary American politics is, by definition, newsworthy on the man-bites-dog principle: It violates a norm. But public insistence—in journalism, punditry, politics, and elsewhere—that incivility is all of a piece, a thing in itself, a beast that must be tamed, gives rise to some curious equations.

Consider, for example, a front-page article in the *New York Times* on October 30, 2011, about an intense fight among neighbors in Cooperstown, New York, over hydraulic fracturing, or "fracking"—the growing practice of injecting vast quantities of chemically treated water underground, under high pressure, in order to access natural gas.[5] The article notes that "dozens of communities" in the Northeast are either passing or considering fracking bans. Many of them are in small towns and rural areas, which, in American lore if not in actuality (or in the writing of Sherwood Anderson, Sinclair Lewis, and Shirley Jackson, among many others), stand for friendly, or at least civil, personal relations. The article singles out Cooperstown, celebrated as the location of the Baseball Hall of Fame—perhaps the definitive celebration of Americans solving their problems with an ingenious combination of teamwork and competitiveness—as a place where "fracking has emerged as the defining, non-negotiable political issue."

The reporter, Peter Applebome, reports in his first two paragraphs that unsigned, computer-generated letters were mailed to about ten local opponents of fracking, comparing them to Nazis and declaring that "they were being watched while picking up their children at school in their minivans." In his third paragraph, Applebome proceeds to describe the "abuse" of a fracking proponent, giving three examples:

> comments online suggesting that people find out where her dairy sells its milk so that they can stop buying it, or the warning that her farm, which has a lease with a gas company, "will fall like a house of cards when your water is poisoned." She and other drilling proponents have also been called "sellout landowners that prostitute themselves for money."

Now, in the first instance, fracking opponents are called "Nazis" and they, and their children, are threatened with possible physical, criminal harm. In the second, fracking proponents are insulted and there is the threat of a consumer boycott. Seized by the conventions of objective journalism—whether because this is the journalist's own preference or because his editors insist—such articles aspire to be evenhanded about the gravity of uncivil conduct. In this case, Applebome balances a call for a consumer boycott with a not-so-veiled threat to harm children. He does not intrude to judge whether these are equivalent.

A NOTE ON COMPARISONS

Now, at least in the eyes of the editors of the *New York Times,* intense community conflict is a phenomenon clear-cut enough to be newsworthy though (or because) it is uncommon enough to be unusual. It is uncommon, but in a common enough way—which can be said to be one definition of newsworthiness.

However, the fact that the Applebome article focuses on this conflict is not to say that the actual practice of incivility in public life, however we define it, is growing—or, on the other hand, that it is steady or even shrinking. Much as we may want to like to know where we stand in the arc of history by declaring that such-and-such phenomenon is either growing, shrinking, or standing pat, such questions are far more easily asked than precisely answered. Is American politics "more uncivil"? Than what, and when? Short of a vast exercise in number-crunching, I do not know how to argue that incivility is on the rise since, say, 2000, 1990, 1980, 1970, 1960, 1950 . . . 1860, 1850 . . . . And yet intuition is continually summoned, in its vivid but less than rigorous way, to testify in behalf of moral panic—the widespread emotional conviction that events are bringing about an apocalyptic decline in standards.

Yet the eruption of moral panics does not mean that standards are *not* declining, or at least changing. Whenever we try to construct meaningful comparisons, we plunge into a wilderness of mirrors. To make a rigorous case one way or the other, we would have to construct a database that lends itself to comparability. We would need evidence from such items as minutes of community council and other local meetings over the years; comparable samples of letters written by members of various communities; and the texts of political speeches from various years—including years when no one recorded, or printed, political speeches. Even when texts survive, or newspaper articles reporting the texts of speeches, we would have to assume that political speeches, or newspaper articles, held comparable significance in their respective times. All such propositions, being comparative, must take care that, when comparisons are made, rotten apples are being compared with rotten apples and not with rotten—or for that matter, plump and juicy—oranges.

So, for example, from the absence of the word "fuck" from officially printed books before 1926,[6] and from mainstream Hollywood movies before 1970,[7] it cannot be inferred that the word was not in common use.

GESTURES AND VEILS

All this said, it would seem altogether self-evident that the American spoken word has coarsened in the course of the past half-century. Vulgar language has become routine on playgrounds, on sidewalks, in TV cartoons, in classrooms, theaters, and virtually every other imaginable public place. Images hitherto considered obscene—and therefore, if to be exhibited at all, only on specialized screens or in the privacy of homes—are now readily available online and in many hotel rooms. Profanity is routine in the movies, on cable TV, in much popular fiction and in magazines. Sexual innuendo is a staple of music videos. Succumbing to road rage and giving the finger to other drivers strikes me—but unsystematically—as far more common than when I began driving fifty years ago. Even the *New York Times* broke its F-barrier when it printed the entirety of the Starr Report on President Bill Clinton's relationship with Monica Lewinsky, on September 12, 1998, quoting Ms. Lewinsky saying that Clinton should "acknowledge . . . that he helped fuck up my life."[8]

In 1995, literary critic Denis Donoghue wrote that "fuckwords" were being "heard in the best-regulated living rooms," as they were not heard, at least in Great Britain, in 1957.[9] But whatever their incidence in private life—if there can even be said to be any such thing—profanities and their attendant gestures have plainly been pouring through public life at an accelerating pace. In mainstream politics, too, the bar has been lowered. When, in 1976, while campaigning for the Ford-Dole ticket in Binghamton, New York, former governor and Vice President Nelson Rockefeller gave the finger to some hecklers, this was considered scandalous. Once again, however, comparisons are hard to mount with any rigor. It is possible that, in earlier years, candidates observed to have gestured similarly would not have been photographed doing so, or, if not photographed, would have been given a pass by friendly reporters who either would have considered it a breach of decorum or a violation of the values of a "family newspaper" to take note of the gesture. It was one thing to give the finger in private, or in a bar—a semi-public, semi-private intermediate place—but quite another to disgrace, to pollute, a public realm with an obscene gesture.

In 1985, the use of a "barnyard" term by the president of the United States was scandalous enough to be itself newsworthy. On July 9, United Press International ran a short dispatch headlined: "Reagan Tiptoes Around Barnyard Term in Speech."[10] Speaking to the American Bar Association, Reagan, according to UPI, was "taking a swipe at the Soviet Union for suggesting that the United States was looking for a 'pretext' to invade Lebanon during the 16-day TWA hostage ordeal." But it was not so unusual for Reagan to "take swipes at the Soviet Union." What occasioned this particular UPI report was that, as the article began, "President Reagan used a lot of verbiage to suggest a barnyard term in his speech Monday to the American Bar Assn." The article went on to specify Reagan's decorous "verbiage":

> Now, ladies and gentlemen of the American bar, there is a non-Soviet word for that kind of talk, an extremely useful, time-tested, original American word, one with deep roots in our rich agricultural and farming tradition.

Reagan's sort of creative phraseology—call it an extended euphemism—was one way of teasing profanity into the public domain: a sort of dance of the seven veils.

It was more elegant, in fact, than the locution that has largely replaced it, namely, the signaling use of the first letter of an unspeakable term, leavened with a suffix. The letter positively identifies the profanity, even if somewhat more daintily than the moment when the 1960s were young, when Lenny Bruce described the prosecutor at his Chicago obscenity trial as having said: "I don't think I have to tell you the term, I think that you recall it . . . as a word that started with a 'F' and ended with a 'K' and sounded like 'truck.'"[11] Shortly after *M*A*S*H* and *Myra Breckinridge* broke the Hollywood barrier, use of "fuck" and its variants soared.[12]

Today, in fact, the single initial letter, as in "the F-word," suffices to indicate the obscenity that is being held just offstage. The suffix then distances the speaker from the unspeakable word itself, and at the same time indicates that the speaker knows that it is considered unspeakable. At one time in the 1980s, liberals started speaking of "the L-word" to declare, half-proudly, that they knew well that liberalism had become the political position that no longer dared speak its name. Such euphemistic though tantalizing locutions, half-evasive, half-teasing—the N-word, the L-word (this time for "lesbian," not "liberal"), the F-bomb, and many others—arose, stylized, delicately indelicate dances of the single veil. There is also the conversion of the letter into the verb, as in *effing,* and the euphemism *four-letter word,* both in use in the 1930s.[13] There is also, of course, the time-tested method of indicating the accursed word through the conspicuous use of asterisks, which gestures toward the revelation of everything via the teasing revelation of something: f***, s**t, a**hole.

Again, it was the very spread of profanity—a phenomenon of the 1960s—that gave rise to the half-revealing euphemism, the one-letter titillation, which became so common as to rise to the level of commonplace itself. Just so, the euphemism "F-bomb" emerged in the late 1980s to make light of the word "fuck" and its derivatives and yet walk right up to the line of the inexpressible. The linguist Jesse Scheidlower has unearthed a 1988 example from *Newsday* of "us[ing] the F-bomb."[14] But the earliest instance of "*dropping* the F-bomb" that comes up in my Lexis-Nexis search occurs in 1993. Only five references in toto occur in American newspapers before 1996— three of them, interestingly enough, attributed to ball players. But the term crops up more regularly in subsequent years.

Such signaling is how our culture has its profanity (or obscenity) and eats it. In a society of rigid censorship, the way to purge discourse is to purge it, period. Certain words will never be used. They will be snipped off the videotape, or bleeped, or, in print, x'd out. Since we do not live in an age of absolute censorship—what we live in is more the opposite, since, to use Rochelle Gurstein's phrase, reticence has long since been repealed—the alternative to outright profanity or pornography is a dance of indirection.

The more common the polluting terms in everyday discourse, the more respectable culture needs recourse to the knowing reference. Thus the prevalence of the not-quite-reference, which permits intermediate cultural figures— those who wish to be conversant with hipness, if not hip themselves, and yet reticent enough to be respectable—to remain in touch with the vox pop without abject surrender. We do not have a culture of repression, nor do we have a culture of openness. Rather, we have a culture of knowingness and snickering—of not-quite-oblique references, euphemisms, strip-teases, veil-dances—punctuated by occasional scandals of scurrility. Knowingness, in other words, arose as public profanity spread.

So did "civility." The culture became preoccupied with civility as it observed ever more frequent transgressions. Geoffrey Nunberg has crunched the numbers for appearances of the words "civility" and "incivility" in *New York Times* articles and editorials during the decades beginning with the 1940s, and has kindly shared his results with me:

	NYT Articles	NYT Editorials
1940s	44	0
1950s	59	0
1960s	179	16
1970s	473	25
1980	845	60
1990s	1581	137

In 1969 [he writes] *civility* and *incivility* appeared in more *Times* editorials than they had in the previous half-century, all of them dealing with campus turbulence.

In a year of major antiwar uprisings, campus turbulence was the most dramatic outward sign of a crisis that would be variously described in the years to come but always revolved around the perception that public life was being damaged by a breakdown in moral restraints. The campaign for civility was rooted in breaches:

Civility and *incivility* [as Nunberg puts it] are the words you reach for when you want to suggest that the behavior you're concerned about isn't simply a breach of manners but a threat to the health of the civil sphere. In subsequent years the *Times* extended the words to cover both inner-city riots and cross-burnings and the everyday courtesies expected between people waiting in line for movies. By the Clinton years, the words were fifteen times as frequent in the press as they had been during Eisenhower's presidency; in 2004, one dictionary web site picked *incivility* as word of the year, ahead of *blogosphere, flip-flop,* and Red States/Blue States.[15]

To stand a chance of reinstating linguistic rectitude, it was no longer enough to appeal to good manners. It was necessary to invoke a crisis in the moral order.

WHEN PRIVATE GOES PUBLIC

Technological enhancement may send hitherto private speech blasting into public, inadvertently leading to eruptions of at least mildly scandalous language. In 2010, for example, a sensitive microphone picked up the voice of Vice President Joseph Biden whispering in President Barack Obama's ear that the health care bill he was announcing was "a big fucking deal."[16] On the ABC daytime talk show *The View*—a women-for-women show—Biden declared that he was only grateful that his mother hadn't been around to hear him.

In this instance, Biden used "fucking" in its sense as a commonplace adjective signaling intensification. There was nothing either sexual or aggressive about it. But an earlier vice-presidential use of "fuck" had a blatantly different import. In 2004, while posing for pictures on the Senate floor, Vice President Dick Cheney got into an argument with Senator Patrick Leahy (D-VT) over Bush's judicial nominees and Cheney's relations with Halliburton. Said Cheney to Leahy: "Fuck yourself."

Cheney never regretted his outburst. Six years later, Dennis Miller, a right-wing radio host, said to Cheney: "I love that move. One of my favorite stories—muttering that." Cheney responded that a lot of people had liked his comment: "That's sort of the best thing I ever did."[17]

In an earlier instance, yet another private chat of presidential and vice-presidential candidates and officials brought out a male-bonding ritual involving the F-word. In 2000, on stage before a Republican Labor Day rally in Illinois, candidate George W. Bush pointed to a *New York Times* reporter covering them and said to candidate Dick Cheney, "There's Adam Clymer, major league asshole from the *New York Times*." Replied Cheney: "Oh yeah, he is, big time."[18] The microphone did the rest. It is highly likely, given right-wing views of the *New York Times,* that the Bush–Cheney ticket benefited from this takedown.

THE UNCIVIL AND THE INCENDIARY

Straightforward incivility—"lack of civility or courtesy; rudeness," in the not altogether helpful words of the *American Heritage Dictionary of the English Language*[19] —is deprecation. It aims to sting. It lowers, or aims to lower, the social standing of its target. Whatever its particular content, the speaker of an uncivil statement declares that the object of the statement is contemptible, unworthy of respect. But a statement about this person's moral unworth is not, by itself, a statement about what ought to be done with, or to, the person, aside, of course, from lowering him or her in the collective estimation.

However, the incivility that has surged up in the United States since the 1980s deserves to be distinguished from rudeness. The tone of attack goes beyond *ad hominem*. It discredits the target not simply on the ground that she is wrong, or even wildly, terribly wrong, but because there is something essential about her that makes her disgusting, loathsome, beyond the pale. Here are some utterances from Rush Limbaugh:

- If Nancy Pelosi "wants fewer births, I have the way to do this and it won't require any contraception: You simply put pictures of Nancy Pelosi . . . in every cheap motel room. . . . That will keep birthrates down because that picture will keep a lot of things down."[20]
- Hillary Clinton couldn't get into the Marines because "they didn't have uniforms or boots big enough to fit that butt and those ankles."[21]
- Mary Landrieu (D-LA) "may be the most expensive prostitute in the history of prostitution."[22]
- "[W]e all know that Barney [Frank] patrols Uranus."[23]
- "Adolf Hitler, like Barack Obama, also ruled by dictate."[24]
- "If Barack Obama were Caucasian, they would have taken this guy out on the basis of pure ignorance long ago." (May 14, 2008)[25]

On the leftward side of the spectrum, abusive loathing is not unknown, either. NBC's Keith Olbermann has used Nazi analogies,[26] and spoken of a rival on the right, Michelle Malkin, as guilty of "mindless, morally bankrupt, knee-jerk, fascistic hatred—without which Michelle Malkin would just be a big mashed-up bag of meat with lipstick on it."[27] A less celebrated liberal radio host, Mike Malloy, has said of the right-wing online aggregator Matt Drudge thus: "Drudge? Aw, Drudge, somebody ought to wrap a strong Republican entrail around his neck and hoist him up about six feet in the air and watch him bounce."[28] But liberal abusiveness is outdistanced, in both scale and intensity, by that of the right.

Piggybacking on the commercial success of Rush Limbaugh have been such talk radio and Fox News stars of recent years as Bill O'Reilly, Sean Hannity, and Glenn Beck. Here, for example, is Beck, who specializes in drawing diagrams displaying what he calls "ties" among liberal groups, not excluding affinities between liberals and Nazis:

- "Al Gore's not going to be rounding up Jews and exterminating them. It is the same tactic, however. The goal is different. The goal is globalization . . . And you must silence all dissenting voices. That's what Hitler did. That's what Al Gore, the U.N., and everybody on the global warming bandwagon [are doing]."[29]

But Beck is remarkable for the alacrity with which he regularly zooms beyond insult and conspiracy theory to hopes for actual or symbolic violence:

- Obama and Democrats generally are vampires "going after the blood of our businesses."
- It would be advisable to "put poison" in Nancy Pelosi's wine.
- "I'm thinking about killing Michael Moore, and I'm wondering if I could kill him myself, or if I would need to hire somebody to do it. . . . No, I think I could. I think he could be looking me in the eye, you know, and I could just be choking the life out."[30]

Beck's rhetoric predicts violence or describes a war that has already been declared, as with such lines as: "The clock is ticking . . . . The war is just beginning . . . . The other side is attacking . . . . Drive a stake through the heart of the bloodsuckers . . . . They are taking you to a place to be slaughtered . . . . They are putting a gun to America's head." Among the ears on which his venomous, incendiary language fell was an unemployed carpenter named Byron Williams. In July 2010, according to the *Washington Post* columnist Dana Milbank,

> When California Highway Patrol officers stopped him on an interstate in Oakland for driving erratically, Byron Williams, wearing body armor, fired at police with a 9mm handgun, a shotgun and a .308-caliber rifle with armor-piercing bullets, Oakland police say. Shot and captured after injuring two officers, Williams, on parole for bank robbery, told investigators that he wanted "to start a revolution" by "killing people of importance at the Tides Foundation and the ACLU," according to a police affidavit. His mother, Janice, told the San Francisco Chronicle that her son had been watching television news and was upset by "the way Congress was railroading through all these left-wing agenda items."

Milbank asks:

> But what television news show could have directed the troubled man's ire toward the obscure Tides Foundation, which sounds as if it's dedicated to oceanography, or perhaps laundry detergent, but which is in fact a nonprofit that claims to support "sustainability, better education, solutions to the AIDS epidemic and human rights"?

A week after the incident, Beck told his radio audience that his trademark blackboard diagrams were inspired, in fact, by his effort to "explain Tides."

> Beck accuses Tides [Milbank continues] of seeking to seize power and destroy capitalism, and he suggests that a full range of his enemies on the left all have "ties to the Tides Center." On [his radio broadcast], he savored the fact that "no one knew what Tides was until the blackboard." For good measure, Beck went after Tides again on Fox that night. And Tuesday night, Wednesday night and Thursday night. That's on top of 29 other mentions of Tides on Beck's Fox show over the past 18 months (two in the week before the shootout) according to a tally by the liberal press watchdog Media Matters. Other than two mentions of Tides on the show of Beck's Fox colleague Sean Hannity, Media Matters said it was unable to find any other mention of Tides on any news broadcast by any network over that same period. Beck declined comment.[31]

More than one impressionable, unbalanced mind might well conclude from Beck's riffs that an armed attack on the Tides Foundation would be a justifiable, indeed excellent way "to start a revolution." Only one of his listeners, so far as we know, was armed, ready, and dangerous. I am not making the claim that Beck bears legal responsibility for Williams' armed mission. I am asserting that we live in a climate in which right-wing broadcasters who view the left (generously defined) as demonic hold the attention of immense audiences while hovering at, or over, the edge of incitement.

It does seem to have been during the presidency of Barack Obama that the tone of public discourse, as Geoffrey Nunberg writes, "started to go completely off the rails." The emblematic moment came when South Carolina's Republican congressman interrupted President Obama's speech on health care by calling out, "You lie!" As Nunberg points out, "The conduct was deemed unbecoming by his own party's leadership—"totally disrespectful," said John McCain."[32]

Here are two other samples of political speech during the Obama presidency: On August 15, 2011, campaigning in Iowa, Texas governor Rick Perry said of Federal Reserve Chairman Ben Bernanke:

> If this guy prints more money between now and the election, I don't know what y'all would do to him in Iowa, but we—we would treat him pretty ugly down in Texas. Printing more money to play politics at this particular time in American history is almost treacherous—or treasonous, in my opinion.[33]

And on May 16, 2008, the Republican former Arkansas Governor Mike Huckabee, having been defeated for the Republican nomination, was in the midst of a speech to the annual meeting of the National Rifle Association when he heard a sudden noise offstage. He ad-libbed: "That was Barack Obama, he just tripped off a chair, he's getting ready to speak." The audience laughed. Huckabee went on: "Somebody aimed a gun at him and he dove for the floor."[34]

But casual, apparently unguarded references to the possibility, or desirability, of physical harm to the president were not unknown during Bill Clinton's presidency either. Consider that, on November 23, 1994, Senator Jesse Helms, the North Carolina Republican, was quoted in the *Raleigh News and Observer* as saying that President Bill Clinton was so unpopular on military bases in North Carolina that: "Mr. Clinton better watch out if he comes down here. He'd better have a bodyguard."

THE DISCOURSE OF EXTENUATION AND APOLOGY

In the wake of the uproar triggered by his statement, Senator Helms confessed to having made "a mistake"—a constructively ambiguous word which, of course, might be used synonymously with "slip of the tongue," "gaffe," "breach of decorum," "error," and one way or the other signals regret without taking on any moral opprobrium. When several senators criticized Helms, he "issued a statement" calling this "an offhand remark" and "a mistake . . . which I will not repeat." An AP dispatch quoted Republican Sen. Bob Dole as saying: "I didn't see the entire statement. My view is that the president of the United States is welcome to come to any state . . . . I think pretty much that Jesse must have said most of this probably in jest."[35] "Most of this." "Probably."

To some of the late Senator's followers, however, Helms' statement remains, if not mainly a jest, in any event a "fiction." The website of the Jesse Helms Center, the official repository of the senator's papers, contrasts what they regard as this fiction with a "truth" it describes as follows:

> When Senator Jesse Helms talked with a reporter from the *Raleigh News and Observer* and mentioned Bill Clinton's unpopularity on military bases in the state, he illustrated his point with an anecdote about a Southern sheriff who had just been defeated in an election. 'He had this big fella with him, about 6 foot 7 and 270 pounds,' said Helms. 'Somebody asked, 'Who's that?' The sheriff answered. 'Any body who can't get more votes than I did better have a bodyguard.' Helms then added: 'Mr. Clinton better watch out if he comes down here. He better have a bodyguard.' The *News and Observer* ran just the Clinton reference without the entire joke that preceded it, and the Associated Press picked up the story. Soon the media were reporting that the Secret Service was investigating Helms' comments, and the editorial page of the *New York Times* called for Helms to step aside as chairman of the Senate Foreign Relations Committee.[36]

Whether the joke boosts the senator's remark out of the realm of incivility and promotes it to civil speech is another matter. In my view, it does not. To the contrary: "Only kidding" is an all-purpose self-justification that attempts to make the opponent look like a killjoy, a sourpuss with no sense of humor. Extenuation might be termed a moral balancing act that distracts from the act, or contextualizes it, with reasons. The extenuator admits a "mistake" and proceeds in the next breath to balance it against a depredation committed by the opponent. The extenuator has not quite seized back the moral high ground, but scrambles to maintain herself on the opponent's level.

As Nunberg points out about Rep. Joe Wilson's "You lie" outburst, Wilson initially apologized and said he had let his emotions get the better of him. But radio hosts celebrated his "guts" and "backbone" and said he had no need to apologize for simply articulating what millions of Americans were saying. Supporters flooded Wilson with campaign contributions, and a bit more alarmingly, a South Carolina gun dealer offered a limited edition component for the AR-15 with "You Lie" etched on the stock.[37]

As for Mike Huckabee's glancing reference to someone aiming a gun at Barack Obama, Huckabee released a statement saying: "During my speech at the N.R.A., a loud noise backstage, that sounded like a chair falling, distracted the crowd and interrupted my speech. I made an off hand remark that was in no way intended to offend or disparage Sen. Obama. I apologize that my comments were offensive. That was never my intention."[38] But no one could have mistaken his remark about "someone aiming a gun" at him as "intended to offend or disparage" Obama—so perhaps, in Huckabee's mental universe, Huckabee meant that "diving under a chair" would be a sign that Obama *deserved* disparagement, presumably as a coward. The point is that the thought of somebody trying to assassinate Obama came easily to Huckabee's mind. Obama, in his mind, was courting assassination. Not exactly deserving it, but courting it. As I was finishing this chapter, it was reported that the president of the College Republicans at the University of Texas, Austin, posted a message on Twitter that the idea of assassinating President Barack Obama was "tempting." It read, in toto: "Y'all as tempting as it may be, don't shoot Obama. We need him to go down in history as the WORST president we've EVER had! #2012." (She later apologized.)[39]

THE WORSE OLD DAYS

Interestingly, the most famous episode of uncivil conduct short of assassination in American political history ended without any retraction or apology at all. In 1856, the Republican Charles Sumner of Massachusetts took to the Senate floor to denounce a number of pro-slavery senators. One of these was Andrew Butler of South Carolina, who, Sumner said, "has chosen a mistress to whom he has made his vows, and who, though ugly to others, is always lovely to him; though polluted in the sight of the world, is chaste in his sight. I mean the harlot, Slavery." Sumner did not skimp at invective ("The senator touches nothing which he does not disfigure") or mockery ("With incoherent phrases discharged the loose expectoration of his speech"). He also declared Stephen Douglas of Illinois "a noisome, squat, and nameless animal."

On May 22, 1856, Rep. Preston Brooks (D-SC) entered the Senate chamber carrying a cane and accompanied by two colleagues from the House, one of them brandishing a pistol. He beat Sumner repeatedly until the cane broke. Sumner took three years to recover.

After the attack, South Carolinians honored Brooks by sending him dozens of new canes. One of them—a gift of the University of Virginia's Jefferson Literary and Debating Society—was gold-headed. The *Richmond Enquirer* called Brooks' attack "good in conception, better in execution, and best of all in consequences," adding: "These vulgar abolitionists in the Senate must be lashed into submission." Speaking to the House two months later, Brooks admitted no fault. In a flourish of legalism, he declared that "if I had committed a breach of privilege, it was the privilege of the Senate, and not of this House, which was violated," and that punishment by the House would constitute "a terrible and insufferable despotism." Then he resigned.[40]

Preston Brooks, Jesse Helms, Mike Huckabee, Joe Wilson, Rick Perry—is it an accident that these gentlemen all hail from the part of America that once seceded to preserve the cruel and casually violent system of slavery? Limbaugh, for his part, comes from southeast Missouri, and Beck from rural

Washington State—both areas where gunplay is routinely considered an emblem of manhood and "the government"—the federal government—has long been viewed as a plague upon freedom, which is held to be synonymous with states' rights. Does it surprise anyone that the incendiary remark thrives in regions where the ideal of unobstructed manhood entails the cutting down of enemies who, by virtue of their dangerous ideas and more, their dangerous and defiling persons, deserve no better?

Running for governor of Mississippi in 1963, Paul Johnson declared that "NAACP" stood for "Niggers, alligators, apes, coons, and possums." By his standard, we would have to say that contemporary politicians are civil.

Endnotes

1. This article benefits from my reading of a not-yet-published, deeply researched manuscript by the linguist Geoffrey Nunberg, Professor in the School of Information at the University of California, Berkeley. Professor Nunberg also commented helpfully on an earlier draft of mine. Any oversimplifications or distortions of his arguments are my own.

2. A brief introduction to the centrality of the public/private distinction, as rooted in Hannah Arendt's *The Human Condition,* can be found in Rochelle Gurstein's *The Repeal of Reticence: A History of America's Cultural and Legal Struggles over Free Speech, Obscenity, Sexual Liberation, and Modern Art* (New York: Hill and Wang, 1996), pp. 9–19.

3. Gurstein, *Repeal of Reticence*, p. 305. On the legal changes of the 1960s, see pp. 281–287.

4. Gurstein, *Repeal of Reticence,* chap. 11.

5. Peter Appelbome, "Drilling Debate in Cooperstown Turns Personal," Accessed at http://www.nytimes.com/2011/10/30/nyregion/in-cooperstowns-fight-over-gas-drilling-civility-is-fading.html?ref=todayspaper.

6. Jesse Scheidlower, ed., *The F Word,* 2nd edition (New York: Random House, 1999), p. xxi.

7. Scheidlower, p. xxiv.

8. Quoted in Scheidlower, p. xxv.

9. Donoghue, "Kicking the Air," *New York Review of Books,* June 8, 1995.

10. Accessed at http://articles.latimes.com/1985-07-09/news/mn-8122_1_president-reagan.

11. Scheidlower, *The F Word,* pp. xxii–xxiii.

12. Scheidlower, *The F Word,* p. xxxvi.

13. Scheidlower, *The F Word,* p. xxxvi.

14. Scheidlower, *The F Word,* p. TK.

15. Nunberg, unpublished ms., p. 19.

16. Accessed at http://www.huffingtonpost.com/2010/03/23/a-big-fucking-deal-bidens_n_509927.htm.

17. Accessed at http://www.huffingtonpost.com/2010/04/23/dick-cheney-patrick-leahy-fuck-yourself_n_549100.html.

18. Jake Tapper, "A 'major league asshole,'" Salon.com, September 4, 2000, Accessed at http://www.salon.com/2000/09/04/cuss_word.

19. Accessed at http://www.thefreedictionary.com/incivility.

20. Accessed at http://mediamatters.org/mmtv/200901260014.
21. Accessed at http://mediamatters.org/mmtv/200909230026.
22. Accessed at http://mediamatters.org/mmtv/200911230018.
23. Accessed at http://mediamatters.org/mmtv/200908190034.
24. Accessed at http://mediamatters.org/mmtv/200908060021.
25. Accessed at http://mediamatters.org/research/200805150008.
26. Accessed at http://www.notablequotables.org/mrc/2006/BestofNQ/ New8/2006-09-25-MSNBCOlbermann.wmv. Accessed November 17, 2011.
27. Accessed at http://mrc-static.s3.amazonaws.com/Newsbusters/static/2009/12/ 2009-10-13-MSNBCOlbermann.mp3.
28. Accessed at http://www.mrc.org/specialreports/radioclips/2007-12-19-Malloy. mp3.
29. "The Glenn Beck Program," May 1, 2007.
30. "The Glenn Beck Program," May 17, 2005.
31. Dana Milbank, "Glenn Beck and the Oakland shooter," *Washington Post,* August 1, 2010, p. 17, Accessed at http://www.washingtonpost.com/wp-dyn/ content/article/2010/07/30/AR2010073003254.html.
32. Nunberg, "Introduction: Cool to Be Cruel," unpublished ms., p. 3.
33. Accessed at http://abcnews.go.com/blogs/politics/2011/08/rick-perry-on-ben-bernanke-it-would-be-almost-treasonous-to-print-more-money-between-now-and-the-ele/.
34. Accessed at http://politicalticker.blogs.cnn.com/2008/05/16/huckabee-jokes-about-obama-ducking-a-gunman/.
35. Accessed at http://www.newspaperarchive.com/SiteMap/FreePdfPreview. aspx?img=104679606.
36. Accessed at http://www.jessehelmscenter.org/jessehelms/fictionortruth. asp#fic7.
37. Nunberg, "Introduction: Cool to Be Cruel," unpublished ms., pp. 3–4.
38. Accessed at http://politicalticker.blogs.cnn.com/2008/05/16/huckabee-jokes-about-obama-ducking-a-gunman.
39. Accessed at http://www.huffingtonpost.com/2011/11/16/obama-assassination-lauren-pierce_n_1098280.html.
40. Quoted in James M. McPherson, *Battle Cry of Freedom: The Civil War Era* (New York: Oxford University Press, 1988), p. 151.

6

Television and Uncivil Political Discourse

Diana C. Mutz

*Words ought to be a little wild, for they are the
assaults of thought on the unthinking.*

JOHN MAYNARD KEYNES[1]

Assessments of the tone of contemporary politics often focus on the words used by politicians, members of the media, and average citizens. From this vantage, things cannot be worse than in the past. Goodness, the things that were said about candidates and elected officials in the nineteenth century! Comparison of this sort can be tricky, however, because the *way* messages are transmitted has changed. Diana Mutz argues that images on television and the Internet violate face-to-face social norms for disagreement. These acts draw greater attention, which means that uncivil conflicts are more likely to be diffused through the population.

Is politics these days really nastier than it used to be? For many casual observers, the answer to this question is obvious. Just turn on the television and watch a few political talk shows, and you have your answer. The participants in televised political discourse regularly link one another to the Nazi party and accuse one another of being un-American, anti-family, and all around evil, demonic beings. But as Dave Barry posed this question,

> Do we truly believe that ALL red-state residents are ignorant racist fascist knuckle-dragging NASCAR-obsessed cousin-marrying

road-kill-eating tobacco-juice-dribbling gun-fondling religious fanatic rednecks; or that ALL blue-state residents are godless unpatriotic pierced-nose Volvo-driving France-loving left-wing Communist latte-sucking tofu-chomping holistic-wacko neurotic vegan weenie perverts?"[2]

I hope not, but one could understandably get this impression from watching political television in the United States these days.

Is political discourse really any meaner and nastier than it used to be? As discussed in the introduction to this volume, many certainly sense this to be true. As Judith Rodin, now president of the Rockefeller Foundation, suggests,

> Across America and increasingly around the world, from campuses to the halls of Congress, to talk radio and network TV, social and political life seem dominated today by incivility, . . . an unwillingness to compromise and an intolerance for opposition. . . . No one seems to question the premise that political debate has become too extreme, too confrontational, too coarse.[3]

But how can we be sure that politicians conversed any differently 100 years ago? In a direct sense, this is not something we can know. We do, however, know that even the much revered founding fathers called one another adulterers, thieves, and liars, and that they sometimes engaged in violence over political differences of opinion. So mudslinging is hardly a recent invention.

There are written records of political discourse from the past, to be sure, but importantly, there is no record of how they would have spoken to one another on television, because the medium did not yet exist. There is good reason to believe that politicians' discourse would have been different on camera and off, just as people behave differently when they are among a small number of friends as opposed to in front of an audience.[4]

To summarize, the argument I make in this chapter is that television has changed the way we experience political discourse while simultaneously changing the discourse itself. We can't say with certainty whether the verbal behavior of politicians and their minions is any more coarse than it used to be. But we can be fairly certain that the way the American public *experiences* this discourse is far different from even how our grandparents and great-grandparents experienced it. In the remainder of the chapter, I first describe research that explains how we experience the images of politicians on television. Second, I discuss how changes in the media industry have altered the demands of political television in ways that encourage still more incivility.

EXPERIENCING PEOPLE ON TELEVISION

There are many popular videos on YouTube that show people's dogs and cats excitedly watching television. What's funny about these videos is that the dogs bark and attempt to chase images of other dogs on the television screen, and the cats salivate and bat at the birds, squirrels, and other prey flitting about the screen. Sometimes they even look behind the television to try and catch the other animal, or knock the television over altogether.[5]

Television, as the old (analog) adage goes, is just a bunch of electrons. As adults, we all know that the people and other animals shown on the screen are not actually in our living rooms. And so we smugly think we're a whole lot smarter than dogs and cats. But research tells us we should not be quite so quick to claim superiority over our furry friends. In fact, in many ways, the human brain responds to representational images of other people on the screen just as it would if real people were physically present in our environment.[6] Cognitively, we know they aren't really there, but we cannot help our own hardwiring, and thus we respond socially to images of other people, particularly when it looks as if they walk, talk, and move just like the people we encounter in real life.

So what do funny animal videos have to do with the way we experience political discourse in a video age? As it turns out, a great deal. Imagine for the moment that we know for certain that politicians and their henchmen and henchwomen today are no more nasty and uncivil than they ever were. I suggest this because the way we now experience that same discourse on television generates the *impression* of far more incivility. When politicians in the pre-television era yelled and screamed at one another or called each other names, there were no television or cell phone video cameras there to cover it. At best, we might have heard about it on the radio or read about such an incident in the newspaper. But because neither newspapers nor radio simulate the impression of real people in our actual environment to the same extent that television does, these exposures would be unlikely to produce the same kinds of visceral reactions that are experienced by viewers of uncivil discourse on television.

At the root of this situation is the fact that most human beings prefer social harmony to conflict, albeit to varying degrees. So although at one level we may know that politics is supposed to involve disagreement and competition among choices, we would prefer that everyone just agreed on things (particularly if they agree with us!). Conflict can be messy and unpleasant, and compromises can disappoint many. Thus when we see or hear about conflict, we are likely to think something is wrong with the system rather than that things are working as they should.

This issue is particularly problematic when it comes to public impressions of Congress. The role of Congress is, after all, to debate controversial issues of the day. These deliberations are open to the public and often televised, though few people are likely to see them except when things get heated and they move from C-SPAN to more widely viewed channels. As some congressional scholars have noted, "When its members disagree, they do so as visibly as they can, seeking publicity for themselves and to discredit their rivals and opponents. As proposals are shaped in Congress, every disagreement is magnified and broadcast, so that when the bargaining and amending are done, the finished product appears not as a coherent whole but as a patchwork of compromises, each of which was controversial and to some extent alienating."[7] Thus, approval of Congress is a function of conflict within Congress as well as the media coverage that the conflict receives. Likewise, when members of the two political parties pull together into a cohesive unit to do battle with one another in Congress, support for Congress as an institution declines.[8] Apparently we do not like to watch them fight, even though this is their constitutionally charged duty.

Watching quarrelsome members of Congress on television is in many ways no different from witnessing any other public fight. As anyone who has ever been at a contentious dinner party knows, conflict can be uncomfortable, even when you are not personally involved in the fight. When the couple across the table starts arguing, it makes most of us tense and uncomfortable even though we are mere voyeurs with nothing to lose and no direct involvement. Research tells us that when conflict is going on around us, our level of tension and emotional arousal automatically increase, theoretically preparing us for fight or flight. Physiologically, emotional arousal means that our hearts pump faster, our level of attentiveness to our environment is enhanced, and we are generally "on alert." What's bizarre is that even though the need for fight or flight is highly unlikely to come to pass there at the dinner table, we prepare for the possibility nonetheless. Evolutionary psychologists suggest that this arousal reaction is a remnant from times when these reactions were highly adaptive; we needed them either to get away from a predator or to be pumped up enough to prepare to duke it out.

This reaction starts to seem even sillier when it comes to televised politics. Politics is, after all, supposed to involve conflicts of ideas about the policies that would best serve the country. Our system of gaining office is purposely set up as a competitive one, so all of the analogies between politics and sports contests are well deserved. Campaigning for office is a contest with winners and losers, and pushing legislation through Congress likewise involves confrontation and conflict. Some extent of conflict is central to democracy.

And even though politics is, for most citizens, a spectator sport, we can nonetheless get revved up, as if ready to do battle, or run for our lives, when we see politicians arguing with one another on television. In a series of my own experiments, I have hooked people up to electrodes that tap their level of emotional arousal while they watch politicians on television, and what I find is that even if they watch the same politicians delivering identical speeches, arousal levels are much higher when the politicians engage one another in a contentious, *uncivil* fashion.[9] So even though we are just watching and it is pretty obvious that no one will come to blows, more intense conflict still causes greater arousal on the part of the passive viewer, just as it does in the real world. There can be conflict without incivility, but conflict that is heated and emotional is even more likely to produce high levels of arousal.

When we witness conflicts in the environment around us, our reaction is naturally conditioned by how close to us the threatening object is. It matters whether the conflict is in the same room, next door, across town, or in another country. A conflict going down across town doesn't necessitate that same level of immediate attention and arousal as one in the same room. People on television can elicit strong reactions from viewers, but some forms of televised faces are particularly likely to do so. In the experiments, not only did the televised uncivil version of the conflict significantly increase viewers' levels of arousal over the televised civil one but also the camera perspective from which viewers witnessed the conflict mattered.[10] Likewise, distance matters on television, even if it is only the *perception of* distance that we have as viewers. Interestingly, when a human being on the TV screen appears to move toward the viewer, the viewer's brain reacts the same way it does when a real human comes closer—arousal goes up, and we pay attention to what appears to be "in our face." But if the person walking (or appearing to walk) toward us is acting in an uncivil or hostile manner, we are particularly likely to react! The impression of close physical proximity logically intensifies our reactions to incivility. Our brains consider incivility to be at its most threatening when it is coming at us, so this kind of television perspective tends to send our arousal levels through the roof. As shown in Figure 6.1, incivility is more arousing than civility, but camera perspective also has an obvious effect. Close-ups elicit systematically more arousal than the identical event shot from a medium camera perspective.

More importantly for purposes of my argument about television, *the appearance of close physical proximity*—which is simulated in our field of vision by larger TV screens or by the close-up camera perspective—intensifies

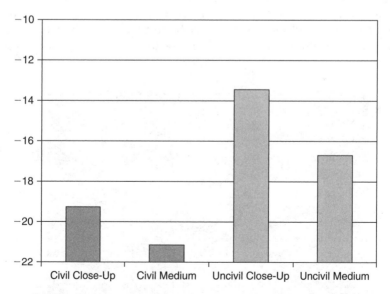

FIGURE 6.1 Emotional Arousal by Civility and Camera Perspective

Reprinted from D.C. Mutz, "Effects of 'In-Your-Face' Television Discourse on Perceptions of a Legitimate Opposition," *American Political Science Review 101*(4): 621–635, 2007.

viewers' reactions to incivility. In the experiment described above, even though people were viewing the same event, those who watched it from a close-up camera perspective experienced far more of the tension and discomfort than those who witnessed it through a more distant camera perspective.

This fact is important because not only has the use of close-ups increased over the years but also our televisions have become bigger. Larger screens have the same kind of effect as close-ups, creating the impression that people on the screen are physically closer to us. In the early days of television, cameras were large and heavy and had to stay in one place as a result. The perspective on the politician was highly static to the audience, screens were smaller on average, and the politician took up a much smaller portion of the TV screen than is common today. Because portable, handheld video cameras did not yet exist, camera footage from outside the studio was also much less common, and the evening news relied primarily on graphics or still photos. When living, breathing humans were shown speaking, it tended to be from a more distant camera perspective that incorporated the whole body of the speaker. Today the norm is a much tighter shot, often close up in the face of the person who is speaking, as illustrated in Image 6.1. On some political talk shows, insistence on the use of close-ups is so persistent that one never even sees where the speakers are in relation to one another. So the same politicians who may have been uncivil before now appear to be "in our faces" with their incivility on a regular basis. In-your-face incivility is especially tension producing, so it is not surprising that so many viewers say they do not like it.

At one point, I took my television-viewing cat on a visit to a friend's home after they had just purchased a huge big-screen TV. I had the idea that it would be very interesting to see how the cat reacted to a five-foot tall

Kevin Lamarque/Reuters/Landov

IMAGE 6.1   George Bush from an Extreme Close-up Camera Angle.

big-screen version of the squirrel from its favorite video. Needless to say, the mega-squirrel was this feline's worst nightmare; rather than chase the squirrel across the screen as usual, he immediately tore out of the room. Large size and close physical proximity are threatening when one's opponent is directly in one's face. Likewise, when people encounter a politician whom they dislike arguing from this kind of close-up camera perspective, arousal levels go up, and they tend to dislike him or her even more than they initially did.

Fortunately, it is highly unusual for humans in everyday life to experience as much incivility "in our faces" as we do when we watch political television. In everyday life, most people are polite to one another most of the time. If they disagree about politics, they do so politely, or they say nothing at all in order to preserve social harmony. But it is also culturally ingrained in us to put greater physical distance between ourselves and those with whom we disagree. "Backing off" is more than just a metaphorical expression. When conflict arises in most settings, without even thinking about it, we put more distance between ourselves and the person with whom we disagree. To move closer to someone with whom we are disagreeing would come across as very threatening. But television routinely violates the social norms that we are accustomed to from face-to-face discourse.

Imagine, for example, a left-wing Democrat experiencing George Bush from the now common close-up perspective shown in Image 6.1. To get this same visual perspective on George Bush in day-to-day life, one in which his visage fills your entire visual frame, you would practically need to be intimate with him. For a left-wing Democrat, this is not likely. And yet via television, that Democrat gets simulated intimacy with someone he undoubtedly hates. This is not "natural," in the sense that it would be unlikely to happen outside of a situation involving representational media. In the real world, people do not generally cuddle up with those with whom they have strong disagreements.

It is for this same reason that it was notable during the 2011 State of the Union speech that Republicans and Democrats were seated next to each other rather than on opposite sides of the aisle. Space conveys meaning, and by sitting next to one another, members of Congress were trying to signal to the American public a lack of animosity and a desire to set aside partisan bickering—at least for the moment.

In short, viewers react to television as an inherently social medium: It puts "people" in our social environments whom we react to in social ways, even though they are not really physically present, and it makes no real sense for us to do this. In many respects, this should not surprise us; we've all seen people in movie theatres pull back in their seats when watching a car appear to come at them, or a fist swing. These reactions make no sense because they are remnants of old brains in the context of high-fidelity representational media. Likewise, when politicians are shown in a manner that makes it seem as if they are up close and in our faces, we respond especially negatively if we do not like them.

Thus far, I have suggested that television brings politicians to our attention in a manner that violates two key social norms that are widely adhered to in face-to-face social contexts: civility and social distance. First, we see more violations of the norms of civility on political television than in real life. Speakers regularly interrupt and talk over one another, raise their voices, and fail to listen respectfully to each other. Second, when conflict and arguments heat up, rather than provide the appearance that the combatants are "backing off," today's TV cameras will tend to dolly in for a close-up of flaring nostrils, sweaty brows, and so forth. Rather than allow us to back away, the camera gives us the impression of being brought still closer to the combatants. Political television provides a very odd and unusual perspective indeed.

Does any of this matter to how we feel about politics and politicians? Some research suggests that it does. In experimental settings, people who view uncivil political programming come away with less trusting attitudes toward politics and politicians in general than they would have if they viewed nothing at all.[11] And in contrast, those who watch civil exchanges among politicians develop more trusting attitudes toward politicians. Apparently, when politicians on television do not violate social norms and act more like the rest of us, people find them more trustworthy. They also come away with generally more positive attitudes toward our system of government.

Television is a highly visual medium, which makes it unique among the various means we have of communicating political information. Print and radio have been around much longer, and they have also been accused of sensationalism in what they choose to emphasize, but I suspect that the effects described above are uniquely powerful in an era of audiovisual media. The effects that I have described do not occur as noticeably through other, non-audiovisual media that less closely approximate "being there." In the experiment described above, I had two actors film a talk show posing as congressional candidates, and they were each restricted so that they had to espouse exactly the same issue positions, make exactly the same political arguments against their opponent and so forth in two different versions of the program. In one version of the program, they stated their positions in a civil and polite manner, without interrupting or raising their voices. In the other, they rolled their eyes as they listened to their opponent, raised their voices while disagreeing, and interrupted one another in ways that violate face-to-face conversational norms in American culture.

Interestingly, when I took the audio portion of this broadcast and had people listen to it in the form of a radio broadcast, they demonstrated only very minor increases in arousal in the uncivil condition relative to the civil one. Those who read a verbatim account of the exchange in the newspaper found it downright soporific and demonstrated no differences in arousal whatsoever. The take-home lesson of these experiments is that regardless of whether politicians are any worse now than they ever were with respect to the civility of their discourse, it matters how the public experiences that discourse. By approximating the physical presence of others in conflict, the audiovisual nature of television makes us respond as if we were actually there. One hundred years ago, a similarly rude and uncivil exchange would be witnessed by very few people, and those reading about it in a newspaper or hearing it on the radio would not have the same reaction.

These readers and listeners rated the civil and uncivil versions as roughly the same in terms of civility because without the nuanced facial expressions, raised voices, and other audiovisual cues, they could not distinguish one version as more or less civil than the other. Unlike print, television is extremely good at conveying the emotional intensity of a conflict, and faces—a staple of political programs that involve talking heads—are particularly good at conveying emotion on television. This is not to say that print cannot be emotionally charged—anyone who has read a good book knows otherwise. But all else being equal, a written account of the same conflict will generally not elicit the same degree of arousal as a televised one.

If everyone hates incivility and it promotes more negative attitudes toward the political system, one has to wonder why political television looks the way it does. I turn next to explaining why television norms have evolved in this direction. If television's perspective on politicians routinely violates what our unenlightened brains are accustomed to and makes us react in illogical ways to representational images, why do television producers insist on doing that?

THE DEMANDS OF POLITICAL TELEVISION

As many of you have undoubtedly noticed, political television programs do not attract Super Bowl-sized audiences, nor do they even approximate *American Idol*. A small subset of Americans enjoys political television a great deal, but this is a distinct minority. Political programming is generally not a big money maker in the television business. Moreover, competition for television audiences has intensified in recent years as a result of the proliferation of program options on cable as well as pay-per-view services. In today's media environment, those who are not interested in politics always have somewhere else to go to be entertained. There are exciting dramas, feature-length movies, and sports on TV 24 hours a day. With more options than ever before, how are political programs to compete for the already sparse political audience?

For producers of political television, one obvious way to compete is to liven things up a bit. There is, after all, a reason that sex and violence sell on television. Even if one is uncomfortable viewing such content, it is difficult to look away. High-arousal content draws viewers. In the experiments discussed above, both incivility and close-up camera perspectives increased viewers' levels of arousal in response to what was otherwise identical content.

For many readers, increased competition may seem like a poor explanation for the existence of so much uncivil discourse on television. After all, people routinely say that they hate this senseless bickering, that it is painful to watch and, in the words of Jon Stewart, that it is "hurting America."

I believe that most of these statements are accurate reflections of how people actually feel. Nonetheless, people watch. The best analogy to this phenomenon is the "rubbernecking" that takes place in highway traffic after automobile accidents. It isn't that humans are inherently sick creatures, enjoying the sight of dead bodies by the side of the road; they know that accidents are unfortunate and sometimes tragic events. But they still look. Evolutionary psychology tells us that we look because it is important information for purposes of our own survival. So *to look* does not necessarily mean the same thing as *to like* or approve of what you see.

Incivility is to political television as violence is to television drama. Many complain about violence on television, but ratings tell us that they watch it a great deal. And just as we are hardwired to pay attention to violence as a means of protecting ourselves, we are also more likely to pay attention to uncivil, rather than civil, discourse as well. Evolutionary psychologists suggest that in the long run, it has simply been more important for human survival to pay attention to negative threats in our environments (the lion might eat us!) than to positive attractions (the berries on that tree look mighty tasty!). So negative events are appropriately more attention grabbing than positive ones. After all, if we miss the chance to eat those berries, it would be too bad, but not fatal. If we overlook the lion, on the other hand, the consequences are more dire. This means that even if most political discourse were civil, we would still pay more attention to the uncivil discourse.

As illustrated in the cartoon in Image 6.2, if people really hated incivility in political media, we could have a political equivalent of the "V-chip" (the technology used in television sets to automatically block children from viewing violent programs). But if the experience of the V-chip is any

IMAGE 6.2   Incivility Is to Politics as Violence Is to Television Drama

indication, few people would use it. We may *say* that violence and incivility are bad things and that we generally disapprove, but that doesn't mean we won't watch them on television.

Likewise, in the research described above, after people were exposed to either the civil or uncivil version of the talk show in my experiments, they were asked at the end of the study how likely they would be to watch this program again at home on their own. Interestingly, although people in the uncivil condition clearly noticed that the candidates were more rude, nasty, and impolite, they were also far more likely to say they would watch the program again than were people in the civil condition. So even though uncivil behavior may seem distasteful, we are drawn to it nonetheless.

Incivility is also entertaining to watch. Some might say that it is inappropriate from the start to expect to be "entertained" by political media, but such is the reality of media consumption. Trying to guilt people into watching boring and polite exchanges of political viewpoints is not likely to be successful. In an age of media plenty, if it isn't entertaining, people will find something better to do with their time. As Bill O'Reilly responded when criticized about the lack of civil political dialogue on his show, "If you want civility, watch PBS . . . "[12]

Of course, even if we didn't have programs like *Hardball*, a small subset of the public would watch political TV regardless of what it is like. They genuinely enjoy politics and will become well informed about candidates and the issues of the day in any format. But for the much larger majority of Americans, politics grabs their attention only occasionally and intermittently. In the old days, when news was limited largely to three simultaneous network news broadcasts (ABC, CBS, and NBC), more people watched the news even though there was much less of it available on the air. If one watched at a certain time of day, news was all that was on. Similarly, when a presidential debate aired, it was on every channel, not just one. Today's media environment, with its huge range of choices, makes it much easier for the casually interested to "opt out" of political television altogether. Thus it is increasingly difficult for political programming to compete for our attention without reinventing itself as something more dramatic and exciting.

Unfortunately, incivility is not without its side effects. In everyday life, most people are civil most of the time, and thus polite behavior tends to be the baseline expectation when we interact with others and when we watch others interact. On television, however, the norm for political discourse is obviously different. The jarring interruptions, raised voices, and barbed sarcasm make it attention grabbing, but viewers get the impression that these people (the political elites) are not like you and me. They don't abide by the same social norms and don't act like decent people should act in social contexts. As a result, viewers often come away with the impression that politicians are real jerks. For the candidates we agree with, we may write off their behavior as righteous indignation, but for the ones with whom we disagree, there is simply no excuse. We come to dislike those politicians we disagree with even more intensely. And rather than come closer together and thus be more likely to compromise, partisans come away with the sense that the "other side" (regardless of which side that is) is downright unreasonable and has no legitimate basis for its views.[13]

In the face-to-face world of interpersonal relations, politeness and etiquette are a means of demonstrating mutual respect. Every culture abides by a certain set of norms for interaction, and by following these rules, we convey a degree of respect toward even those we may dislike. On television, however, the "norm" is precisely the opposite; television uses norm violations as a means of getting viewer attention, and it appears to work well toward that end. The problem is that incivility also decreases respect for the opposition and makes political compromises more difficult for the public to accept.

In addition to drawing the attention of viewers, getting people hot and bothered and perhaps even outright angry when they watch political television may serve a secondary purpose as well. As it turns out, people are particularly likely to tell others about things they experience while in a state of heightened arousal.[14] The social transmission of information from person to person extends the impact of whatever content people view on television, and it also encourages others to watch. Experiments have shown that people are more likely to share stories, news, and information if physiological arousal levels are high when they watch. So, for example, if what a politician says on TV leaves you extremely angry, anxious, or excited, then you are more likely to tell your friends about it. Interestingly, this remains true even when the information itself is not what caused the high level of arousal. So, for example, jogging while you're watching TV would also make you more likely to pass the information on to friends! This social transmission of information—through people's personal and online networks, for example—is extremely important in an era when so much of what we read, view, and pay attention to is determined by what people in our social network recommend to us.

Now that television is online along with printed news stories, researchers have been studying what it is that makes some content go "viral" while other content does not. An analysis of which *New York Times* stories were most likely to be shared showed that as with television, strong arousal and intense emotional responses to stories predict the extent to which they will be re-transmitted to others. Stories likely to evoke strong feelings, whether positive or negative, compelled people to share articles with others. This finding persists even after taking into account factors such as how practical an article is, how prominently it is placed on the Web page, and for how long it is featured. All of this suggests that understanding emotional reactions is central to explaining why people react the way they do to mass media.

IF WE BUILD IT, WILL THEY COME?

It is easy for us as observers of the political process to sit back and decry both the extent of incivility in political discourse and the overall quality of political television today. But it is worth pondering whether, given the constraints of the contemporary media environment, we would really want political television to consist of excruciatingly polite, civil discourse—assuming we had the power to make it so. What would be the consequences? Personally, I doubt many of us would watch it. Bill O'Reilly was correct: The ratings received by very civil, high-quality news shows on public broadcasting do not suggest there is a huge unmet demand for this kind of content.

But some obviously argue otherwise. In a now infamous exchange between *The Daily Show* host Jon Stewart and Tucker Carlson, then-host of the political talk show *Crossfire*, Stewart lambasted the *Crossfire* hosts for their "knee-jerk, reactionary talk." As he admonished, "You have a responsibility to the public discourse, and you fail miserably." Stewart was widely cheered for his attack on *Crossfire*, and the heated exchange was itself intense and uncomfortable to watch.

But just how fair is this criticism? Stewart differentiates his own show from real news, and thus denies that he has any similar responsibility to public discourse. As the main commentator for a "comedy news" program, he does not need to worry about serious public discourse. Moreover, Stewart has his own gimmick—comedy—to bring viewers to his program. And thus, as he readily acknowledges, he can make fun of politicians with impunity, and is not expected to present a full or accurate account of the day's events. So-called "serious" journalists are unlikely to get away with the same approach.

But if these programs became calmer, more civil, and less emotional, would their audiences dwindle further? Based on what Americans say in response to how they feel about incivility, audience size should increase because, "Americans clearly don't want a reality show food fight when it comes to politics. They want civil discourse of the issues."[15] But is their viewing behavior really consistent with this idea? And what might serious journalists do to draw in viewers?

These are important questions to consider that have not been satisfactorily answered. Some have argued that the current state of affairs will be self-correcting because "we'll reach a tipping point when people will demand more civil discourse."[16] I'm not so sure. If uncivil political programs were punished with lower viewership, this argument would make perfect sense and the market would drive political television toward more civil programs. But instead, it may be precisely the reverse; that is, uncivil discourse gets a much larger audience than civil discourse. This is what is widely believed by talk show hosts and their producers. Incivility can be entertaining and lively to watch, just like extreme sports. So even though Americans claim to hate it, their level of attentiveness to uncivil conflict suggests that they can't look away.

Ultimately, this chain of events gives politicians an even greater strategic incentive to act uncivilly. If they want to get their message out, they are more likely to do so if they scream at another politician than if they calmly explain their viewpoint. Perhaps I'm naïve, but I think that most politicians in face-to-face situations are no more uncivil and impolite than the average person discussing politics. They only act like jerks on television because they know it will reap benefits such as more media coverage, more public memory, and more people who talk about their message with others.

In an era of many choices on television, the Internet, and elsewhere, traditional news audiences are already shrinking. For people who are not political junkies, there are many more entertaining options than simply talking heads blathering on about politics. So if the norm on television were civil public discourse, it's not clear how many people would actually be watching. The highly politically involved would probably still tune in, but those looking for entertainment value would change the channel and go elsewhere.

To summarize, conflict is an integral part of the political process. Our political system is supposed to be competitive, but conflict is not something we're all necessarily comfortable with as human beings in social situations. Conflict produces physiological arousal when we observe it, just as it would in a real-world social situation, even though we are not actual participants in the conflict. Much of the conflict on television violates our face-to-face social norms for disagreement by failing to maintain polite discourse and by appearing to come too close to us in the context of these disagreements. These norm violations produce strong emotional reactions, and they are particularly likely to get covered by the media. In addition, once such a conflict is covered by the media, it is highly likely to grab our attention. When we watch it, it is likely to boost levels of physiological arousal that in turn make us more likely to tell others about it, to e-mail the link to our friends, and so forth. The sum total effect of this process means that uncivil conflicts are much more likely to be diffused through the population to still larger numbers of people, creating the impression of still more political incivility.

Endnotes

1. *New Statesman and Nation,* July 15, 1933.
2. Dave Barry, December 18, 2004.
3. See Judith Rodin and Stephen P. Steinberg (Eds.), *Public Discourse in America: Conversation and Community in the Twenty-First Century* (Philadelphia: University of Pennsylvania Press, 2003).
4. See Erving Goffman, *The Presentation of Self In Everyday Life* (New York: Doubleday, 1959).
5. Do not try this at home. Particularly if you use your computer screen to play the video, you risk damage to the screen.
6. See Byron Reeves and Clifford Nass, *The Media Equation: How People Treat Computers, Television, and New Media Like Real People and Places* (New York: Cambridge University Press, 1996).
7. See Robert H. Durr, John B. Gilmour, and Christina Wolbrecht, "Explaining Congressional Approval," *American Journal of Political Science 41*(1): 175–207, 1997, p. 182.
8. See Mark D. Ramirez, "The Dynamics of Partisan Conflict on Congressional Approval," *American Journal of Political Science 53*(3): 681–694, 2009.

9. See Diana C. Mutz, "Effects of 'In-Your-Face' Television Discourse on Perceptions of a Legitimate Opposition," *American Political Science Review 101*(4): 621–635, 2007.

10. Ibid.

11. See Diana C. Mutz and Byron Reeves, "The New Videomalaise: Effects of Televised Incivility on Political Trust," *American Political Science Review 99*(1): 1–15, 2005.

12. Lecture at Fairfield University, as reported in *The Connecticut Post*, September 18, 2006.

13. Ibid, Mutz, 2007.

14. See Jonah Berger, "Arousal Increases Social Transmission of Information," *Psychological Science 22*(7): 891–893, 2011.

15. Pam Jenkins, President of Powell Tate, in comments on *Civility in America 2011*.

16. Jack Leslie, Chairman of Weber Shandwick, in comments on their 2011 report, *Civility in America 2011*.

7

Our Tribal Nature and the Rise of Nasty Politics

Daniel M. Shea

This chapter takes a somewhat different tract. Rather than laying the blame for declining civility merely on the backs of the media or on the nature of party politics, the author explores cognitive psychology and the weight of "tribal" instincts. Americans have always gathered with like-minded citizens, but new data suggests dramatic demographic changes are underway. This shift, coupled with the self-selection of information on the Internet, has invigorated the idea of politics as a struggle of "us vs. them." It is little wonder that respect for different points of view and willingness to compromise are increasingly rare.

From the very beginning, it seemed that Virginia Republican George Allen stood a good chance of winning his 2006 reelection bid to the U.S. Senate. He was popular, good looking, articulate, and an excellent fundraiser. There was even some talk of Allen running for the White House, perhaps two years down the line at either the top of the ticket or as a vice-presidential candidate. Certainly, he was a rising star in the Republican Party.

But a racial slur, captured on video, derailed his campaign and evaporated his chances of being on any national ticket. Allen delivered his off-hand remark at an event in rural Virginia, where he called a volunteer of his opponent's campaign "macaca." (The macaque is a monkey, and the young man had dark-colored skin.) Allen also greeted the volunteer sarcastically, saying, "Welcome to America and the real world of Virginia. . . . My opponent has never been here and will probably never come." Scholars point to Allen's "macaca moment" as evidence of when the new and old media merged. A video clip of the slur was quickly posted on YouTube, and soon Allen was apologizing on *Meet the Press*. But the event highlighted another aspect of politics—a feature that is being played out writ-large in contemporary politics. It is a development that may help us better understand the growing vitriol in modern political rhetoric.

This chapter will attempt to merge elements of cognitive psychology, new data on economic and demographic changes in the United States, and a bit of what we know about patterns of voting behavior throughout American history. It will be argued that humans confront contradictory impulses. On the one hand, we have an innate sense of empathy, a deep-seated concern for the well-being of our fellow citizens. On the other hand, we have a strong defense mechanism, which can push us to strike at perceived opposition in stunningly forceful ways. The balance between these forces is tipped toward defense when we confront perceived threats, particularly when the source of those threats is thought to be from other "tribes." The more we draw distinctions between "us" and "them," the easier it is to berate opponents. Americans have tightened their circle of friends and have reinforced their tribal networks. There also have been disturbances that propel our desire to create party and ideological enclaves. As such, we should not be surprised that the tone of politics has taken a turn for the worse, or that there is less willingness to find compromise solutions to our most pressing problems.

OUR CONTRADICTORY IMPULSES

One could not possibly overstate the breadth of scholarship, research, and analysis devoted to understanding the root of human motivations. Attempts to summarize this material are risky. With that disclaimer, we might say that early thinking about altruism, also called human benevolence, centered on self-interest. All that we do, the logic goes, is in the name of self-interest. We may choose to aid a person in need, lend a hand to a family who lost their house in a fire, or give a fellow student our notes, but we do so because we receive a reward. We get a sense of satisfaction, praise from others, and maybe even a warm, fuzzy feeling. Robin Hood worked diligently for the poor because he got a charge out of his work. "What a great guy you are, Robin. You are so special . . . so awesome!" Taking this line of reasoning a bit further, we automatically move quickly to keep a child from falling into a fire because *we* do not want to experience the pain of watching her die. Simply stated, it's all about us!

Yet research in the new field of social-cognitive neuroscience is shedding a different light on empathy, or the act of perceiving, understanding, and responding to the needs of others. As the story goes, in 1992, researchers studying the brains of monkeys (coincidently, macaque monkeys) discovered that the section of a monkey's brain that is activated when the monkey eats a treat also "lights up" when it watches another monkey eat a treat. In other words, part of a monkey's brain seems to experience another monkey's sensations.

Ultimately, neuroscientists identified a class of cells in the brain (both animal and human) called "mirror neurons." These cells fire when an individual observes another person or animal having an experience or feeling a sensation. As noted by a team of researchers, the discovery of mirror neurons shows that the phrase, "I feel your pain" may be literally true—not that the speaker is actually experiencing the other person's feelings, but that the speaker's brain creates very real sensations in response to another person's experience.[1] Mirror neurons appear to be the primary physiological mechanism of empathy. Or, as David Brooks notes in, *Social Animal,* "Scientists believe that the ability to unconsciously share another's pain is a building block of empathy, and through that emotion, morality."[2]

But how does that help our understanding of civility in politics? One could argue that we are hard-wired to feel compassion or to appreciate the validity of other points of view. As noted by Jeremy Rifkin in, *The Empathetic Civilization,* "[I]t is the extraordinary evolution of empathic consciousness that is the underlying story of human history."[3] We can be passionate about our politics, but also understand that those on the other side are also thoughtful and well-meaning.

But, of course, that is not the end of the story. Humans are *also* hardwired to respond to perceived threats in powerful, physical ways. Researchers have long understood that our "fight or flight" response is instinctive. When we sense danger, our body responds in a host of ways: the release of adrenalin, endorphins, and hormones; a quickening of our heart beat and a surge in blood pressure; the dilation of pupils and the swell of acid in our stomach. Evidence also suggests our hair stands on its end—literally.

This outlook, perhaps more primal, would be consistent with the Hobbesian view of human nature. Humans engage in ongoing competition for resources, a relentless struggle for domination and material well-being. Government is introduced to mitigate these more base instincts. "His only answer to the nightmare of human existence was to call for the right hand of government authority to keep people from killing each other in a way of 'each against all.'"[4]

We are left with a balancing act—a desire to protect, defend, and get ahead, and to extend a helping hand. We realize that a colleague's promotion might jeopardize our own career advancement, but we put a smile on our face and say, "Well done!" We want our team to win, but we know that rubbing it in after the game will make the loser feel even worse. We want to give to charitable causes, but are fearful that we will run out of money before our next paycheck. When it comes to politics, or at least politics that we admire, we believe our view is best. We still, however, understand that those on the other side, while misguided perhaps, have a right to air their concerns. Make no mistake, the balance is precarious. "Empathy orients you toward moral action, but it doesn't seem to help much when that action comes at a personal cost." It is a "fragile flower," easily crushed by self-concern.[5]

THE REEMERGENCE OF TRIBALISM IN AMERICAN POLITICS

On top of our contradictory impulses is an inclination to bond with like-minded humans—what we might call our tribal instinct. One of the earliest extensive looks at the importance of group dynamics in society and politics was conducted in 1906 by William Graham Sumner. Using the term "ethnocentrism" instead of tribal instincts, Sumner suggested one's group identity is the "center of everything."[6] He writes, "Each group nourishes its own pride and vanity, boasts itself superior, exalts its own divinities, and looks with contempt at outsiders."[7] Scores of other works have drawn similar conclusions. As for the sources of our alliances, the line demarcating one group from another can shift with circumstances—from one's neighborhood, occupation, alma mater, and economic class to one's preference in beer and allegiance to sports teams (as any member of the Red Sox Nation could attest). Of course, political lines are also drawn based on policy preferences, religion, ideology, party identification, candidate allegiance, and much else. As noted by scholars Donald Kinder and Cindy Kam, "Which of our tribal associations is salient depends on what is happening around us."[8]

Indeed, tribalism is an old tune in politics. The call of "us vs. them" has been a handy strategic tool for political operatives, and it is at the center of myriad bigoted policies and countless private prejudices. At the turn of the twentieth century, New York City party boss George Washington Plunkitt made this point clear when he suggested that upstate politicians were "natural born hayseeds, and can never become real New Yorkers."[9] There is also plenty of scorn for bookworms and college professors.

Given that our allegiances spring from "what's happening around us," it should come as no surprise that disturbances trigger tribal behaviors. Demographic changes and economic transformations, in particular, seem to prompt group impulses. In America, a powerful nativist movement in the 1840s was prompted by a flood of German and Irish Catholic immigrants. Several violent encounters boiled up between immigrants and native-born Americans in the 1830s and early 1840s. A riot in Philadelphia in July 1844, for instance, left more than 20 people dead. This movement coalesced into the Native American Party, commonly known as the Know Nothings. (The party's proceedings were often secret. When asked about their plans, members often responded with, "I know nothing.")

Spurred by similar disruptions, a second nativist movement emerged in the 1920s. At this time, immigrants were mostly from Italy and Poland. At about the same time, the Ku Klux Klan surfaced as a powerful tribal force in the Deep South in response to social tensions of urban industrialization and vastly increased immigration. Klan membership grew rapidly in cities across the nation. And, of course, the Civil Rights movement in the 1950s and 1960s spurred white, nativist organizations.

But one should not assume that tribalism inflames only nativist politics. Kinder and Kam, for instance, present detailed case studies of contemporary "tribes" centered around the women's rights movement, the gay rights movement, welfare policy, and other progressive causes.[10] Again, our tribal associations are dependent upon what we care about and what is happening around us.

TROUBLE IN KANSAS AND THE BIG SORT

Many scholars and journalists have been exploring political trends for decades, but journalist Thomas Frank wrote an especially telling book titled, *What's the Matter with Kansas?* Frank, a native of Kansas, charted the stunning transformation of the state's politics from progressive, sometimes radically liberal, to hard-core social conservatism and steadfast pro-business. At the heart of his inquiry is how low-wage, blue-collar voters would jettison economic policies that might benefit them in favor of social concerns like abortion, gay marriage, evolution, school prayer and gun control. He writes,

> [In the past], when business screwed farmers and workers—when it implemented monopoly strategies invasive beyond the Populists' furthest imaginings—when it ripped off shareholders and casually tossed thousands out of work—you could be damned sure about what would follow. Not these days. Out here the gravity of discontent pulls in only one direction: to the right, to the right, further to the right. Strip today's Kansans of their job security, and they head out to become registered Republicans.[11]

Frank argues that conservative leaders in his state (and elsewhere) made a determined effort to move voter concern from economic policies by raising the specter of massive cultural decay, and by suggesting that we are in a quasi-civil war. Pitted against the "real Americans" are the liberal elite: the high-taxing, government-spending, latte-drinking, sushi-eating, Volvo-driving, *New York Times*-reading, Hollywood-loving, left-wing freak show.[12] The nation is divided between "red states" and "blue states," easily evident by looking at an Electoral College map from the past few elections. Red states are the heartland; blue states are at the coastal extremes. And, goodness, there is so much red! This view, according to Frank, allowed conservatives to present their views as the philosophy of a region that Americans venerate—a repository of national virtue and down-home family values. It also brought majoritarian legitimacy to a president who had actually lost the popular vote (George W. Bush in 2000).[13]

"Us vs. them" (or should we say, "red vs. blue") rhetoric became commonplace by the early 1990s. In 1992, the chair of the Republican National Committee proclaimed to a national television audience that "we are America [and] those other people are not."[14] Former Speaker of the House Newt Gingrich described Democrats as "the enemy of normal Americans."[15] A few years after George Allen's macaca incident, when he welcomed the young man to "real America," Sarah Palin proclaimed at a campaign stop in North Carolina, "We believe that the best of America is in these small towns that we get to visit and these wonderful little pockets of what I call the real America, being here with all of you hard-working, very patriotic, very pro-America areas of this great nation." About the same time, John McCain stated, "Western Pennsylvania . . . is the most patriotic, most God-loving part of America," and Robin Hayes, a Republican congressman from North Carolina, extolled, "Liberals hate real Americans that work, and accomplish, and achieve, and believe in God."[16]

Frank used Kansas as a microcosm of a national trend, a broad consensus, particularly among conservatives, that the nation is being divided into two distinct tribes. Cultural grievances and moral concerns have replaced economic policy disputes as the dividing line between the parties, and, by doing so, the "us vs. them" is made vivid. And, of course, this in turn shapes the tone and outcome of contemporary politics. As noted by scholar Morris Fiorina, "The symbolic nature of many contemporary political issues is another factor that makes compromise more difficult and contributes to the nasty quality of contemporary debate."[17]

While this might have been true a decade ago, or even when McCain and Palin stumped for the presidency in 2008, perhaps the Great Recession put economic concerns back at the fore. The oft-told narrative regarding the rise of the Tea Party movement, for example, seems to challenge Frank's supposition. Surely job loss, bank bailouts, huge deficits, and wasteful government spending pulled activists to the streets and to the ballot box. Drawing on 3,000 interviews in 2006 and again in the summer of 2011, scholars Robert Putnam and David Campbell were able to uncover the motivations spurring those who would later back the Tea Party movement. "Next to being a Republican, the strongest predictor of being a Tea Party supporter today was a desire, back in 2006, to see religion play a prominent role in politics." They continue, "The Tea Party's generals may say their overriding concern is a smaller government, but not their rank and file, who are more concerned about putting God in government." Indeed, in the fall of 2011, as threats of a double-dip recession seemed all too real, a prominent Baptist preacher and key backer of Texas Governor Rick Perry called it "a spiritual imperative" to oust President Barack Obama.[18]

It should be noted that some scholars question the general thesis that voters no longer focus on economic issues. A few years after the publication of Frank's book, a team of scholars headed by Andrew Gelman published an important article dubbed, "Rich State, Poor State, Red State, Blue State: What's the Matter with Connecticut?"[19] Using different sets of data, they find that economic voting continues to shape voter choice and that, generally speaking, poor voters support Democrats and rich voters back Republicans. They also find that income matters more in red states than it does in blue states. Nevertheless, this work and others admit that there is a great deal of slippage (poor people voting for Republicans) and that much of economic voting can be explained by race. That is, black Americans, who on the whole are poorer than white Americans, vote for Democratic candidates in overwhelming numbers. Stated a bit differently, the percentage of poor, white, rural voters—the group Frank writes about—who support GOP candidates is quite robust. In 2008, for instance, we know that Barack

Obama won the presidential contest quite handily, but he was victorious in just 870 out of 3,111 counties. In many counties the percentage of votes for John McCain actually increased.[20] Counties that changed their majority vote from Republican in 2004 to Democratic in 2008 had an average per capita income of $25,587. Counties flipping Republican had an average per capita income of only $18,555. Stated a bit differently, average incomes in counties turning from Republican to Democratic were 38 percent higher than average incomes of counties turning from Democratic to Republican.

Another important book to help in our understanding of contemporary tribal politics is *The Big Sort: Why Clustering of Like-Minded America is Tearing us Apart*, by William Bishop, also a journalist. With help from an empirical social scientist and using truckloads of data, Bishop discovers an important transformation: the steady, systematic migration of voters to homogenous communities.

> Over the past thirty years, the United States has been sorting itself, shifting at the most microscopic levels of society. . . . When they look for a place to live they run through a checklist . . . Those are now political decisions, and they are having a profound effect on the nation's public life.[21]

Since the 1970s and spurred by more opportunities to move, Americans have been forming tight-knit political tribes. In 1976, for example, 33 percent of congressional districts produced presidential landslides (where the difference between candidates was more than 20 percent). By 2004 that figure had jumped to 60 percent. Bishop demonstrates that the mere redrawing of district lines is not central to the story. Other forces are at work, including the conscious decisions of citizens to move to communities where residents share their values, culture, and politics.

The novel part of Bishop's analysis is the weight afforded to place of residence. There is nothing new about thinking about partisanship and support for policies in group terms. Do Evangelicals support environmental protection? Are young voters concerned about Social Security reform? Will Hispanic Americans back pro-choice candidates? What Bishop discovers, however, is that traditionally important demographic categories, like age, gender, religion, and occupation, are often washed out when a person's place of residence is considered. He found that women in Democratic landslide counties were strongly against the war in Iraq, but Democratic women in Republican blow-out counties were strongly supportive of the war, for example. Democrats in Republican landslide districts were much more likely to attend church than were Democrats in Democratic landslide districts. "The partisanship of place overpowered the categories that research normally uses to describe durable voting blocks."[22]

But how would the transformation of policy disputes into symbolic, value-centered differences—combined with the tendency to live with like-minded citizens—shape the conduct of politics? For one, this tribal behavior has led to a rejection of compromise. According to Bishop, social psychologists began studying the effects of group dynamics on individual perceptions more than 100 years ago. "That people living in homogeneous groups would be loath to compromise—or even exhibit a bit of ideological 'road rage'—would not surprise the researchers in the slightest." Brooks suggests much the same: "Once politics became a contest pitting one identity group against another, it was no longer possible to compromise. Everything became a status war between my kind of people and your kind of people."[23]

Is it not the case that modern technologies mitigate tribal tendencies? We are constantly flooded with information and our circle of "friends" (through social networks) is vastly broader than in the pre-digital age. Might changes in the flow of information and our ability to connect with diverse citizens shrink these tribal instincts? Roger Cohen of the *New York Times* suggests this is probably not happening: "The Internet opens worlds and minds, but also offers opinions to reinforce every prejudice. You're never alone out there; some idiot will always back you. The online world doesn't dissolve tribes. It gives them global reach."[24]

Moreover, there is a growing consensus that partisan media outlets, made possible by cable television, satellite radio, and websites, fostered tribal instincts and a refutation of compromise. As citizens of all ideological stripes escape to an enclave of concordant news information, they become reluctant to hear opposing points of view. While noting the possibility of some positive developments with the rise of partisan media "echo chambers," scholars Kathleen Hall Jamison and Joseph Cappella suggest audiences are often held to a station or commentator by value-centered politics, with consequences: "A steady diet of moral outrage feeds the assumption that the opponent is the enemy." Partisan news pundits encourage their audiences to see the world as "unburdened by either ambiguity or common ground across the ideological divide."[25] Law and political science scholar Cass Sunstein also has written on this subject. He argued that the ability to self-sort through the media is nothing new. We have always picked different newspapers and magazines, and to some extent television and radio programs, to reduce the likelihood of cognitive dissonance (hearing discordant points of view). The great difference with modern technologies is the power to "fence in and to fence out." We live increasingly in an era of enclaves and niches, once again leading to more extreme positions. He calls this "enclave extremism," with the outcome being "serious problems of mutual suspicion, unjustified rage, and social fragmentation."[26]

As politics moves from disputes over precise policy questions to notions of values and rights, compromise becomes difficult and rhetoric becomes more heated. Mary Ann Glendon charted the rise of "rights" politics in the 1970s—a tendency to frame nearly every social controversy in terms of a clash of rights (a woman's right to her own body vs. a fetus's right to life), which impedes compromise, mutual understanding, and the discovery of common ground.[27] There is no middle ground on issues of right, as anyone opposed to your rights is an oppressor.

A somewhat different approach has been used by those on the right in recent years. It has become common to challenge policy questions by calling into question their constitutional validity. If a policy dispute about an issue involving health care reform, the national debt, gun control, federal mandates to states, or even the entire Social Security system is deemed unconstitutional, then compromise becomes unlikely and efforts to find a middle ground may be deemed unpatriotic. This helps explain why most GOP House and Senate candidates in the 2010 election proclaimed their intention to "uphold the Constitution," a rather strange and ambiguous assertion prior to that election. The implication is that those on the other side of the policy dispute are not simply wrong-headed, but are willing to throw the nation's sacred document out the window. The other side's position is not legitimate because it is not constitutional.

Scholars Theda Skocpol and Vanessa Williamson have penned an important new book on the formation of the Tea Party movement.[28] At the center of the movement, the authors say, is a direct link between Christian doctrine and constitutional principles, as well as a tribal notion of "us" and "them." They write,

> A splendid depiction of the fundamentally religious understanding of the U.S. Constitution prevalent in many Tea Party circles appears in a painting by Utah artist Jon McNaughton, entitled "One Nation, Under God." In the painting, Jesus Christ is shown holding up a copy of the United States Constitution, while American historical figures from Abigail Adams to Ronald Reagan stand admiringly behind him. The crowd in the foreground is divided into two groups. On Christ's right, people including a Marine, a farmer, and the mother of a disabled child look admiringly towards the Constitution and Savior. A college student is shown holding a copy of *Five Thousand Year Leap*. On the left of Jesus, however, one finds a less pious crowd, with faces turned away from Jesus and the Constitution.

There is also a professor (with wire-rimmed glasses, of course), turned away from Jesus. He is holding a book: Darwin's *Origin of the Species*. There is a depiction of an entertainer and a liberal reporter, all turned away. Clearly, there is a group on the stage with Christ and the Constitution, and there is a group on the floor, turned away from both.

Finally, there is evidence to suggest like-minded groups not only reinforce conformity, but foster extremism. Social psychological research has identified what is called the "risky shift phenomenon."[29] Whereas we might expect group decisions to reflect the average opinions of those in the group, since the 1970s researchers have found that group positions have become more extreme than the average position of their members. In other words, our positions become more radical as we merge with others. In politics, the implication is that a group's policy position will become more extreme over time, particularly if these positions are symbolic, continually reinforced by a partisan media, and rarely challenged. Writing of Supreme Court Justice Clarence Thomas' propensity to only work and socialize with like-minded conservatives, Harvard Law Professor Charles Fried, who served with Thomas in the Reagan Administration, suggests, "The effect has been to harden his point of view and to make him more and more extreme and isolated in his ideas . . ."[30]

THE JARRING IMPACT OF ECONOMIC AND SOCIAL DISTURBANCES

One could argue that a storm has been brewing for the past few decades; it was not until 2008 that the hurricane hit land. Our defense impulse and tribal instincts are most acute when there are perceived disturbances—a jarring of the established order, for example. Several pressures have been building, and by 2008 they seemed to reach a crescendo. As one observer noted,

> A cultural revolution had decimated old habits and traditional family structures. An economic revolution had replaced downtowns with big isolated malls with chain stores. The information revolution had replaced community organizations that held weekly face-to-face meetings with specialized online social networking where like found like. . . . Out-of-wedlock birth skyrocketed. Crime rose. Trust in institutions collapsed.[31]

Clearly, the impact of the economic crisis had a significant impact. Midway through the 2008 presidential election, news of a massive economic disaster made headlines. A mix of a sub-prime mortgage crisis, global inflation, high oil and food prices, a declining dollar value, and a horrible housing market sent shockwaves across the system. Several major financial institutions collapsed, others were absorbed, and still others were taken over by the U.S. government. This led to a dramatic tightening of credit and a precipitous decline in the stock market. Housing values tumbled, retirement accounts plummeted, small businesses folded, factories slowed, and unemployment soared. In January of 2008, Gallup reported that 32 percent of Americans suggested that economic conditions in the country were either "excellent" or "good," but by the end of the year that figure had dropped to just 7 percent. Since then, this figure has not moved above 13 percent. The percentage of Americans who noted economic problems are the "most important" issues facing the nation went from 16 percent in 2008 to 86 percent in 2011. By October of 2008, the number of Americans "struggling" surpassed the number "thriving." As disturbances go, the economic crisis of 2008 was a whopper. Some 1.4 million Americans filed for personal bankruptcy by 2009, a jump of 32 percent from the previous year.[32] Simply stated, confidence in our nation's long-term prosperity has been shaken.

This disturbance added to growing worries about the decline in the middle class. New data on the disparity between the affluent and the middle class began to pile up by 2010. It was estimated, for instance, that the top 20 percent of Americans controlled 93 percent of the country's financial wealth.[33] Some 66 percent of the nation's income growth between 2001 and 2007 went to the top 1 percent of all Americans. In 1950, the ratio of the average executive's paycheck to the average worker's paycheck was about 30 to 1. Since 2000, that ratio has exploded. It is now between 300 to 500 to 1.[34]

Statistics are one thing; kitchen table concerns are another. In 2007, some 43 percent of Americans told pollsters that they lived "paycheck to paycheck." Three years later that figure had jumped to 61 percent. Surely the rising cost of higher education, the disappearance of the retirement pension system, anemic 401K retirement plans, the escalating cost of health care, declining middle-class wages, and, of course, the disappearance of good manufacturing jobs have deeply worried the nation for more than a decade. Gone, too, is the belief in American exceptionalism. By 2008, we began to hear a steady stream of stories about how China's economy will overtake us within a few decades. For perhaps the first time in American history, parents have begun to fret that their children will not have it as good as they did.

But other changes were also underway. By 2008, the U.S. Census had reported that for the first time in American history, most births in the United States would be of minority children. As recently as 1990, some two-thirds of births were of non-Hispanic white children. While some people welcome our growing diversity, others surely find these changes unsettling. On a related note, the ascendance of a much more diverse group of prominent public officials seemed to highlight broader transformations. Although some think columnist Frank Rich takes things a bit too far, his assessment is note-worthy: "The conjunction of a black president and a female speaker of the House—topped off by a wise Latina on the Supreme Court and a powerful gay Congressional committee chairman—would sow fears of disenfranchise-ment among a dwindling and threatened minority in the country no matter what policies were in play."[35]

We might add that there have been dramatic changes in attitudes to-ward homosexuality. Again using Gallup data, a majority of Americans be-lieve homosexuality to be morally wrong (53 percent to 40 percent) in 2000. That figure steadily declined through the decade, and by 2008 there was parity between the two positions (48 percent). Similarly, the percentage of Americans who believe homosexuality should be considered an acceptable alternative lifestyle went from 34 percent in 1983 to 57 percent in 2008.[36] Of no little consequence, the greatest change was among the younger genera-tion. Pew Research Center found, for instance, that in 2007 some 47 percent of 18- to 29-year-olds believed that gay couples should not raise children. Within four years that figure had dropped to just 28 percent.

Finally, there was our never-ending war against terrorism. Unlike other times of adversity, a sense of shared purpose faded rather quickly after September 11, 2001. With past military conflicts, when the enemy was ob-vious (like Germany and Japan in World War II), our goals were clear and the mission defined. We fought a nation or regime within a prescribed geo-graphic area. But 9/11 was an attack by a fluid network of terrorists spread out across several nations. As part of an aggressive effort to fight terror-ism and prevent future attacks, President George W. Bush decided to attack Saddam Hussein and the Iraqi military, even though there was no evidence linking them to the 9/11 attack. The wisdom of the war in Iraq will be de-bated for decades, but we do know that the war created a deep divide in American politics. Most scholars agree that the 2004 election, just three years after the attack, was one of the most partisan contests in generations.

ENTER BARACK OBAMA

It was within this context that the nation was introduced to Barack Obama. To say that Obama was "different" would be a vast understatement. He had only modest experience in politics, and very little of it was in the Washington arena. He was a professor and a self-described "community organizer," and his early family life was, well, "complicated." Obama's father was born of Luo ethnicity in Kenya, spending his childhood years herding goats. He won a scholarship that allowed him to leave Kenya for the University of Hawaii in Manoa, where he met Obama's mother, Ann Dunham. The couple married and later divorced when Obama was two. His mother remarried a few years later and the entire family moved to Jakarta, Indonesia. By the time Obama was 10, he was back in Hawaii living with this grandparents and his mother was once again divorced. Needless to say, this is not your typical presidential biography.

Obama is half black and, of course, there is that unique name: Barack Hussein Obama. It was different, hard to pronounce, and the middle name became quite controversial considering we were at war with Saddam Hussein in Iraq. According to a *Time* article in February of 2008, it was deemed contentious to even say Obama's middle name. At the Oscars in 2008, host Jon Stewart joked by saying that "Barack Hussein Obama running today is like a 1940s candidate named Gaydolph Titler."[37]

It is hard to imagine a presidential candidate that better represented America's increasingly complex, diverse society than the senator from Illinois. For many, this difference is at the heart of Obama's appeal. He represented change, a new direction, a new America. As captured in an *Atlantic* article in 2007, "Obama's candidacy in this sense is a potentially transformational one. Unlike any of the other candidates, he could take America—finally—past the debilitating, self-perpetuating family quarrel of the Baby Boom generation that has long engulfed all of us."[38] His message of change and transformation was particularly potent for younger voters, as they preferred him over John McCain by 68 percent to 30 percent —the highest share of the youth vote obtained by any candidate since exit polls began reporting results by age in 1976.[39]

It is also fair to say that to many others Obama's politics, message of change, and biography represented a radical departure from the status quo. "As a new president of diverse heritage promised to 'transform America,' perceived threats to the very nature of 'our country' spurred many people, and particularly older people, to get involved with the Tea Party."[40] Whereas many on the left were giddy with the prospects of a transformational president, many on the right were springing to action to "take back their country." For Tea Party activists, especially, Obama was somehow outside or beyond comprehensible categories.[41]

"RAW AND BITTER AND DANGEROUS"

We have established that humans confront the contradictory impulses of empathy and defense, and that we have a natural tendency to merge with like-minded citizens. As suggested, our empathetic impulses can be weakened in group settings, and there is evidence to suggest our tribal behavior has grown in recent years. We are in homogeneous groups, fed a steady diet of congruent partisan information. Further, it can be argued that when we perceive threats from the "other" tribe, our aggressive impulses overwhelm our empathy and we are more likely to respond in visceral, spiteful ways. That is to say, when we determine the opposition is from the other tribe, a nasty slur becomes acceptable. It becomes easy to use mean-spirited language and violent imagery.

Beyond tagging Barack Obama as an intellectual, liberal, and a socialist, implicit in the Birther Movement (the assertion by some that Obama is not a natural-born citizen) is the claim that he cannot be part of "real America" because he is not a citizen. One has to wonder what the birthers expect to gain by pushing the issue. Could they imagine that the election would be reversed years later, or that Congress or the federal courts would somehow throw Obama from office? Could they see the majority of Americans who sent him to the White House quietly acquiescing to his removal? More likely, these activists intuitively understand that by pushing the issue they buttress the notion that Obama is of another tribe, and thus his policies are a threat to traditional American values. His positions cannot be legitimate because, after all, he is not one of us.

The same could be said about the persistent false claim that Obama is a Muslim. Even after two years into his presidency, the percentage of Americans who either do not know the president's faith or who believe he is a Muslim stood at 62 percent. In 2010, a full one-third of conservative Republicans believed the president was a Muslim.[42] The odd thing is that the percentage who believe the president is a Muslim has actually grown, even though his attendance at Christian church events and participation in Christian prayer meetings is widely covered in the media. How could this be true? Those who say he is a Muslim overwhelmingly disapprove of his job performance, but a majority of those who think he is a Christian approve of his performance.[43] We might understand why partisan news commentators would perpetuate this myth (Throw some red meat to the audience!), but why would Republican leaders, knowing full-well that Barack Obama is both a citizen and a Christian, parse their words when asked about these issues? The tribal instinct is powerful.

For many on the right, Obama lacks legitimacy because he could not have taken up residency in the White House without the overwhelming support of minorities and young voters. According to *New York Times* exit polling, Barack Obama netted 95 percent of the black vote, 67 percent of the Hispanic vote, and 68 percent of the youth vote.[44] He received a whopping 69 percent of first-time votes! Conversely, Obama netted just 34 percent of white Protestant votes and 45 percent of votes in rural areas. He received just 30 percent of white Southern votes. And the percentage of white, Southern men that backed Obama? Negligible. Stated differently, without the support of youngsters and non-whites, John McCain would be president. This certainly did not get lost on Tea Party activists, as reported by Skocpol and Willimson.

During an interview for the book, an activist noted, "The 'young generation' is all 'Obama, Obama, Obama,' says Bonnie [Sims], but she dreads where he is leading the nation. 'I am not a racist,' she assures us, but Obama is 'a socialist' who 'got a lot of it from his father.'"[45] Stated simply, Obama lacks legitimacy because "others" brought him to power.

It is worth brief mention that following the 2008 election roughly two dozen states, all controlled by Republicans, began considering policies to tighten voting regulations. Several states moved to jettison same-day voter registration and others passed legislation to require voters to present state-issued voter identification cards at polling places. There is overwhelming evidence to suggest these measures, and others, would disproportionately impact poor, minority and young citizens. Turnout among these groups would decline, but of course that is the implicit, sometimes explicit goal of these efforts. The GOP speaker of the New Hampshire State House commented that students' access to the ballot box should be blocked because young people tend to "vote their feelings," which leads them to vote "as a liberal."[46]

CONCLUSION: ONE NATION?

If the president is perceived as "different," certainly not of the "heartland," and if we confront a new set of challenges and transformations, then shouldn't we expect empathy to be overpowered by our defense instinct? The balance is always precarious, but when we confront new dangers, our ability to relate to others, to find well-meaning intentions in the opposition, is stunted—and it is shattered when we see the others as members of a different tribe. To many, it is little wonder that the conduct of our politics has become nasty, rude, and stubborn. Few would be surprised to hear that a U.S. Senate candidate called a volunteer of his opponent a macaca.

But is it really fair to blame the rise of nasty politics on these developments? How do we even know, with certainty, that things have actually gotten worse? Have we not seen nasty politics at many times in our nation's history? If so, what is new about this period? These are all important questions. Two points might be raised. First, regardless of whether or not there has been an actual increase in nasty, mean-spirited politics, numerous polls suggest the public believes things have gotten worse. We might say that assessing the tone of politics is necessarily a subjective endeavor. If the public believes things are worse, then they are. Second, we know that important forces have aligned, such as our movement to homogenous communities, the polarization in Congress and state legislatures, and the growing popularity of hyper-partisan news. These forces would surely suggest the tone of politics has, or will, change for the worse. In fact, the struggle might be to explain how the tone of our politics has *not* deteriorated, given these conditions.

So we should not have been surprised at the vitriol spewed during health care reform town hall meetings or to hear a member of the House of Representatives shout, "You lie!" during a State of the Union address. It might even be expected that pundits and elected officials would assail the President of the United States as a traitor and unpatriotic because he espouses policy positions they oppose. It might be unsightly, but not entirely unexpected, to see violent, racist imagery at political rallies, or to hear a statewide candidate suggest a "2nd Amendment remedy" to bring Congress under control. Seasoned GOP operative and political commentator Peggy Noonan got it right when she described our politics as "raw and bitter and dangerous."[47] Our better angels are nowhere to be found.

Is this merely the result of conservative outrage? Political tectonic plates have shifted in such a way that the change has fostered conservative fury. Yes, much of what we have noticed about the rough nature of politics in the past few years springs from value-centered politics, economic and social disturbances, and the election of Barack Obama. We also know, for instance, that conservatives seem much less inclined to seek compromise solutions than do those on the left. A poll conducted by the Center for Political Participation at Allegheny College found, for instance, that 78 percent of Republican Party county chairs believe elected officials should stick to their principles and not seek compromise solutions, while 12 percent of Democratic chairs said the same. Conversely, 88 percent of Democratic chairs thought politicians should find compromises, but just 22 percent of GOP leaders held a similar view.[48] But make no mistake. Tribal politics and misplaced empathy are not the sole providence of the right. The so-called liberal blogosphere has been particularly rabid for more than a decade, too. George W. Bush and Sarah Palin, both certainly not of the liberal tribe (Can you believe she hunts?), have been the targets of ceaseless attacks.

It would be assuring to suggest our mean-spirited politics is but a passing phase, perhaps little different than other rough patches in our political history (there have been many). This may be true, but it is unlikely. The challenges we confront, particularly economic transformations, are massive and, for some, frightening. Coupled with our tendency to live in communities of like-minded citizens and to draw a comfortable information cocoon around ourselves, rough waters are ahead. Partisan media outlets, which seek to draw greater ratings by giving their readers and listeners ever-shocking commentary, are not going anywhere. But there is our sense of empathy—that uniquely human characteristic that allows individuals to relate, care, and connect. Beyond our politics, religion, values, sexual orientation, race, and all our other differences, our capacity to care remains. Are Americans more empathetic than citizens in other nations? Probably not. Yet a vast majority of Americans believe respectful politics is important for the long-term stability of our democracy. Civil discourse is part of our political culture—even if we do not always practice what we preach. We may cluster with our ideological pals, but we also understand that all are part of the American fabric.

Perhaps we will recognize that "otherness" need not be demeaned in order to satisfy tribalism. The ancients recognized that we each need the other in order to fully know ourselves. Our interests, well-being, and success are wrapped up in the interests, well-being, and success of others. We are connected—one to the other—not hidden from or immune to their well-being. Acts, rhetoric, and contexts that devalue others limit what the tribe can become. Recognizing our complexity is essential to the whole unit . . . the one tribe. Otherness is a necessary condition of us. One tribe.

Endnotes

1. J. T. Kaplan, "Getting a Grip on Other Minds: Mirror Neurons, Intention Understanding, and Cognitive Empathy," *Social Neuroscience*, Vol. 1 (3–4), pp. 175–183.
2. David Brooks, *Social Animal: The Hidden Sources of Love, Character and Achievement* (New York: Random House, 2011), p. 41.
3. Jeremy Rifkin, *The Empathic Civilization* (New York: Penguin, 2009), p. 10.
4. Ibid., p. 7.
5. David Brooks, "Empathy's Limits," *New York Times,* September 30, 2011.
6. William Graham Sumner, *Folkways: The Study of Mores, Manners, Customs and Morals* (Mineola, NY: Dover Publications, 1906), p. 13.
7. Ibid.
8. Donald Kinder and Cindy Kam, *Us Against Them* (Chicago: University of Chicago Press, 2010), p. 71.
9. William L. Riordon, *Plunkett of Tammany Hall* (New York: Signet, 1995), p. 41.
10. Ibid., Part II: Empirical Case Studies.
11. Thomas Frank, *What's the Matter with Kansas: How Conservatives Won the Heart of America* (New York: Metropolitan Books, 2004), pp. 67–68.
12. Ibid, p. 17.
13. Ibid.
14. Ibid, p. 13.
15. Ibid.
16. Bernd Debusmann, "Real verses Unreal Americans," Reuters.Com, October 29, 2008. Accessed at: http://blogs.reuters.com/great-debate/2008/10/29/real-vs-unreal-americans/.
17. Morris Fiorina, *Disconnect; The Breakdown of Representation in American Politics* (Norman, OK: University of Oklahoma Press, 2009), p. 38.
18. Joe Scarborough, "Jeffers Throws Jesus Under the Bus," Politico.Com, October 11, 2011. Accessed at: http://www.politico.com/news/stories/1011/65562.html.
19. Andrew Gelman, et.al., "Rich State, Poor State, Red State, Blue State: What's the Matter with Connecticut?" *Quarterly Journal of Political Science*, 2007: 345–367.
20. Center for Rural Strategies, "The 2008 Election: State by State." Accessed at: http://www.dailyyonder.com/2008-election-state-state/2008/12/05/1789
21. Bill Bishop, *The Big Sort: Why Clustering of Like-Minded America is Tearing us Apart* (Boston, MA: Houghton Mifflin, 2008), p. 5.
22. Ibid., p. 48.
23. Brooks, *Social Animal*, p. 319.
24. Roger Cohen, "Tribalism Here and There," *New York Times*, March 10, 2008.
25. Jamison, Kathleen Hall and Joseph N. Cappella, *Echo Chamber: Rush Limbaugh and the Conservative Media Establishment* (New York: Oxford University Press, 2008), p. 245.
26. Ibid.

27. Mary Ann Glendon, *Rights Talk: The Impoverishment of Political Discourse* (New York: Free Press, 1991), p. xi.

28. Theda Skocpol and Vanessa Williamson, *The Tea Party and the Remaking of Republican Conservatism* (New York: Oxford University Press, 2012).

29. Bishop, *the Big Sort*, p. 66.

30. Nina Totenberg, "Thomas Confirmation Hearings Had a Ripple Effect," National Public Radio, October 11, 2011.

31. Brooks, *Social Animal*, p. 318.

32. Michael Snyder, "22 Statistics that Prove the Middle Class is Being Systematically Wiped Out of Existence in America," *Business Insider*, July 15, 2010. Accessed at: http://www.businessinsider.com/22-statistics-that-prove-the-middle-class-is-being-systematically-wiped-out-of-existence-in-america-2010-7#.

33. Bruce Watson, "Disturbing Statistics on the Decline of America's Middle Class," DailyFinance.Com, October 17, 2010. Accessed at: http://www.dailyfinance.com/2010/10/17/disturbing-statistics-on-the-decline-of-americas-middle-class/.

34. Snyder, "22 Statistics . . ."

35. Frank Rich, "The Rage is Not About Health Care," *New York Times*, March 27, 2010.

36. Gallup.Com, "Americans Evenly Divided on Morality of Homosexuality," June 18, 2008. Accessed at: http://www.gallup.com/poll/108115/Americans-Evenly-Divided-Morality-Homosexuality.aspx.

37. Nathan Thornburgh, "Why Is Obama's Middle Name Taboo?" *Time*, February 28, 2008. Accessed at: http://www.time.com/time/politics/article/0,8599,1718255,00.html.

38. Andrew Sullivan, "Goodbye to All That: Why Obama Matters," *The Atlantic*, December 2007. Accessed at: http://www.theatlantic.com/magazine/archive/2007/12/goodbye-to-all-that-why-obama-matters/6445/.

39. CIRCLE Staff, "Young Voters in the 2008 Presidential Election," December 19, 2008. Accessed at: http://www.civicyouth.org/PopUps/FactSheets/FS_08_exit_polls.pdf.

40. Skocpol and Williamson*, The Tea Party and the Remaking of Republican Conservatism*, p. 7.

41. Ibid., p. 79.

42. Pew Research Center, "Growing Number of Americans Say Obama is a Muslim," August 18, 2010. Accessed at: http://pewforum.org/Politics-and-Elections/Growing-Number-of-Americans-Say-Obama-is-a-Muslim.aspx.

43. Ibid.

44. *New York Times*, "National Exit Polls Table," November 5, 2008. Accessed at: http://elections.nytimes.com/2008/results/president/national-exit-polls.html.

45. Skocpol and Williamson, *The Tea Party and the Remaking of Republican Conservatism*, p. 46.

46. Editorial, "Keeping Students from the Polls," *New York Times*, December 26, 2011.

47. Peggy Noonan, "The Heat is On: We May Get Burned," *The Wall Street Journal*, March 25, 2010. Accessed at: http://www.peggynoonan.com/article.php?article=516.

48. Center for Political Participation, "Local Parties Healthy, But Differences Emerge Over Compromise," September 13, 2011. Accessed at: http://sites.allegheny.edu/cpp/2011/09/13/local-political-parties-healthy-but-differences-emerge-over-compromise/.

8

Presidents, Partisans, and Polarized Politics

Gary C. Jacobson

In this chapter, Jacobson introduces a concept—party sorting—that features prominently in several of the chapters that follow. Party sorting refers to the fact that although the American citizenry as a whole is no more polarized than it was decades ago, the issue positions and ideological stances of citizens have become more closely tied to their party affiliations. As a result, presidents increasingly depend on electoral coalitions based primarily on their own partisan supporters rather than draw support from a broader range of the political spectrum. Prevailing political conditions force presidents to govern as dividers, not uniters.

The president holds a uniquely prominent place in modern American political life. As head of the world's most powerful state, commander of its armed forces, agenda setter for its national legislature, head of its vast bureaucracy, and leader of one of its two main national parties, the president is always at the center of political attention. Any shift in the tenor of public political discourse is therefore certain to encompass the presidency. Insofar as "rude, nasty, and stubborn" politics has become the order of the day, we will see it surface in the way presidents are regarded and treated by rival politicians, the news media, the commentariat, and the public at large. But presidents are not merely passive victims of changing political etiquette. A president's leadership style, objectives, policy decisions, and public rhetoric have a direct bearing on the temperature and tone of political discourse during his administration; his legacy continues to shape the structure and idiom of political conflict long after he has left office.

Every newly elected president aspires to be, as G.W. Bush put it, "a uniter, not a divider" and pledges to be "president of all the people," not just those who voted him in. No president fully achieves this goal, of course. As the winner of a contest between candidates chosen by rival parties, and as his party's top leader, the president is inevitably a partisan figure, always better regarded by his own side than by rival partisans in government and in the public. Partisan reactions to presidents are quite variable, however, and, more to the point, have grown much stronger and more discordant over the past half-century or so. This change shows up in the uglier rhetoric and more rancorous conflict that now marks the president's relations with rival politicians. But, as I show in this chapter, it also shows up in the way ordinary Americans have come to regard their presidents. The actions and discourse of political leaders have primed citizens to react as partisans, while a more pervasively partisan electorate has increased the payoffs for (or at least reduced the costs of) partisan intransigence in Washington. The Republicans' victory in the 2010 midterm elections provides a case in point; its aftermath also illustrates the corrosive effects of strategic polarization on governance and presidential leadership. Under present conditions, a president who tries to govern by building public consensus and cross-party coalitions is almost certain to fail.

The growing strength of partisanship in shaping elite and popular reactions to presidents did not occur on its own. It reflects a gradual but profound ideological realignment that over the past four decades has transformed the Republican and Democratic parties into much more homogeneous and divergent coalitions than they had been in the 1970s. I therefore begin with a brief account of this realignment and its consequences before considering how it has affected the way Americans have come to regard and treat their presidents.

THE WIDENING PARTISAN DIVIDE

After reaching historically low levels in the 1970s, the ideological differences between the Republican and Democratic parties grew steadily wider and deeper for the next 40 years. The growing ideological divide between rival party politicians and activists is abundantly documented and not in dispute; according to the standard DW Nominate measure derived from roll call votes, for example, ideological differences between the congressional parties widened steadily over this period, leaving them further apart in the 111th Congress (2009–2010) than at any time since the Civil War.[1] The extent to which ordinary Americans have participated in this polarizing trend is disputed, but even skeptics acknowledge that except among the politically inert—people who generally ignore politics and do not vote—partisan identities, ideological identities, and issues preferences have moved into closer alignment.[2] Although ordinary partisans have not moved as far apart ideologically as those more active in politics, their political opinions have become more internally consistent and more distinct from those of partisans on the other side.[3]

The sources of this ideological realignment are too many and too complex to cover in detail here, but the most important include the movement of white Southern conservatives into the Republican Party following the Civil Rights Act of 1964 and the Voting Rights Act of 1965; the emergence of new partisan divisions on social issues—epitomized by abortion—in the 1960s and 1970s; and sharpened differences on taxes and spending provoked by the economic stagnation of the 1970s. Presidents played no small part in these developments. Lyndon Johnson championed civil rights legislation knowing full well that its passage would alienate conservative white Southerners, eroding their historic allegiance to the Democratic Party.[4] Ronald Reagan, who had signed a bill legalizing abortion while he was governor of California, helped to make a pro-life position Republican orthodoxy during his 1980 campaign. While in office, Reagan sought to slash taxes on the wealthy and eliminate government programs dear to Democrats, initiating partisan battles over taxes, spending, and budget deficits that have continued (with a brief respite during the second Clinton administration) to this day. More generally, partisan leaders, especially presidents and presidential candidates, have gradually redefined and clarified what their parties stand for, making it easier for people to choose the party that better fits their political views—or, alternatively, to adopt their favorite party's positions as their own.[5]

As a result of this realignment, political cleavages that once divided up the public in diverse ways now tend to coincide, leaving ordinary Democrats and Republicans in disagreement on a growing range of issues and beliefs, to the point where, according to some scholars, they now appear to inhabit separate cognitive and moral worlds.[6] The emergence of social issues contributed to this trend by driving religious traditionalists, particularly white evangelical Christians, toward the Republican Party, and religious modernists and seculars toward the Democratic Party.[7] To the extent that they view the other side as wrong—even morally wrong—on a lengthening list of public issues, people will be disposed to scorn their partisan adversaries as "them" rather than "us" and to demonize their leaders.

Stronger partisan identities also have increased people's propensity to engage in what psychologists term "motivated reasoning," enlisting cognitive biases to protect current attitudes and beliefs from information that might undermine them. Motivated reasoners absorb, uncritically, messages that confirm their opinions but deflect discordant information through some combination of avoiding, disbelieving, misperceiving, misremembering, or forgetting.[8] Partisanship is a potent inducer of motivated reasoning; stronger partisanship produces greater biases in political perceptions and, hence, wider differences in how ordinary Republicans and Democrats judge political actors and events.

The information environment has been changing in ways that facilitate motivated political reasoning. The sources Americans rely on for political news are increasingly fragmented, ideologically diverse, and openly biased.

Mainstream news sources—the network news programs and the prestige press—have lost audiences to tendentious radio talk shows, Internet bloggers, and Fox News. Fox News is unique among national television news outlets in adopting a transparent ideological and partisan identity, staffing its shows with conservative pundits and once and future Republican presidential candidates. Indeed, most of the innovations in political media have come from the right side of the political spectrum, often with the avowed purpose of countering the alleged liberal bias of the mainstream media. Fanning the flames of partisan and ideological conflict is central to the business plan. Imitators on the left have not been nearly as successful in attracting audiences, but not for want of trying. Media fragmentation, partiality, and competition for niche audiences have clearly coarsened public discourse; they also have enabled people to find information outlets that can be counted on to reinforce rather than challenge their political beliefs and opinions.

THEN AND NOW: FOUR COMPARISONS

To get a flavor of how these developments have affected the way politicians, the media, and the public treat presidents, consider the following four comparisons.

1. In 1960, John F. Kennedy defeated Richard Nixon in the closest presidential election in history.[9] He would have lost the electoral vote had it not been for narrow victories in Illinois and Texas, both tainted by charges of vote fraud sufficiently serious to convince Nixon and other Republican leaders that the election had been stolen from them. Yet Nixon decided against challenging the results and demanding a recount, even asking a reporter who was writing a series of articles reporting evidence of vote fraud to stop because, Nixon said, he did not want to provoke a constitutional crisis at the height of the Cold War.[10] The story soon faded from public attention; neither Gallup nor any other polling outfit even bothered to ask Americans if they thought Kennedy had won the election fairly, and his legitimacy was not questioned by any prominent Republican leader. During his first three months in office, an average of 59 percent of Republican identifiers approved of Kennedy's performance, and their ratings remained at this high level through Kennedy's entire first year in office.

In 2000, Al Gore won the major party popular vote, 50.26 percent to George W. Bush's 49.74 percent, but election night found Bush with a tiny lead in Florida, which, if sustained, would give him an Electoral College majority and thus the White House. The close Florida vote triggered an automatic recount amid revelations of balloting irregularities that left the accuracy of any final count forever in doubt. Teams of lawyers for both candidates fought bitterly over whether and how to conduct a recount, and the dispute was not settled until five weeks after the election when a majority of five Supreme Court justices, all Republican appointees, stopped the recount, effectively handing the presidency to Bush.

From election night onward, and ignoring the real uncertainties about what had occurred, partisan elites and activists rallied to their party's candidate with heated rhetoric and, on one occasion, a mini-riot (among Republican staffers). Ordinary Americans also split along party lines in responding to polling questions about the controversy; in surveys taken in the two months following the election, an average of 87 percent of Republicans thought Bush was the legitimate winner, while 74 percent of Democrats thought he was not; four years later when Bush was running for reelection, the proportion of Democrats thinking he had not been the legitimate winner in 2000 had grown to an average of 83 percent.[11] Bush entered the White House in 2001 with only about 30 percent of Democrats approving his performance. His rating remained at that level or lower until the great rally following the terrorist attacks of September 11.

2. The Vietnam War became increasingly controversial and unpopular over the course of Lyndon Johnson's administration (1963–69). It spawned an extensive anti-war movement, complete with mass demonstrations that sometimes turned violent, and split a nation accustomed to unity in wartime into quarreling "hawks" and "doves." Reactions to the war contributed to the profound changes in American social mores and behavior that defined the 1960s, initiating social and ideological cleavages that continue to divide Americans decades later. Johnson became a figure of hatred and scorn for many in the anti-war camp and endured some of the vilest personal attacks imaginable.[12]

The Vietnam War certainly polarized the country, but not along party lines. In Congress, hawks and doves could be found on both sides of the aisle. In the public, Democrats, Republicans, and independents grew disaffected with the war at similar rates over time. The average partisan gap in polls probing support for the war was a mere 5 percentage points, the smallest for any of the post–World War II American military actions,[13] with Democrats slightly more supportive while Johnson was president and Republicans slightly more supportive when Nixon took over in 1969. The decline in approval of Johnson's performance was also bipartisan. The war cost Johnson's party the presidency, but it did so by splitting his coalition rather than by shifting popular support to the Republican Party.

The war in Iraq also became increasingly divisive and unpopular during George W. Bush's presidency.[14] This time, however, the parties were divided over the wisdom and necessity of the war even before it began, and they became even more divided as the war dragged on (Figure 8.1). Within a year of its onset, the partisan gap in support for the war had grown to more than 60 percentage points and it remained above 50 points for the remainder of Bush's presidency, the widest partisan division by far on any post-war military action. From the start, Bush's approval ratings were tightly bound to opinions on the war; as partisans grew increasingly divided on the war, they became increasingly divided in their views of the president. Republican support for the president and the war declined only slowly and never dipped

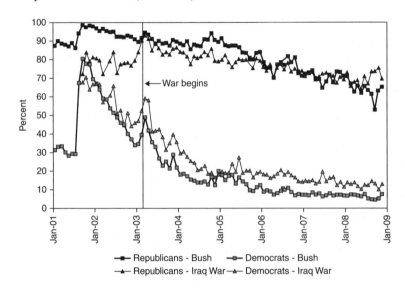

FIGURE 8.1 Approval of GWB's Performance and Support for Iraq War, by Party

below a majority; Democrats soon grew thoroughly disillusioned with both, and Bush became the most divisive president on record.[15]

3. The Watergate scandal, involving break-ins and other illegal activities targeting Richard Nixon's supposed enemies, and the administration's efforts to cover them up, led to Nixon's resignation in 1974 under the threat of almost certain impeachment and conviction. Nixon gradually lost public and elite support among both Democrats and Republicans as the scandal unfolded, although he always had more defenders among his own partisans; just before his resignation in August, 64 percent of Americans, including 42 percent of Republicans, thought he should be impeached. Nixon gave up when Republican senators told him he did not have enough support in his own party to avoid conviction in the Senate if, as expected, the House voted to impeach him.

In 1998, the Republican-controlled House actually did vote to impeach Bill Clinton for lying and obstruction of justice in trying to cover up his tacky affair with Monica Lewinsky, a White House intern. All but four Republicans voted for at least one of the four articles of impeachment; only five Democrats voted for any of them. In what was billed as a "conscience" vote, 98 percent of the Republican consciences dictated a vote to impeach the president, while 98 percent of the Democratic consciences dictated the opposite. After the Senate's impeachment trial, every Democrat voted for acquittal, while 91 percent of Republicans voted for conviction on at least one article.

Although Americans on the whole opposed impeachment, popular partisan divisions on the issue were also huge, with a large majority of Republican identifiers favoring impeachment and an even larger majority of Democratic identifiers opposing it. In the end, 68 percent of Republicans wanted the Senate to convict and remove Clinton, with only 30 percent favoring acquittal; among Democrats, 89 percent favored acquittal, while only 10 percent favored conviction.[16] Clinton's approval rating among Democrats peaked at 90 percent in January 1999 while the Senate was deliberating his fate; Republican ratings were 56 points lower.

4. That John F. Kennedy was an enthusiastic womanizer was no secret to his colleagues in the Senate or to reporters covering his presidential campaign. Yet this never came up either in the Republican campaign against him or in press coverage of the election. In 1992, in contrast, Bill Clinton had to deal with charges of infidelity first raised during the primary. He then spent most of his presidency under continuing Republican-sponsored probes of his personal life, culminating in the exposure of his dalliance with Lewinsky that eventually led to his impeachment by the House.

Of course, each of these comparisons involves situations that differ in important respects. Unlike the Cold War premise of Vietnam, the Bush administration's main justification for the Iraq War—that Iraq was producing and hiding weapons of mass destruction—was discredited within a year of the U.S. invasion. Nixon's transgressions involved the abuse of power aimed at harming political opponents and attempting to cover it up; Clinton was trying to conceal an embarrassing sexual indiscretion. Moreover, in 1974, the economy was in recession; in 1998, it was booming. In 2000, a machine recount was, under Florida law, automatic in a close election; in 1960, Democrats controlled the counting process in Texas and Illinois and could block a recount. Public and private life were still considered separate domains in 1960; by the 1990s, the distinction had virtually disappeared, with parties routinely hiring investigators to dig up dirt on the other side's candidates (opposition research, it is called), and media outlets trafficking in scandal, real or imagined, spreading like kudzu. Nonetheless, these anecdotes suggest that partisanship now plays a much larger role in shaping elite and popular reactions to presidents and their actions than it once did, a conjecture that is amply supported by more systematic evidence.

PRESIDENTIAL APPROVAL

One indisputable sign of the growing strength of party in shaping reactions to presidents is the widening partisan divide in popular evaluations of the president's job performance. The trend is documented in Figures 8.2 through 8.5, which display the quarterly averages of the share of identifiers with president's party and the rival party who said they approved of the president's job performance in Gallup Polls taken between 1953 and 2011. Two things stand out when we compare the first two figures, covering the Eisenhower through Carter administrations, to the second two figures, covering the Reagan through Obama administrations. First, the partisan trends move more consistently in parallel in the earlier than in the later period. During the Johnson, Nixon, and Carter administrations, for example, ordinary Democrats and Republicans clearly reacted in very similar ways to whatever was driving popular evaluations of the president (mainly disillusionment with the Vietnam War for Johnson, the Watergate scandal for Nixon, and economic problems for Carter). This was not true for either of the Bush administrations, during which job approval ratings offered by Republicans tended to remain quite high even while those offered by Democrats were plummeting.[17]

Second, and more importantly, partisan differences tend to be much wider in the later period than in the earlier period. The gross trajectory of

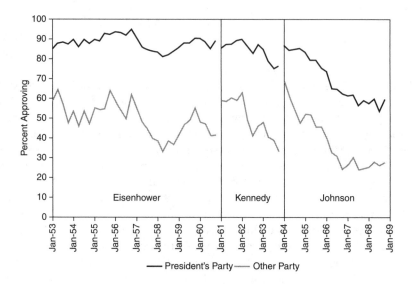

FIGURE 8.2   Presidential Approval, By Party, Eisenhower through Johnson

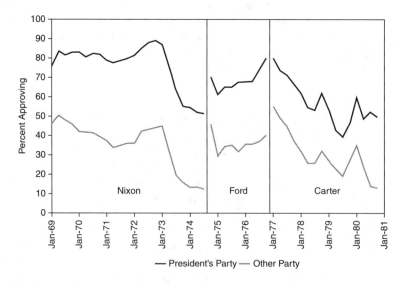

FIGURE 8.3   Presidential Approval, By Party, Nixon through Carter

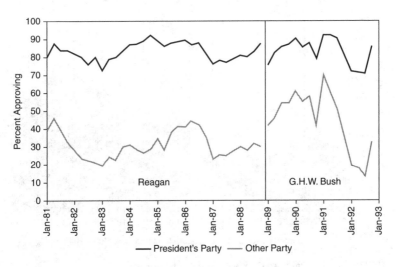

FIGURE 8.4   Presidential Approval, By Party, Reagan-G.H.W. Bush

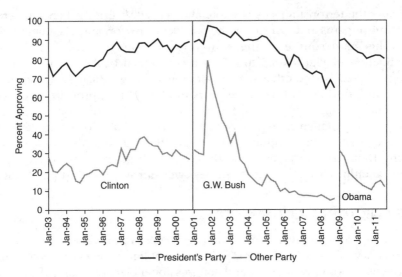

FIGURE 8.5   Presidential Approval, By Party, Clinton-Obama

the partisan approval gap (measured by annual averages) suggests that it expanded in two fairly distinct steps (Figure 8.6). From the Eisenhower through the Carter administrations, partisan differences were comparatively modest, averaging about 35 percentage points; from the Reagan through the Clinton administrations, the average gap jumped to 51 points; since G.W. Bush took office in 2001, the average gap has risen again, to an average of 63 points. The rise is not unbroken; Reagan and Clinton were more divisive than the president they bracket, G.H.W. Bush, at least until his final year in office, and G.W. Bush enjoyed a period of strong bipartisan support when the public rallied to his

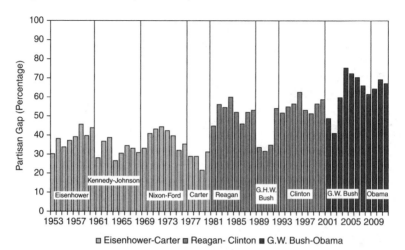

FIGURE 8.6 The Partisan Gap in Presidential Approval

side after the terrorist attacks of September 11, 2001. But the general increase over time in partisan dissensus on the president's performance is unmistakable.

The main source of the widening partisan gap, evident from an examination of Figures 8.3 to 8.5, is a substantial decline in the approval ratings offered by the other party's adherents.[18] G.W. Bush set the record in this regard; during his final three years in office, his approval rating among Democrats averaged 8 percent, hitting an all-time low of 3 percent in three Gallup surveys taken in September and October 2008. For comparison, this figure is 8 percentage points lower than Richard Nixon's worst showing among Democrats just before he resigned in disgrace in 1974. Republican approval ratings from these three surveys were an average of 61 points higher.

THE ELECTORAL CONNECTION

The increasing influence of party on presidential approval echoes the growing potency of party in electoral politics. Party-line voting has become more prevalent in both presidential and congressional elections since the 1970s.[19] So have partisan electoral consistency and coherence; since 1972, the rates of ticket splitting (voting for a president of one party and a senator or representative of the other) and split outcomes (states and congressional districts delivering majorities to different parties' presidential and congressional candidates) have fallen sharply, while correlations between the presidential and congressional votes at the state and district level have grown to their highest levels in 60 years.[20]

One consequence is that electoral coalitions assembled by winning presidential candidates have become increasingly dominated by the president's own partisan. Table 8.1 displays the percentage of each successful presidential candidate's electoral coalition—those respondents who reported

| TABLE 8.1 | Partisan Composition of Presidents' Electoral Coalitions, 1952–2008 |

	Republican Presidents			Democratic Presidents		
	Own Party	Other Party	Independents	Own Party	Other Party	Independents
1952	65	29	6			
1956	65	22	13			
1960				86	6	8
1964				80	14	6
1968	68	23	10			
1972	58	33	10			
1976				80	10	10
1980	65	24	11			
1984	73	17	10			
1988	79	14	8			
1992				84	8	8
1996				85	12	4
2000	80	12	8			
2004	86	9	5			
2008				85	8	7

voting for the winning candidate in that year's American National Election Study—who were from the president's party, the rival party, or were pure independents.[21] For much of this period, the Democratic Party enjoyed a large advantage among people who identified with a party, so Republican presidents necessarily had to attract a lot of Democrats to get elected. Their cross-party appeal has obviously diminished: G.W. Bush's second electoral coalition was easily the most homogeneously partisan of any in the Republican series. Democratic presidents have never attracted as much cross-party support as Republicans, but Clinton and Obama's coalitions were more partisan than any since Kennedy's, which had been assembled at a time when party loyalty was at an earlier peak.

The growth in party-line voting and decline in ticket splitting have also sharply reduced the proportion of electoral constituents presidents share with members of Congress from the other party. At the peak in 1972, about 50 percent of the voters for the winning Senate and House Democrats had also voted for Nixon; in 2008, only 10 percent of voters for the winning Republican senators also voted for Obama, as did only 21 percent of voters for the winning Republican representatives.[22] To an increasing extent, then,

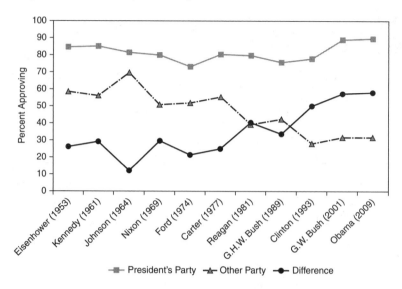

FIGURE 8.7   Partisanship and Approval of Newly Inaugurated Presidents

Source: Gallup Polls taken during the first quarter of each administration (average).

senators and representatives in the party not controlling the White House have owed their election to people who voted against the president.

That recent presidents have entered office with relatively little support from voters identifying with the other party has no doubt contributed to the decline in approval ratings among its partisans—but this cannot be the whole story. Although Kennedy won relatively few votes from Republicans, they did not immediately turn critical of his performance (Figure 8.7). At one time, newly elected presidents could expect to enjoy a "honeymoon" period during which many voters on the losing side were willing to give them the benefit of the doubt before going into opposition. From Eisenhower through Carter, a majority of out-party identifiers approved of the president's performance during his first three months in office. Since Reagan, the honeymoon has become a thing of the past, with the partisan gap in approval during the supposed honeymoon period growing from an average of 23 percentage points prior to 1980 to 58 points for G.W. Bush and Obama. Presidents are thus now dividers rather than uniters as soon as they enter office.

ATTACKS ON THE PRESIDENT'S LEGITIMACY

Some partisans on the losing side have now moved beyond mere disapproval to full-scale attacks on the president's legitimacy. Bizarre conspiracy theories about a president's ascension to power have never been entirely absent among his more fervent detractors, but until recently such theories have been confined to crackpots operating on the more remote fringes of political life.

No respectable politician or reporter thought it worth pursuing the claims that Eisenhower was a communist agent or that Johnson had arranged the assassination of his predecessor, although both notions had their fevered proponents. Bill Clinton, in contrast, was dogged by investigations not only of his past sex life and real estate dealings, but also whether the suicide of his wife's aide, Vincent Foster, had actually been a murder arranged or covered up by the Clintons. Suspicions fanned by journalists financed by Clinton's Republican enemies led to three years of investigations by the Department of Justice, the FBI, Congress, and two independent counsels (all concluding that Foster's death was a suicide).[23] The legitimacy of George W. Bush's election was questioned not only in 2000, when the Florida debacle gave the idea some plausibility, but also in 2004, when charges of election-rigging in Ohio, a state Bush won by nearly 119,000 votes, drew attention from congressional Democrats and investigators and led to some on the left to argue that the election had been stolen.[24]

The most sustained attacks on a president's legitimacy, however, have been directed at Barack Obama. During the 2008 Republican presidential campaign, John McCain, Sarah Palin, and their allies sought to define Obama as a '60s-style radical plotting to turn the United States into a socialist country.[25] The campaign failed to win the election, but it did succeed in shaping perceptions of Obama among people who did not vote for him, a large proportion of whom came to view him as a dishonest leftist radical with a socialist agenda.[26] Hostility to Obama left many of his detractors susceptible to spurious claims that he was not even born in the United States and was therefore constitutionally barred from the presidency. In eight surveys taken between April 2010 and April 2011, an average of 40 percent of Republicans said they thought Obama was foreign born, 17 percent said they did not know, and only 43 percent said he was American born.[27] Several Republican members of Congress implied that Obama's citizenship could legitimately be questioned, and some Republican state legislators introduced legislation to compel presidential candidates to prove their citizenship to get on their state's ballot.[28] Even after the administration had delivered the proof demanded by the so-called "birthers," the belief persisted; in May of 2011, about a quarter of Republican partisans still said that Obama was probably or definitely foreign born.[29]

A substantial proportion of Republicans also refused to acknowledge that Obama is a Christian; in four surveys taken during 2009 and 2010, an average of 31 percent of Republicans said he was a Muslim; 38 percent, a Christian; and the rest did not know.[30] An August 2010 a *Newsweek* poll found a majority of Republicans believing that it was definitely (14 percent) or probably (38 percent) true that "Barack Obama sympathizes with the goals of Islamic fundamentalists who want to impose Islamic law around the world."[31]

The balance of sincere belief and opportunistic Obama-bashing measured in these survey responses is uncertain,[32] but they do stand as clear evidence of both motivated reasoning (in this instance, uncritical acceptance of highly dubious information consistent with one's biases) and the eagerness of so many of Obama's opponents to declare him un-American. G. W. Bush and his policies also provoked some strongly biased partisan takes on reality. A solid majority of Republicans, for example, continued to believe that Iraq possessed weapons of mass destruction (WMD) at the time the U.S. invaded years after the Bush administration had conceded that none could be found. Meanwhile, half of the Democrats who had once believed Iraq possessed WMD and had initially supported the war evidently forgot they had done so after they had turned against it.[33] During Bush's second term, about 80 percent of Democrats came to believe that Bush was not merely mistaken about the WMD but had deliberately misled the public to justify going to war.[34] No one knows for sure how confident the president and his advisors were in their judgment that Iraq was making and hiding WMD, but they did seem totally unprepared for the search to come up so empty. Most Democrats, however, chose to resolve any uncertainties about Bush's candor in his disfavor. A couple of surveys even found a surprising proportion of Democrats saying that Bush knowingly let the terrorist attacks of September 11, 2001, on New York City and the Pentagon happen, or even planned them.[35] Like some Republican "birthers," some Democrats evidently took the opportunity offered by a survey question to vilify a president they detested.

GOING TO FURTHER EXTREMES: THE TEA PARTY

Although both Bush and Obama provoked extraordinarily strong partisan reactions, particularly from rival partisans, Obama is unique in inspiring a self-conscious political movement among his partisan detractors: the Tea Party. Some Tea Party activists claim to disdain the Republican establishment, but the vast majority of Tea Party activists and supporters are Republicans (or independents leaning toward the Republican Party) who voted for John McCain in 2008. They form the populist right wing of the Republican coalition, sharing the political beliefs and opinions typical of other Republicans, only with more consistent conservative orthodoxy. Tea Partiers have been especially eager to question Obama's origins and legitimacy; the 2010 Cooperative Congressional Election Study found 53 percent of respondents with positive opinions of the Tea Party, saying that Obama was either foreign born or a Muslim, with only 15 percent acknowledging the reality that he is an American-born Christian.[36]

Tea Partiers led the rhetorical assault on Obama at rallies and demonstrations, protesting his health care reform legislation and other initiatives. To the movement's more unhinged adherents, Obama is not simply an objectionable liberal Democrat, but a tyrant (of the Nazi, fascist, communist, socialist, monarchist, or racist variety, depending on the critic)[37] intent on subjecting Americans to, variously, socialism, communism, fascism, concentration camps, or control by United Nations, Interpol, international bankers, the Council on Foreign Relations, or the Trilateral Commission.[38] To be sure, far from all Tea Party supporters (about a quarter of the public) or sympathizers (about a third of the public, but a solid majority of Republicans) entertain such bizarre notions, but they are nearly unanimous in their disdain for Obama and believe that his policies are moving the country toward socialism.[39]

Conservative voices on talk radio, Fox News, and the Internet have encouraged the Tea Party movement in its bitterly anti-Obama stance, sticking to a business model in which outraged denunciation, unconstrained by any fetish for accuracy, is the stock in trade. Glenn Beck, a demagogic conspiracy theorist with the rant of a street-corner crank, became for a time a star performer on Fox, with a nightly audience of millions.[40] According to the April 2010 CBS News/*New York Times* survey, Fox News was the preferred news source for 60 percent of the Tea Party supporters, and 58 percent of them viewed Glenn Beck favorably (the comparable figures for other Americans were 13 percent and 8 percent, respectively).[41]

STRATEGIC POLARIZATION

Tea Party sentiments and rhetoric epitomize the "rude, nasty, and stubborn" aspect of contemporary American politics. They also identified a source of partisan passion and energy that Republican congressional leaders were eager to encourage and exploit for the 2010 elections. Thus, soon after Obama took office, they adopted a strategy of reflexive rejection of almost anything the administration and Obama's Democratic allies in Congress proposed, exemplified by their unanimous opposition to changes in the health care system that, as its Democratic defenders were fond of pointing out, look very much like those Republican presidential aspirant Mitt Romney had pushed through when he was governor of Massachusetts and that Republicans had proposed as alternatives to Bill Clinton's plan in 1993. Republican leaders even adopted some of the Tea Party's apocalyptic rhetoric in denouncing the legislation: House minority leader John Boehner called the struggle over the final vote "Armageddon" because the bill would "ruin our country."[42] His Republican colleague, Devin Nunes of California, declared that with this "Soviet"-inspired bill, Democrats "will finally lay the cornerstone of their socialist utopia on the backs of the American people."[43]

Republican leaders adopted this oppositional stance and hyperbolic rhetoric because they figured it would revive their electoral fortunes, which had taken a beating in the 2006 and 2008 elections. It turned out to be shrewd strategy for several reasons. First, their attacks on the president and refusal to allow him any bipartisan legislative victories helped erode his standing with the public, which had the effect of tarnishing the Democratic Party's image and weakening its appeal as an object of individual identification.[44] As Figure 8.8 shows, opinions of the president and his party are now closely related; the fewer people with positive opinions of the president, the fewer with positive opinions of his party.[45] And as Figure 8.9 shows, the president's approval ratings are also strongly related to the share of partisans who say they identify with the president's party.[46] The lower the president's approval ratings, the smaller his party's share of identifiers, an effect that is especially consequential in an era of strong party-line voting. Thus, anything

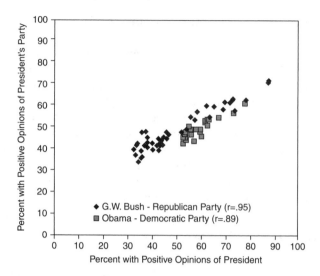

FIGURE 8.8 Positive Views of the President and His party, Obama and Bush Administrations

Source: NBC News/*Wall Street Journal* Polls.

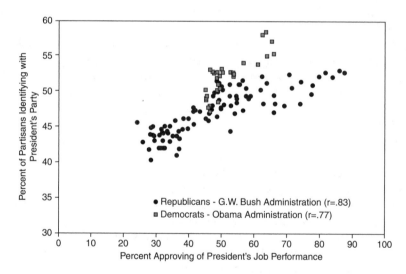

FIGURE 8.9 Presidential Approval and Party Identification, GWB and Obama Administrations

Source: Gallup Polls.

the opposition can do to diminish the president's standing with the public pays additional electoral dividends by diminishing that of his party as well.

Second, the Republican attack strategy was well suited to an era in which opinions of the president have an increasingly powerful influence on voting in midterm elections. The growing connection between evaluations of the president's performance and midterm voting is clear from Figures 8.10 and 8.11, which display the percentages of survey respondents in elections from 1974 through 2010 whose House and Senate votes were consistent with their evaluations of the president's job performance: voting for the president's party's candidate if they approved, or voting for the rival party's candidate if they disapproved.[47] The upward trajectory is obvious, with both series reaching their highest points yet in 2010, when an average of 88 percent of House voters and 91 percent of Senate voters reported casting a vote in line with their assessments of Obama's performance.

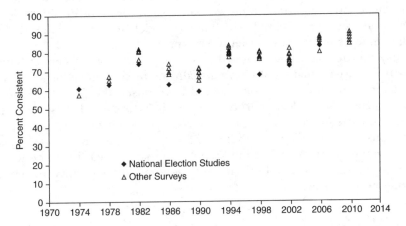

FIGURE 8.10 Consistency of Presidential Approval and the House Vote in Midterm Elections

Source: See Endnote 47.

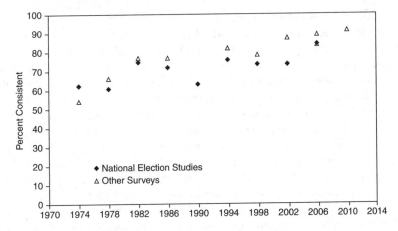

FIGURE 8.11 Consistency of Presidential Approval and Senate Voting in Midterm Elections

Source: See Endnote 47.

Third, the strategy helped to generate comparatively high Republican turnout, particularly among the Tea Party faction. Republicans reported much greater enthusiasm about participation in the 2010 midterm, with Tea Party supporters the most enthusiastic of all.[48] Differences in enthusiasm translated into differences in participation, with Republicans voting at higher rates than Democrats and Tea Party sympathizers voting at higher rates than other Republicans. [49]

The result was not only a historic Republican victory[50] but also proof of the strategy's potency, assuring its continuation in the new Congress. Just before the election, Senate minority leader Mitch McConnell had declared, "The single most important thing we want to achieve is for President Obama to be a one-term president."[51] The battle over deficit reduction and the debt ceiling in the summer of 2011 left no doubt that he meant it. McConnell and his Republican colleagues refused to consider any sort of comprehensive bipartisan bargain that would have actually addressed the nation's long-term fiscal problems, for such a deal would have raised the president's stature as a problem-solving leader. They also could focus on reducing the federal deficit rather than creating jobs and spurring economic growth. Indeed, they could push for spending cuts that might well reduce demand and thus slow the economy, in the comfortable knowledge that Obama would be the one to suffer politically if employment and economic growth failed to rebound before the 2012 election.

CONCLUSION

In the current era of evenly balanced, strongly opposed national parties, campaigning never really stops because the stakes are so high and every electoral victory or defeat is reversible in the next election. And partisan divisions in the public ensure that any politician sufficiently appealing to his or her own party's voters to win a presidential nomination will have little appeal to the voters on the other side. Under such conditions, presidents will always find bipartisan support from politicians and the public elusive, except, perhaps, in the face of dire emergencies, such as the one provoked by the terrorist attacks of September 11, 2001. Obama's pursuit of Republican votes for his health care reform and comprehensive deficit reduction proposals proved futile, attracting no Republican support while disappointing his party's liberals. The president's only alternative is to concentrate on mobilizing his own side while peeling off enough votes from the opposing party to overcome a Senate filibuster if one cannot otherwise be circumvented. G.W. Bush achieved several such victories,[52] as did Obama on the passage of his health care reforms. These are, however, polarizing victories. When the parties square off, no matter who wins, political rhetoric heats up, professional ideologues fulminate, and most ordinary citizens, while professing to detest the partisan squabbling, reflexively take their party's side. Until something interrupts this polarizing dynamic, "rude, nasty, and stubborn" presidential politics will continue to be the order of the day.

Endnotes

1. The most recent update of the DW Nominate series was undertaken by Jeffrey B. Lewis, Keith T. Pool, and Howard Rosenthal and is available at http://voteview.com/downloads.asp (accessed August 8, 2011).

2. Alan I. Abramowitz, *The Disappearing Center: Engaged Citizens, Polarization, and American Democracy* (New Haven: Yale University Press, 2010); Morris P. Fiorina with Samuel Adams, *Disconnect: The Breakdown of Representation in American Politics* (Norman, OK: University of Oklahoma Press, 2009); Matthew Levendusky, *The Partisan Sort: How Liberals Became Democrats and Conservatives Became Republicans* (Chicago: University of Chicago Press, 2009); Morris P. Fiorina, Samuel J. Adams, and Jeremy C. Pope, *Culture War? The Myth of a Polarized America* (New York: Longman 2006).

3. Gary C. Jacobson, "The Electoral Basis of Partisan Polarization in Congress," presented at the Annual Meeting of the American Political Science Association, Washington, D.C., August 31–September 3, 2000; Larry M. Bartels, "Partisanship and Voting Behavior, 1952–1996," *American Journal of Political Science* 44 (January, 2000): 35–50; Levendusky, *Partisan Sort*, 39–52; Abramowitz, *Disappearing Center*, 34–61. The electoral units in which people find themselves have also grown more politically homogeneous; see Jeffrey M., Stonecash, Mark D. Brewer, and Mach D. Mariani, *Diverging Parties: Social Change, Realignment, and Party Polarization* (Boulder, CO: Westview Press, 2003), and Gary C. Jacobson, *The Politics of Congressional Elections*, 8th ed. (New York: Longman, 2013), pp. 258–274.

4. Johnson is reported to have said upon signing the Civil Rights Act of 1964, "We have lost the South for a generation."; see Richard Cohen, "The Election that LBJ Won," *Washington Post*, November 4, 2008.

5. Levendusky, *Partisan Sort*, Ch. 6.

6. Marc J. Hetherington and Jonathan D. Weiler, *Authoritarianism and Polarization in American Politics* (New York: Cambridge University Press, 2009), p. 11.

7. John C. Green, "The Fifth National Survey of Religion and Politics: A Baseline for the 2008 Presidential Elections," Ray C. Bliss Institute of Applied Politics, University of Akron, September 19, 2008.

8. Ziva Kunda, "The Case for Motivated Reasoning." *Psychological Bulletin* 108 (3) 1990: 636–647; Milton Lodge and Charles S. Taber, "Three Steps toward a Theory of Motivated Political Reasoning," in Arthur Lupia, Mathew D. McCubbins, and Samuel L. Popkin (eds.), *Elements of Reason: Cognition, Choice, and the Bounds of Rationality* (Cambridge: Cambridge University Press, 2000), 183–213; Charles S. Taber and Milton Lodge, "Motivated Skepticism in the Evaluation of Political Beliefs". *American Journal of Political Science 50* (July 2006): pp. 755–769.

9. Official returns gave Kennedy 50.09 percent of the major-party vote, Nixon, 49.91 percent.

10. Peter Carlson, "Another Race to the Finish," *Washington Post*, November 17, 2000, A1.

11. Gary C. Jacobson, *A Divider, Not a Uniter: George W. Bush and the American People*, 2nd ed. (New York: Pearson Longman, 2011), pp. 48–53.

12. Theodore H. White, *The Making of the President 1968* (New York: Atheneum Publishers, 1969), pp. 103–104.

13. Jacobson, *Divider*, pp. 101–107.

14. Because it was fought with an all-volunteer military, the Iraq War did not provoke anything like the level of mass protest that occurred during the Vietnam era, when millions of young American men faced the prospect of being drafted into the fighting.

15. Jacobson, *Divider*, pp. 6–7.

16. Gallup/*USA Today* Poll, February 12–13, 1999, reported at http://www.pollingreport.com/scandals.htm (accessed February 15, 1999).

17. The correlation between partisans' approval ratings is .89 for the Eisenhower–Carter period, and .61 for the Reagan–Obama period.

18. The partisan gap is correlated with the out-party's approval ratings at –.05 for the Eisenhower–Carter period, and –.89 for the Reagan–Obama period.

19. In the American National Election Study, from 1952 through 1976, partisans voted loyalty for their party's presidential candidate an average of 82 percent of the time; between 1980 and 1988, the loyalty rate was 85 percent; since then, it has averaged a little over 90 percent; for evidence of increased party loyalty in House and Senate elections, see Jacobson, *Politics of Congressional Elections*, Figures 6.2 and 6.3.

20. Jacobson, *Politics of Congressional Elections*, Figures 6.3 to 6.5.

21. The NES classifies partisans on a seven-category scale: strong Democrats, not strong Democrats, independents leaning toward the Democratic Party, pure independents, independents leaning toward the Republican Party, not strong Republicans, and Strong Republicans. Because independent leaners generally vote like not strong partisans, I include them here among the partisans.

22. Ibid., Figures 7–13 and 7–14.

23. The House inquiry was led by Dan Burton, an Indiana Republican who tried to show that Foster was murdered by reenacting the supposed crime in his backyard, firing his pistol into a pumpkin representing Foster's head. See "Fool on the Hill," Time.Com, May 8–10, 1998, at http://www.time.com/time/daily/special/look/burton/ (accessed July 28, 2011).

24. Mark Crispen Miller, "None Dare Call It Stolen: Ohio, the Election and America's Servile Press," *Harpers Magazine*, August 2005, at http://harpers.org/archive/2005/08/0080696 (accessed July 28, 2011).

25. Scott Conroy, "Palin: Obama's Plan Is 'Experiment with Socialism,'" CBS News, October 19, 2008, at http://www.cbsnews.com/8301-503443_162-4532388.html (accessed June 21, 2010); Bob Drogan and Mark Barabak, "McCain Says Obama Wants Socialism," *Los Angeles Times*, October 19, 2008; Alex Johnson, "McCain Hammers Obama on Ayers Ties," MSNBC, October 23, 2008, at http://www.msnbc.msn.com/id/27343688/ (accessed March 20, 2010); Kate Kenski, Bruce W. Hardy, and Kathleen Hall Jamieson, *The Obama Victory: How Media, Money, and Message Shaped the 2008 Election* (New York: Oxford University Press, 2010).

26. Gary C. Jacobson, "Obama and the Polarized Public," in *Obama in Office: The First Two years*, ed. James A. Thurber (Boulder, CO: Paradigm Publishers, 2011), pp. 19–40.

27. Only 10 percent of Democrats, on average, thought Obama was foreign born; the surveys are from CBS News/*New York Times*, April 5–1, 2010, June 1–3, 2010, and April 15–20, 2011; ABC News/*Washington Post,* April 22–25, 2010; CNN, July 17–20, 2010; Fox News, April 3–5, 2011, Gallup, April 20–23, 2011, and the 2010 Cooperative Congressional Election Study.

28. See the references at http://en.wikipedia.org/wiki/Barack_Obama_citizenship_conspiracy_theories (accessed August 2, 2011).

29. Gallup Poll, May 2–8, 2011; CNN Poll, April 29–May 1, 2011.

30. Pew Research Center for the People & the Press, March 9–12, 2009 and July 21–August 5, 2010; *Time*/SRBI Poll, August 16–17, 2010; 2010 Cooperative Congressional Election Study, Harvard-UCSD Module.

31. Seventeen percent of Democrats and 27 percent of Independents were of the same opinion; *Newsweek* Poll, August 25–26, 2010, at http://nw-assets.s3.amazonaws.com/pdf/1004-ftop.pdf (accessed August 2, 2011).

32. There is certainly some of the latter; as disapproval of Obama's performance increased, so did the proportion of respondents thinking he was a Muslim; about 95 percent of those saying he was a Muslim disapproved of his performance (from data in the polls referenced in note 31).

33. Gary C. Jacobson, "Perception, Memory, and Partisan Polarization on the Iraq War," *Political Science Quarterly 125* (Spring 2010): 31–56.

34. That was the average in 26 surveys that asked the question during this period; only about 16 percent of Republicans held this view; see Jacobson, *Divider*, p. 114.

35. A Zogby survey taken in August 23–27, 2007, found 36 percent of Democrats saying that Bush had knowingly let the attacks happen, with 6 percent saying he made them happen. The respective figures for Republicans were 16 percent and 4 percent; at http://www.911truth.org/images/ZogbyPoll2007.pdf (accessed August 4, 2011).

36. Gary C. Jacobson, "The President, the Tea Party, and Voting Behavior in 2010: Insights from the Cooperative Congressional Election Study," paper presented at the Annual Meeting of the Political Science Association, Seattle, September 1–4, 2011.

37. Google, "Obama" in conjunction with any of these labels to see how routinely they are used—and defended—on the Internet.

38. David Barstow, "Tea Party Lights Fuse for Rebellion on Right," *New York Times*, February 16, 2010.

39. Only 5 percent of Tea Party supporters in the April 5–12 CBS News/*New York Times* poll approved of Obama's performance; 90 percent disapproved, and 94 percent said his policies were leading the country toward socialism (author's analysis of the survey supplied by the Roper Center, University of Connnecticut, survey USCBSNYT2010-04). Also see "Tea Party Movement: What They Think," at http://www.cbsnews.com/htdocs/pdf/poll_tea_party_041410.pdf (accessed April 15, 2010). For summary data on Tea Party support, see http://www.pollingreport.com/politics.htm (accessed August 9, 2011).

40. For a sample of Beck's flights of rhetoric, see http://politicalhumor.about.com/library/bl-glenn-beck-quotes.htm (accessed March 24, 2010); by one count reported in July, 2010, since Obama's inauguration, Beck transcripts included "202 mentions of Nazis or Nazism, . . . 147 mentions of Hitler, 193 mentions of fascism or fascist, and another 24 bonus mentions of Joseph Goebbels. Most of these were directed in some form at Obama—as were a majority of the 802 mentions of socialist or socialism"; see Dana Milibank, "The Tea Party Makes Trouble with a Capital T," *Washington Post*, July 18, 2010.

41. "Tea Party Movement: What They Think," at http://www.cbsnews.com/htdocs/pdf/poll_tea_party_041410.pdf (accessed April 15, 2010).

42. "Boehner: It's "Armageddon," Health Care Bill Will "Ruin our Country," The Speaker's Lobby, Fox News, March 20, 2010, at http://congress.blogs.foxnews.

com/2010/03/20/boehner-its-armageddon-health-care-bill-will-ruin-our-country/comment-page-3/?action=late-new (accessed April 2, 2010).

43. Speech on the House floor, March 21, 2010, video available at http://vodpod.com/watch/3280104-devin-nunes-health-care-the-ghost-of-communism-a-socialist-utopia (accessed April 10, 2010).

44. Gary C. Jacobson, "The Effects of the George W. Bush Presidency on Partisan Attitudes," *Presidential Studies Quarterly* 39, June, 2009: 173–209.

45. The relationship between positive views of the president and positive views of the rival party is much weaker; it was actually positive (r=.35) during the G.W. Bush administration, but is negative (r=-.45) during the Obama administration.

46. The data include independents who lean toward a party as partisans.

47. The data are from the American National Election Studies, Cooperative Congressional Elections Studies, national exit polls, and CBS News/*New York Times*, Gallup, *Newsweek, Time,* ABC News/*Washington Post*, CNN, NBC News/*Wall Street Journal*, and Pew surveys taken just before or after the election; exit poll and media survey data were acquired through the Roper Center, University of Connecticut. The number of surveys for each year for House elections ranges from two to twelve, with an average of six; the number of surveys per Senate election ranges from 1 to 3, with most having only two observations. The NES tends to report lower consistency, so I have highlighted the NES entries in the figures; I found no systematic difference among the other types of surveys either by timing (pre- or post-election) or survey organization.

48. In Gallup's final pre-election survey, 58 percent of Republicans and 76 percent of Republican Tea Party supporters (comprising 54 percent of Republicans in this poll) said they are "very enthusiastic" about voting. By comparison, only 41 percent of Democrats and only 46 percent of Democratic Tea Party opponents (comprising 57 percent of all Democrats surveyed) were very enthusiastic about voting; see Gallup/*USA Today* Poll: Final Midterm Pre-Election Poll 2010 [USAIPOUSA2010-TR1028], available through the Roper Center, University of Connecticut.

49. Jacobson, "President, Tea Party, and Voting," 20–22.

50. Republicans gained a net 63 House seats to win a 242–193 majority, their best showing since 1946; they gained 6 Senate seats to raise their total from 41 to 47 and to put them in reach of a majority in 2012, when 23 of the 33 seats at stake will be defended by Democrats.

51. Gerald F. Seib, "The Potential Pitfalls of Winning Big," *Wall Street Journal*, October 29, 2010.

52. Jacobson, *Divider,* pp. 58–62.

9

Partisan Polarization and Satisfaction with Democracy[1]

John H. Aldrich

John Aldrich points out that the responsible parties (unified parties that have clear and distinct platforms) wished for by some mid-twentieth century political scientists have contributed to the current era of contentious politics. Marshaling an impressive amount of data, he argues that unrepresentative political activists, enabled by the rise of a partisan media, have played an important role in the evolution of today's parties. But he questions whether the broader public has been much affected by the partisan polarization that prevails today.

Our politics today can be described as Hobbesian—nasty, brutish, and short-tempered. While ill-tempered politics is neither unique to the U.S. nor to these times, it seems to have reached a level that is both more extreme and more worrisome than in recent memory. While there are many possible culprits to explain both the level of vituperation and its apparent increase, most attention has focused on the contemporary political parties and on the degree of partisan polarization, in particular.

Both the strength and influence of the two major political parties and the degree of polarization between them are dramatically different than a generation ago. Those of us who have lived through the two eras are convinced that politics today is more Hobbesian than in the earlier era. That is particularly clear among our national politicians, both those elected to office themselves and those who assisted in getting them there by virtue of being the activists and group leaders whose support made their electoral victories possible. So, there is certainly a *prima facie* case that the growing strength of our parties and the (related) policy, ideological, and cultural differences between them are the driving forces behind today's vituperation.

We should not jump to conclusions prematurely, however. As we will soon see, there may be a difference between the 1970s and today in our parties and our presentation of politics, but that pairing may be a coincidence. Looked at in broader historical terms or in comparative perspective, today's parties and their polarization are not novel configurations. Rather, they have been the norm for the U.S. and other nations (particularly the UK) that are among the most similar institutionally. Secondly, there are especially strong similarities in many of these regards between American politics of the late nineteenth century and these early years of the twenty-first century. And, while there is much *not* to emulate in that period, it was prolegomenon to the emergence of the U.S. as a world leader economically, militarily, and politically. Thus, at least the worst fears of a looming collapse of the republic need not necessarily follow solely from the presence of strong, polarized politics. That is, strongly polarized political parties are not necessary for mean-spirited politics, and indeed they may not be sufficient either. But, of course, this leaves open the question of just why our politics is so apparently Hobbesian, what that explanation itself is likely to portend, and how, if at all, we might repair the ills that do affect our body politic.

ARE RESPONSIBLE PARTIES RESPONSIBLE?

There has long been a strong strain of Anglophilia in the U.S. (naturally enough, given our origins) and this was as true in academia as anywhere and was especially true in political science. One of its primary manifestations was an admiration for the English party system. Hopes for a party system more in the British mold came to be summarized as a call for a more "responsible" party system. Such appeared almost immediately after the first truly democratic emergence of the British system itself.[2] Woodrow Wilson's famous and still influential book *Congressional Government* (1881) included a set of hopes that the congressional parties of the 1870s and 1880s (when he wrote) could become more like their British cousins.[3] These views peaked in the immediate post-war period. E.E. Schattschneider was a leading scholar of American politics in general and of its political parties in particular.[4] He developed his point of view so effectively (in 1942) that he was named chair of a committee created by the American Political Science Association, issuing a report titled "Toward a More Responsible Two-Party System" (1950).[5]

In the 1970s and 1980s, there was a sustained literature on the weakness of our political parties. Indeed, the opening chapter of a book I wrote (1995; but compare with the newer version, 2011) looked back over that literature and argued that, if it were ever appropriate, it was (in the early to mid-1990s) a misplaced lament of weakness, for, weak or strong, they had not changed much since World War II.[6] If there were any exception, however, it was an exception for showing increased signs of vitality, and consequently was moving in the opposite direction. Thus, in a special issue of *Perspectives on Politics*, David, Herrnson, and White (each 1992) reflected differing viewpoints on how things had changed over the preceding 40 years since the APSA Committee's Report.[7] In a most thoughtful account during this period, Fiorina reflected on the apparent weakening of the parties in response to the kinds of arguments that underlay Wilson, Schattschneider, and others. He argued that the decline at the time was a decline in the taking of collective responsibility by elected politicians and the institutions in which they served. The culprit in this was the political party—"the only way collective responsibility has ever existed, and can exist, given our institutions, is through the agency of the political party; in American politics, responsibility requires cohesive parties."[8]

Here, I will begin with the observation that the political elites have, indeed, polarized along party lines and that this polarization has mattered in terms of their voting behavior in Congress. Indeed, elite polarization is usually measured by roll-call voting patterns on the floor of the House and Senate. I then show that the public in fact perceives this polarization; that doing so affects their evaluations of political figures; and that it also shapes their behavior. However, I also show that there is good evidence that, at least on some important measures on which elites have polarized, the public has polarized only to an extent that is a very weak reflection of the degree of elite polarization. I illustrate that, while the public might find that elites in both parties have moved away from where the public stands at least as rapidly as the public has moved toward the elites, this has not dramatically affected the extent to which the public is satisfied with their democracy—nor is there much difference between our satisfaction with our two-party political system and that of our cousin across the Atlantic, the UK. This in turn re-raises the original question: If it is not the polarization that has caused our Hobbesian politics, then just what might it be? I end by considering two claims to guide future research. One possibility is that it is not how elites vote that matters, but what they say, on what media (and what media personnel say, as well), and with what effect that has done the trick. The other possibility is elites are not talking to the public in general but to the relatively narrow slice of voters who nominate them and/or to the activists who support their campaigns.

THE POLITICAL PARTIES POLARIZE, AT LEAST IN CONGRESS, AND AT LEAST SINCE THE 1940s

The last half of the twentieth century opened with the two political parties internally divided. The Republicans had been contesting over just how to respond to their loss of majority status to Franklin Roosevelt and the New Deal Democratic majority that had emerged in the early 1930s, at the height of the Depression and public rejection of the Republicans who had held the majority through the crisis to that point. This majority held through the Depression and World War II, but Republicans could imagine defeating the New Deal Democrats, as they had briefly in the 1946 midterm elections and so narrowly missed doing in the 1948 presidential elections. Their question was just how to do so. On the one hand, economic conservatives, led at that time by Sen. Robert Taft of Ohio, believed presenting a distinct contrast to New Deal liberalism was the best way to reestablish majority status, and argued strategically that the massive defeats of Hoover in 1932 and Landon in 1936 were not likely to be repeated, as the country was no longer as deeply in the Depression. These were sometimes called the "Main Street" Republicans who were conservative on economics and on social considerations. "Wall Street" Republicans argued that presenting the opposite extreme was exactly the problem, and that a more moderate conservativeness, often expressed as conventionally conservative economic positions coupled with a more moderate or even a moderately liberal stance on social issues and a more active internationalism, would hold a position closer to the center and thus where more votes would be won in the fall. Unfortunately, while these views led to nominations of Wilkie in 1940 and Dewey in 1944 and 1948, they also led to losses in the general election. The 1948 contest, especially, was very close indeed. It was, however, also one that everyone thought—up to election day itself—was going to Dewey and the Republicans, only to witness what became the most storied electoral comeback in presidential election history. This tension was resolved in 1952 by turning conservative Taft aside and choosing a moderate Republican war hero, General Eisenhower, and with it carrying Republicans to victory in the House and Senate.

If this split in the Republican Party was real and divisive, it was nowhere near as deep or lasting as the division of Democrats between North and South. Nor was it nearly as important, because after a short time of unified control of government under Eisenhower, the Republicans lost both congressional chamber majorities in 1954. They would not hold a majority in the Senate until after the 1980 elections, and in the House until 1994, an historic 40-year span of minority status.

Not only was the Democratic division central due to its long run as the majority party, but the division was deep. North and South had been divided since the Founding, and the division that led to the Civil War had not been resolved. In fact, it was the thrusting of civil rights—of the at-long-last successful legal resolution of these racial issues—to the forefront of public attention during the Eisenhower years and onward that highlighted just how very different northern and southern Democrats were from one another. This salient division within the majority party and a less salient division within the opposition would shape national party and congressional politics over the 1950s, 1960s, and 1970s. The resolution of those deep intra-party divisions and clarifying of just which wing of the party would come to all but dominate each congressional party is what we call *party polarization*. And it is the near completion of this polarization that defines the national parties and the politics they play today.

Figure 9.1 gives a detailed look at this process of polarization of the parties—in this case in the U.S. House from the 1970s to 2008 (the picture in the Senate is identical in all important respects for this account). I focus on this measure because it is the central measure of polarization in most accounts in political science; that is, most accounts of polarization are built off these or similar data. The figure graphs a scaled measure of how Democrats and Republicans compare in their records of casting roll-call votes on the floor of the House (or Senate). It is drawn from a statistical procedure by Poole and Rosenthal (e.g., 2009) that uses roll-call votes to determine dimensions of choice, with one dimension of choice (often interpreted as "liberal-conservative") dominating all others.[9] An important part of the story, not captured in this figure, is that this dimension was less dominant in the 1950s, 1960s, and 1970s and has become so overwhelmingly significant in the last few decades as to be effectively the only dimension in town, as it were. But even not observing that part of the story, Figure 9.1 illustrates how the average Democrat and the typical Republican member of Congress (MC) have diverged from one another over even the relatively shorter period depicted in this graph.[10] Another way to put this is that the two parties started clearly but not massively different from one another in the graph. Over this time, there were Republicans who voted more "liberally" than at least some Democrats (or, one might say, some Democrats who voted more conservatively than some Republicans). By the early 2000s, there was no overlap in the Senate at all (that is, the most "liberal" Republican voted more conservatively than the most "conservative"

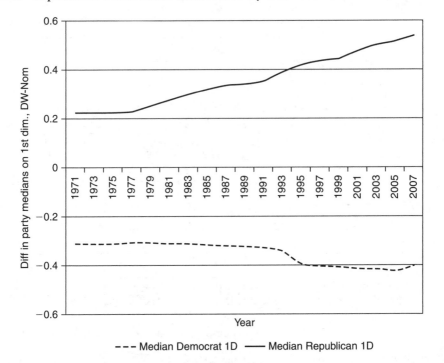

FIGURE 9.1 Party Differences, "Ideology," U.S. House

Source: Voteview.com, compiled by author.

Democrat). By the end of that decade, that was essentially true in the House as well. There is no missing the fact that, by the current period, Democrats and Republicans not only say they differ from each other, but also they act on it in Congress in the most important way—by voting differently on what bills are to become the law of the land.

Does this make the current period unusual? It appears not. It seems, rather, that the 1950s and 1960s stand out as the more unusual period. Consider Figure 9.2. In that figure, I report a different but similar summary measure based on this major dimension of the Poole–Rosenthal scaling procedure that I call "CPG." This stands for "conditional party government," an account of the dynamics of political parties and the effects on the Congress that Dave Rohde and I have offered.[11] The details of that explanation are not important to the present story, but the measure in Figure 9.2, developed with Tofias, is important because it combines not only how different the two parties are, but also how similar the voting choices of MCs within each party are.[12] That is, it combines how homogenous each party is with how different the parties are from one another. In that sense, it is a fuller measure of polarization. In addition, it is reported over the entire period from the end of Reconstruction (1877), when the South and hence southern Democrats were fully reincorporated into the Union and the Congress, to the most recent period.

FIGURE 9.2 Conditional Party, U.S. House and Senate

Source: Aldrich, Rohde and Tofiasn, (2007; http://www.uwm.edu/~tofias/research/), compiled by author.

The point of this figure is that in the House (and also in the Senate), the current polarization is nearly up to the levels of the turn of a different century, that is, at around 1900, and that the middle of the twentieth century stands out as a particularly low degree of polarization. It is harder to make comparison to even earlier periods because there are different parties involved, but it appears that these earlier periods also were typified by polarization at least as high as today's, punctuated only with the collapse of one of the major parties or of the Union itself during the era around the Civil War (see voteview.com).

That establishes two major points. One is that today's congressional parties are very different from those of the 1950s (without telling us why that is, of course), but it also tells us that today's congressional parties are not unique in this regard, nor do they seem to be the most extreme in this regard either. That leads us to our next question: Is this confined to the Congress?

OTHER PARTISAN ELITES POLARIZE; DOES THE PUBLIC?

It is certainly true that the Congress is one of the most important places to look for the existence of polarization, for if the two parties are voting for different laws, then that is likely to be a fact of great importance that reverberates throughout the political system. But it remains at least potentially possible that polarization is some unique characteristic of congressional parties, not general to the system.

If MCs reflect partisan divides in their choices, where else might we turn? One step removed might be other political elites central to electoral democracy. Two more are considered here. I start with a first glimpse at delegates to our two parties' national conventions. At the conventions, the delegates write the rules for the national party for the next four years, adopt the party's platform for the coming general elections, and nominate the presidential and vice presidential standard bearers for that campaign. That is, it is the most important venue for the party as a party.

In all surveys, as reported in Figures 9.3 and 9.4, delegates were asked to evaluate the opposition party on a scale running 0–100 (hence they are called *thermometer scales*), that measure how warmly (toward 100 degrees) or coolly (toward 0 degrees) they feel toward the other party. We would expect such high-level partisan activists (many of them officeholders) to feel warmly toward their own party and its candidates, but just how coolly/negatively do they feel about the opposition? In these figures we divide the hundred points into deciles (that is, 10 units, the first of which runs from 0 to 10, the second from 11 to 20, etc.). This way, we can look at the proportion of delegates who fall in the most negative 10-point unit for evaluations, and so on. We might have no idea what to expect about any one year, but we do expect to find out whether the delegates are, like their partisan peers in Congress, polarizing over the last few decades, with an increasingly large percentage of delegates gravitating toward the negative end of the scale, year

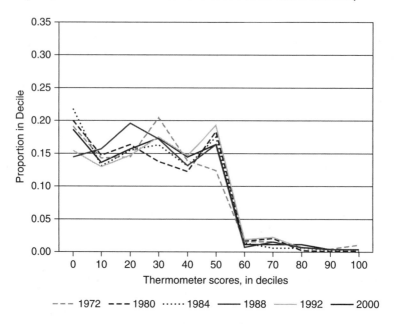

FIGURE 9.3 Democratic Delegates Evaluate Republicans

Source: National convention delegate survey (ICPSR), various years, compiled by author.

after year. That is, if delegates in 2000 are more polarized than those in 1972, they should be more stridently negative in their evaluations of the opposition. Figure 9.3 reports the graphs for delegates to the Democratic Party conventions; Figure 9.4 reports the graphs for the Republicans, for the years 1972, 1980, 1984, 1988, 1992, and 2000. To aid in viewing, the earliest three elections are the dotted or dashed lines and the latter three are solid lines, where we should expect to find lower and higher levels of negativity, respectively.

The first and most obvious points are that the two graphs are largely very similar and that the delegates are not positively inclined toward the opposition party. Little distinguishes the two parties from each other.[13] Indeed, while there is fluctuation across the negative ranges (roughly speaking, below the neutral point of 50 degrees), it is not too far from uniformity—20 percent-plus are in each of the first four categories in both parties.

More importantly, however, there is no sign that I can detect of systematic change over time. Perhaps the Democrats have become somewhat less negative toward Republicans over time, but certainly not strongly more so. Republicans also differ little from year to year and show no pattern at all. The two parties' national delegates have been polarized the whole time, but not increasingly so. In this, they appear to differ from their congressional counterparts. Little evidence of changing levels of polarization can be found among national convention delegates.

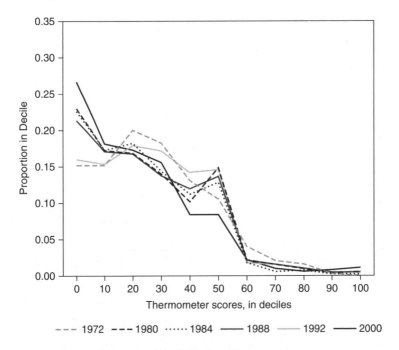

FIGURE 9.4 Republican Candidates Evaluate Democrats

Source: National convention delegate survey (ICPSR), various years, compiled by author.

Perhaps, then, we are looking in the wrong place. Perhaps polarization appears in congressional voting and among other groups of elite political actors. Indeed, this does seem to be the case. To see this, we turn to a comparison across groups over time, as reported in Figure 9.5, taken from Aldrich and Freeze (2011; as modified in Aldrich, 2011).[14] In this figure we report the differences between Democrats' and Republicans' average self-placements on a scale that runs from 1, "extremely liberal," through a midpoint of 4 and then to 7, or "extremely conservative." Every one of the sets of actors reported in that figure put themselves on the same scale, with the same question. The groups include two sets drawn from surveys of the general public, so this figure provides a transition and a bridge between political elites and the general public. There is a new set of "high-level" activists in partisan politics, those who give substantial amounts of money to presidential campaigns. We can define that "club" as those who give sufficient money to require that their donation be reported by name (and address) to the Federal Election Commission, and then to be reported to the public. Surveys have been conducted among this elite set of actors giving to presidential candidates four times—in 1972, 1988, 2000, and 2004—and liberal-conservative self-placements were gathered each time. This gives us a set of elite political figures of high relevance to political parties, and we have two elections in which there should have been relatively low levels of partisan

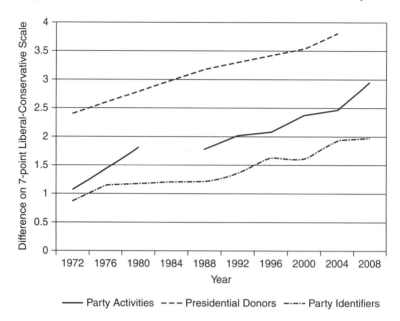

FIGURE 9.5   Ideological Polarization of Partisan Identifiers and Party Activists

Source: Aldrich and Freeze (2011), compiled by author.

polarization and two in which there should have been high levels. And of course, by looking at the changes over time we can make comparisons to the different sort of data we have for partisans in Congress.

But we can also compare them to the general public. So, in Figure 9.5 I include two measurements taken from the ANES surveys.[15] One measurement is where those respondents in the general public who identify themselves as Democrats place themselves, compared to where those who call themselves Republicans place themselves. This is the broadest possible look at partisan polarization in the public. But some of those (often around 20 percent in ANES surveys) are more than just citizens and voters. These individuals are part of the public who engage in campaigning, such as by wearing buttons, putting up yard signs, attending campaign rallies, and so on. They have distinguished themselves from the typical member of the public, but they hardly could be considered at the same level of involvement in campaign politics as national politicians, national convention delegates, or those who write large checks to partisan candidates.

The data in Figure 9.5 reveal two important things. First, there has been an increase in polarization almost continually, year after year. This is true for all three sets of people in that figure. For presidential donors, the average difference in placement between Democrats and Republicans started in 1972 at a substantial 2.5 point difference (out of a possible 6 points if every Democrat claimed to be "extremely liberal" and every Republican said he or she was "extremely conservative"). By 2004, partisan differences had increased to over 3.5 points. For more conventional party activists, those who ring door bells, stuff envelopes, and so on, the difference started at 1 point in 1972 and increased steadily to over 2.5 points (and slightly greater than 2 in 2004, when contributor data end). Conversely, for those who identify with one of the two parties, ideological differences started at a bit less than 1 point and increased by less than a full point by 2008. Second, and more importantly for our discussion, presidential donors started out more polarized than party identifiers ended up in 2008 (and 2004), and the gap between activists of either sort and party identifiers grew over time. Thus, while the general public has either polarized somewhat by this measure or, perhaps, "sorted" more cleanly by party, this polarization is less in magnitude and of a more modest increase than it is among those actively involved in campaigns, and much less so than high-level activists.[16]

THE PUBLIC SEES ELITE POLARIZATION

Before returning to the question of how polarized the public may be, we can observe that, no matter what the effect of elite polarization may be on the preferences and beliefs of the public, it is evident that they observe the increasing elite polarization clearly. In Figure 9.6, for example,

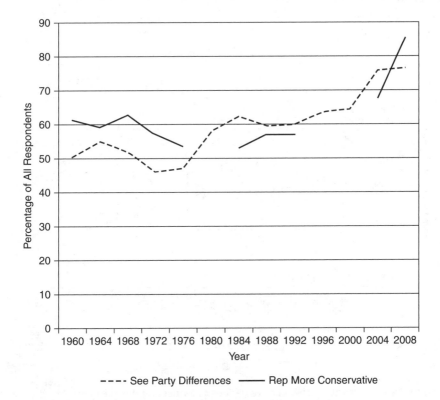

FIGURE 9.6 Perceptions of Party Differences By the Electorate

Source: ANES surveys, various years, compiled by author (Aldrich, 2011, 181).

I present the percentages of the public who report, from 1960 through 2008, that they see a difference between the two parties and (for available years) the proportion that reports seeing the Republican Party as the more conservative party. In 1960, about 3 in 5 reported seeing differences, and this grew to nearly 4 in 5 by 2008. And, in 1960, half the respondents perceived the Republican Party to be the more conservative party, essentially a coin flip between the two options, whereas in 2008, 7 in 8 perceived the Republicans' conservative stance.

One could point to a number of such indications of public perceptions of increasing "clarity" of the two parties' positions and of observing polarization among partisan elites. Instead, in Figure 9.7, I report a summary of these kinds of views, based on thermometer evaluations of a large variety of Democratic candidates, parties, and figures, along with their Republican counterparts (for details, see Aldrich and Sparks, forthcoming).[17] This figure uses the same data as Figures 9.3 and 9.4, presented as, in effect, an averaging (actually a scaling) of how divergent respondents' evaluations are, and the data in the figure give a very clear answer. Respondents do, indeed, evaluate the candidates of one party as more and more alike, and they evaluate the opposition party's candidates as increasingly unlike their opponents. When these questions were first asked in the 1968 ANES survey, the fact that a respondent reported liking a Democrat gave virtually no clue at all

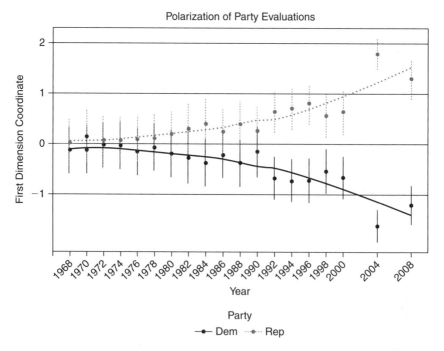

FIGURE 9.7 Polarization of Public Evaluations of Parties and their Leaders

Source: ANES surveys, various years, compiled by the author and David Sparks.

as to whether that respondent would like or dislike a Republican. By 2008, respondents who liked one Democrat tended to like all Democrats—and to dislike all Republicans. Republicans were just as likely to feel as positively toward their own candidates and as negatively toward the Democrats. And the gap has widened to a gulf in the most recent decade. It is, of course, entirely uncertain whether these changes are because of the differences in preferences in the electorate, or differences among the elites. The latter would mean increasing similarity among Democrats and among Republicans, with increasing differentiation of the parties' leaders from one another. We know the second has happened. Has the first?

IS THE PUBLIC POLARIZED?

In Figure 9.5, we saw that partisans have become, by at least this one measure, a bit more divergent in ideology from the opposition than they were in the 1970s. But this observation could have come about either because the public is more extreme in ideology than they once were, or because conservatives left the Democratic Party and instead became Republicans (and vice versa for liberals), without changing the balance of liberals, conservatives, and moderates. The former case would be polarization; that is, the moderate center is losing support, and more citizens are inclined toward the extreme end points of ideology than they once were. The latter would be what is called "sorting" (championed particularly by Levendusky, 2009).[18] In the first case, we might say that the public appears to be following political elites. That is, as MCs vote in a more polarized manner on legislation, and as major financial contributors place themselves at more extreme ideological positions, so does the public. The sorting hypothesis would indicate, instead, that parties may be more consistently filled with people from the same range of ideological positions, but it does not mean that there are an increasingly large number of extreme liberals and extreme conservatives in the electorate. Their divergent evaluations, as in Figure 9.7, would follow from the increased similarity among Democratic leaders to be evaluated and of comparably increased consistency among Republican candidates and officeholders—not from changes in the electorate.

One way to examine this question is to look at the distribution of responses in the electorate to the ideological scale, as is reported in Figure 9.8. The figure shows the actual distribution of responses to the 7-point ideology scale for every presidential election in which the question was asked. The idea is that, if there has been increasing ideological polarization from 1972 to 2008, there would be substantially more respondents in the "1" and "2" and the "6" and "7" response categories in 2008 than earlier, and fewer in the three middle categories. To aid observation, the responses in 2008 are in the darkest shade. What one can see is that there is only a small degree of change over time. It is the case that there are more at the extremes and fewer in the middle categories in 2008 than earlier, and thus there is a degree of ideological polarization in the electorate. However, this is a modest degree

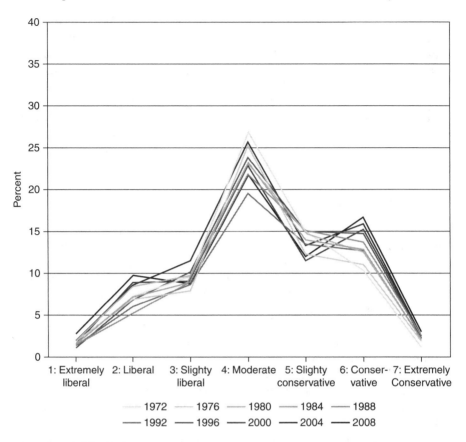

FIGURE 9.8 Public Ideology

Source: ANES surveys, various years, compiled by author.

of polarization, and it is mostly near but not at the end points of "extremely liberal" and "extremely conservative" (that is, it is mostly due to increases in responses of "2" and "6" rather than of "1" and "7"). It thus appears that the major dynamic in Figure 9.5 is that of the sorting of partisans into ideological categories. What ideological stance the citizens report does not appear to be affected very much by the increasingly strident, "Hobbesian" character to elite positioning and presentation to the public.

IS THE PUBLIC DISAFFECTED IN A POLARIZED DEMOCRACY?

To this point, the argument is that the elites in both parties have become increasingly ideologically divergent, or what is popularly referred to as "polarized." The public clearly perceives this elite polarization. But the public, at least to date, has not itself polarized very much at all. Ideology does appear more relevant to partisan politics in the public, but this appears primarily through increased sorting—Democrats are increasingly likely to be liberal in their expressed ideology, and the same is true for Republicans and con-servative ideological stances. However, there are not many more liberals or many more conservatives than there were a generation ago. There is a slight increase in polarization in the public, but it is quite slight. If the public is not tracking the polarization of their partisan elites, they may well react nega-tively to the increasing stridency of elite discourse. The worry is that they may be becoming increasingly disaffected by that sort of politics and hence disaffected from their own democracy. We look briefly at this question in this section. We consider two ways in which we can examine public reac-tions to an increasingly polarized government in the U.S. over time, and then we turn to a comparison of the U.S. with the UK.

The first question is whether the American public is responding less positively to their government as the partisan elites have become more polarized—and more strident. Figures 9.9 and 9.10 present two relevant measures. Figure 9.9 shows the percentage of the electorate who report positively in response to the question of whether public officials care what the public thinks. Since the public is viewing elected officials as diverging from positions similar to those held by the public to more extreme ones, it might follow that they would view these same officials as not caring as much about what that public thinks. Instead, if anything, the reverse is true. The percentage agreeing with that statement was low in the 1950s, dipping under 1 in 4 in agreement in 1960. That percentage climbed, reaching 1 in 2 in the 1970s and it has hovered in the 50–60 percentage range ever since.

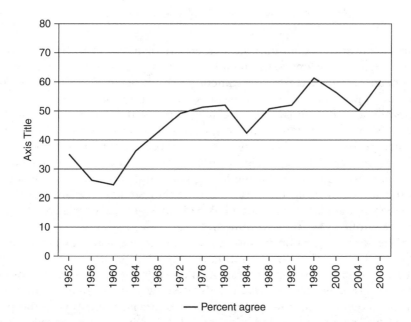

FIGURE 9.9 Perceptions that Public Officials Care About What the Public Thinks

Source: ANES surveys, various years, compiled by author.

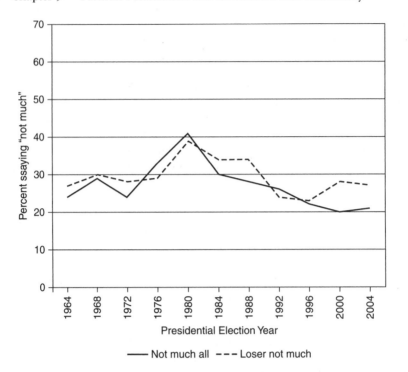

FIGURE 9.10 Perceptions of Government, Listening to People

Source: ANES surveys, various years, compiled by author.

A similar question examining the percentage of those who think the (federal) government listens to the people is presented in Figure 9.10. Here, the percentage saying that the government does not listen much at all peaked at about 40 percent in 1980, but has been in decline since then. The dotted line examines the comparable percentage among those reporting that they voted for the losing party, on the grounds that perhaps those who back winners are always more content with the government than those who lose elections. As we can see in Figure 9.10, however, there is little difference between those who voted for the losing party and the public as a whole in this regard. In short, in these (and many other similar) measures, there is no evidence that elite polarization has had any significant negative effect on how the public views its government.

The second question is how the U.S. compares with other nations, in this case, the UK. The UK is a relevant point of comparison because it has long had a primarily two-party system, and, while there have been ebbs and flows, the two major parties have mostly been divergent from each other over most of its democratic history. Indeed, it was precisely this point—the presence of two major parties with clear and distinctive positions enacting large parts of their particular platform upon winning election—that led so many in the U.S. to desire to become more like the UK in their calls for a more responsible party system, as was described earlier. The difference is that, although there certainly are times and places in which the partisan elite in the UK engage in strong partisan attacks and there are other features of the sort I have characterized as "Hobbesian" politics—question time in Parliament most evidently—the dominant feature is less one of partisan attacks than one in which the party out of office serves as the "loyal opposition." In any event, we are fortunate to be able to compare U.S. and UK public responses to survey questions to give us a small degree of comparison.

American elections run on a strict calendar. Elections to the British parliament need to be held every five years at the latest, but an election can be called at virtually any time. We are therefore fortunate that the UK held elections relatively shortly after the U.S. presidential elections of 1996 and 2004 (in 1997 and 2005, respectively). In addition, the national election studies in both nations asked the same question in each of the four elections.[19] In particular, in each survey, respondents were asked the degree of their satisfaction with democracy, with responses that ranged from *very* through *fairly* and *not very* to *not at all satisfied with democracy*. The responses are reported in Figure 9.11 for the four instances. First, note that there are essentially no differences in responses in the 1996–97 and the 2004–05 periods. Second, there are slight differences between the two nations, but they are

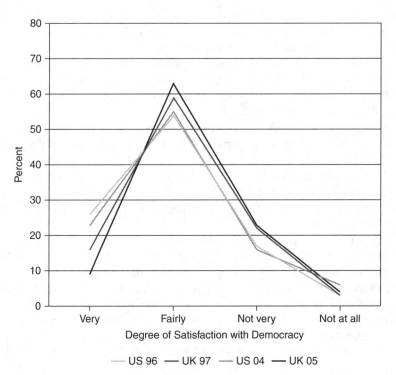

FIGURE 9.11   Public Satisfaction with Democracy in the U.S. and UK

Source: CSES, various surveys, compiled by author.

slight indeed. A few more in the UK than in the U.S. say they are fairly satisfied with their democracy, but more in the U.S. report being very satisfied and fewer report being not very satisfied in the UK. Again, these are slight differences, and the overall conclusion is that respondents in the U.S. and the UK are essentially identical on this dimension.

In both nations, more than 3 in 4 are fairly or very satisfied with their democracy, and this response spans over a decade. Of course, these measures were taken before the Great Recession and the consequent dissatisfaction with the incumbent administrations in both countries that led to their defeat at the polls in 2008 and 2010, respectively. While it therefore may be true that major negative shocks could still shake these high degrees of satisfaction with their respective democracies, the most important point for our purposes here is that there is no evidence that the American electorate is dissatisfied with their democracy and therefore that increasing polarization of elites away from the kinds of ideological views held by the public cannot have been causing such dissatisfaction.

CONCLUSION

The evidence in this chapter implies the following chain of reasoning:

1. Members of Congress and those who give large amounts of money to presidential candidates have always been differentiated, but they have become increasingly polarized over the last generation. They began this era more polarized than the public and their increase has been even greater than that of the public. And, of course, for MCs in particular, this is based on the "bottom line," that is, the data are of voting for different public policies for the U.S.[20]

2. The public accurately perceives this increasing polarization, and their reactions and evaluations reflect their viewing of a more polarized partisan elite.

3. The public also has reacted to that polarization, but only by sorting themselves by party more cleanly. That is, Democrats are now more uniformly on the left and Republicans are more consistently on the right than earlier.

4. The public has not, however, become more polarized. Or, at least, the extent of polarization is a quite pale imitation of that at the elite level.

5. Finally, while this might have been driving the public away from its political elites and perceiving its government as less responsive to people's concerns, such does not appear to be the case. The public is largely satisfied with its democracy; if anything, the perception of responsiveness of the government has increased, and certainly has not decreased, and the American public is quite like its British cousins in this regard.

The argument, therefore, is that polarization, per se, is not the culprit in explaining the stridency of contemporary American politics.

Where, then, might the fault lie? One option is that the changing nature of the mass media and the dramatically different technologies of the contemporary world of political communication have served as culprits. To be sure, it is the partisan elites who are the actual culprits, but it may be the new media that have enabled them to do so. First, the mass media may be something of an oxymoron. From the 1950s to the 1970s, news was dominated by a few central sources (the three major television networks, a few national newspapers and news services, etc.), and large numbers attended to these few outlets. Today, the news media are highly fragmented. Network news is attended to by a much smaller proportion of the public than 40 years ago, and cable news shows draw small fractions of what the networks can still draw. Perhaps this fragmentation has encouraged more partisan, strident, and even "Hobbesian" politics from these elites. The idea here is that the small markets of Fox, MSNBC, and others are drawing disproportionately from those few in the public who enjoy hearing partisan "gotcha" accounts. They are the loyal listeners and will be lost if more polite discourse is followed—without the cable news show being able to pick up less rabid followers.

The major alternative is that the partisan elite are not speaking to the general public.[21] Rather, they are speaking to those who tend to be more polarized. That is, they are speaking to those who are likely to give large amounts of money to their campaigns, are likely to work for their election and reelection, and are more likely than typical Americans to vote in primary elections or, even more, attend caucuses where candidates win nominations. These two explanations are not exclusive, of course. They are complementary and mutually supportive.

The final question is rather different. If the data in Figures 9.9–9.11 are taken at face value, it may well be worth asking whether the concern that motivates this chapter (and this author) and, indeed, this project may be misplaced. Perhaps the public is the grown-up in this account, and the tempertantrum-like behavior of our political elites is just so much sound and fury. It may, in fact, signify nothing.

Endnotes

1. I would like to thank Eric Schmidt for serving as research assistant for this project. I would also like to thank the ANES, BES, and CSES for use of their data. All analyses and interpretations are strictly the responsibility of the author.
2. Gary W, Cox *The Efficient Secret: The Cabinet and the Development of Political Parties* (London: Cambridge University Press, 1987).
3. Woodrow Wilson, *Congressional Government: A Study in American Society* (Baltimore: Johns Hopkins University Press, 1881).
4. E. E. Schattschneider, *Party Government: American Government in Action* (New York: Farrar and Rinehart, 1942).
5. APSA Committee on Political Parties, Toward a More Responsible Two-Party System: A Report of the Committee on Political Parties (NewYork: Rinehart & Co., 1950).

6. John H. Aldrich, *Why Parties? The Origin and Transformation of Political Parties in America* (Chicago, IL: University of Chicago Press, 1995).

7. Paul T. David, "The APSA Committee on Political Parties: Some Reconsiderations of Its Work and Significance," *Perspectives on Political Science, 21,* (2), 1992, Spring: 70–79; Paul S. Herrnson, "Why the United States Does Not Have Responsible Parties," *Perspectives on Political Science, 21* (2), 1992, Spring: 91–98; John Kenneth White, "Responsible Party Government in America," *Perspectives on Political Science, 21* (2), 1992, Spring: 80–90.

8. Morris P. Fiorina, "The Decline in Collective Responsibility in American Politics," *Daedalus 109*(3), 1980, Summer: 25–45.

9. Keith T. Poole, and Howard Rosenthal, *Ideology and Congress* (New York: Transaction, 2009).

10. This period was chosen to align with the availability of other data to come.

11. John H. Aldrich and David W. Rohde, "Theories of Party in the Legislature and the Transition to Republican Rule in the House." *Political Science Quarterly 112,* (4), 1997–98, Winter; Ibid., "The Republican Revolution and the House Appropriations Committee," *Journal of Politics, 62* (1), February, 2000a, 1–33; Ibid., "The Consequences of Party Organization in the House: The Role of the Majority and Minority Parties in Conditional Party Government," in *Polarized Politics: Congress and the President in a Partisan Era,* edited by Jon R. Bond and Richard Fleisher. (Washington, DC: CQ Press, 2000b); Ibid., "The Logic of Conditional Party Government: Revisiting the Electoral Connection," in *Congress Reconsidered,* 7th ed., edited by Lawrence C. Dodd and Bruce I. Oppenheimer, 2001 (Washington, DC: CQ Press, 2001); Ibid., "Consequences of Electoral and Institutional Change: The Evaluation of Conditional Party Government in the U.S. House of Representatives," in *New Directions in American Political Parties,* edited by Jeffrey M. Stonecash (New York: Routledge, 2010), pp. 234–250.

12. John H. Aldrich, David W. Rohde, and Michael Tofias, "One D Is Not Enough: Measuring Conditional Party Government, 1887–2002," in *Party, Process, and Political Change in Congress: Further New Perspectives on the History of Congress,* edited by David Brady and Mathew D. McCubbins (Stanford, CA: Stanford University Press, 2007).

13. There is more negativity among Republicans than among Democrats, but it is not greatly different.

14. John H. Aldrich and Melanie Freeze, "Political Participation, Polarization, and Public Opinion: Activism and the Merging of Partisan and Ideological Polarization," in Paul Sniderman and Ben Highton, ed., *Facing the Challenge of Democracy: Explorations in the Analysis of Public Opinion and Political Participation* (Princeton, NJ: Princeton University Press, 2011), pp. 185–206; John H. Aldrich, *Why Parties? A Second Look* (Chicago, IL: University of Chicago Press, 2011).

15. The American National Election Studies (ANES) are face-to-face interviews of the public that have been conducted in presidential election years since 1948, and are the highest quality academic surveys about politics.

16. Two other points: First, the 1984 ANES failed to have comparable usable measures and so could not be included here. Second, while there are too few delegate surveys for me to include them here, the few there are indicate little change over (a short) time, but their polarization was at about the same level as the presidential campaign contributors.

17. John H. Aldrich and David Sparks. forthcoming. "The American Public Observes and Evaluates a Polarized Partisan Elite" (tent. Title).

18. Matthew S. Levendusky, *The Partisan Sort: How Liberals Became Democrats and Conservatives Became Republicans* (Chicago, IL: University of Chicago Press, 2009).

19. The question analyzed in Figure 9.11 is actually a part of the Comparative Study of Electoral Systems project, in which national election studies agree to run exactly the same module of questions (here, modules 2 and 3 for the two election periods, respectively, were run by the ANES and the British Election Survey). The idea is to facilitate cross-national comparisons, precisely as employed here.

20. The data are presented for the U.S. House, but the U.S. Senate supports exactly the same conclusions. Note, however, that insofar as we can judge, this is not true for all partisan elites. At least by some measures, delegates to the party's national conventions have not displayed increased levels of polarization.

21. That is, this is the major alternative flowing from elite polarization. It may well be that a wholly different explanation is called for. One obvious candidate is the remarkable transformation of the American economy, the massive dislocations that accompany it, and the dramatic increase in income inequality in America.

10

Party Homogeneity and Contentious Politics

Morris P. Fiorina

Morris Fiorina continues the discussion of party sorting, arguing that it is the principal cause of the contentious politics of our time. He discusses how partisan sorting weakens the incentives for politicians to compromise. Furthermore, he argues that greater disagreement on the issues—and on more issues—encourages the kind of uncivil talk and behavior we see today. Starker choices mean that elections matter more, and as the stakes rise, civility falls.

Many of the articles in this volume were drafted during the great political battle over the Debt Ceiling Extension in July 2011. Under the banner of the Tea Party, Republican fiscal conservatives in the House of Representatives refused to budge from their announced principles and took the country to the brink of default on its debt. In reaction, Democratic politicos and pundits charged that the Tea Party Republicans were "extortionists" and worse: "this small group of terrorists," "the Republican Taliban wing," "the GOP's Hezbollah faction," and the "tea terrorist party." The Tea Party Caucus was a "nihilistic caucus" that "waged jihad on the American people." Tea partiers donned political "suicide vests," "strapped explosives to the Capitol" and engaged in other "terrorist tactics," which ultimately forced the entire nation to eat a "sugar-coated Satan sandwich."[1] About all that was missing were the Hitler comparisons.

While Tea Party Republicans were on the receiving end of most of the incivility during the debt extension fight, as noted in our introductory chapter, they had engaged in their share of incivility during the two-year run-up to the August 2 deadline. An Iowa Tea Party billboard compared Obama to Hitler and Lenin.[2] Tea Party posters depicted President Obama as the "Joker" in the popular

Batman movies.[3] Somewhat later, a Tea Party heckler called Massachusetts Democratic Senate candidate Elizabeth Warren a "socialist whore" with a "foreign-born boss."[4]

To those of us who have living memories of the middle decades of the twentieth century, there is no question that politics today in Washington and many of our state capitals is more contentious and less civil than a generation ago. Indeed, a tremendous irony is that partisan politics in the halls of government in the 1960s was more civil than it is today, even though that was a time when popular passions may well have been more greatly inflamed: the Vietnam war protests raged, campuses were convulsed by strikes and demonstrations, racial conflicts ignited summer conflagrations in American cities, and prominent political leaders were murdered. As I have shown in earlier work, today's electorate is no more divided on the issues—and perhaps even less so—than the electorate of a half-century ago, while the politicians voters send to office are far more divided.[5]

Still, as skeptics have pointed out, the endpoints chosen for comparisons make a great deal of difference. As a number of authors in this volume note, there have been other eras in American history when contentious politics matched or exceeded that of today. While it would certainly be premature to posit cycles of civility and incivility, we can at least recognize historical variation. And that variation enables us to begin to identify the factors that contribute to more or less contentious politics. I will situate the discussion in this brief chapter by first contrasting the less polarized politics of the 1960s to the more polarized politics of today.

POLITICS THEN AND NOW

Studies of the U.S. Congress written during the 1950s and 1960s often likened the institution to a gentlemen's club, especially the Senate.[6] Donald Matthews discussed the "folkways" of the Senate—norms guiding appropriate senatorial behavior. Among them were elaborate rules of courtesy, such as never questioning another senator's motives, campaigning against another senator, or attacking another senator's state. Another was institutional patriotism:

> A senator whose emotional commitment to Senate ways appears to be less than total is suspect. One who brings the Senate as an institution or senators as a class into public disrepute invites his own destruction as an effective legislator. One who seems to be using the Senate for the purposes of self-advertisement and advancement obviously does not belong.[7]

Similarly, in his classic treatise on the House Appropriations Committee, Richard Fenno discusses committee norms, including subcommittee and committee "unity" (e.g., no minority reports allowed). Unity was achieved by "compromise," which in turn was supported by "minimal partisanship." Of course, even in the 1960s some committees such as Education and Labor were recognized as particularly contentious, but these were regarded as exceptions to the general pattern.[8] According to John Manley, the Ways and Means Committee, perhaps the most powerful committee in the House, which dealt with a host of important issues, followed a norm of "restrained partisanship."[9] Juliet Eilperin's description of the contemporary Congress in Chapter 11 of this volume stands in sharp contrast with these older descriptions of congressional operations.

The first signs of fracture in the old order were associated with political pressures generated by the Civil Rights movement and the Vietnam War. Congressional scholars began to notice comments in debates that sounded more strident and more personal than we were accustomed to. And by the time of the fractious 1968 Democratic national convention it was clear that the old order was changing. Still, during the presidency of Ronald Reagan (who was the target of considerable incivility) a Republican president and Senate majority leader and a Democratic speaker of the House could come together in 1983 and put Social Security on a sound actuarial footing for 20 years—and repeat the feat in 1986 to reform the tax code. As late as 1990 a Republican president and Democratic congressional leaders cut a deal that contributed to a balanced federal budget later in the decade (although it may have cost President George H.W. Bush a second term). In 1993, however, the Clinton budget passed the House without a single Republican vote, and as the Clinton presidency went on, the rising political decibel level made it clear that the modern era had arrived.

The most precise way to measure the ups and downs of congressional polarization is by using the roll call voting record. Perhaps surprisingly, at most times in history congressional voting divisions tend to fall along a single dimension. This is often interpreted as an economic left-right dimension, although Francis Lee has shown that a significant part of it is pure partisanship with little or no substantive basis.[10] Figure 10.1 contrasts three Congresses spanning a century's time.

Both Republicans and Democrats in today's House are more concentrated on their side of the spectrum than they were in the early 1960s; their centers of gravity have moved outward toward the poles on their sides of the continuum, and as a consequence the overlap between Democrats and Republicans has all but disappeared. But if one were to contrast the Congress of the early 1960s with that of the early 1900s, one would make precisely the opposite observations. Indeed, the 1900s House looks quite similar to the 2000s House. Research to date suggests that the most likely explanation of these variations in roll call polarization is the degree of similarity within the parties' electoral coalitions and the degree of dissimilarity between them.[11]

PARTY SORTING AS THE UNDERPINNING OF POLARIZED POLITICS

In his classic study of the McKinley congresses (1897–1900), David Brady points out that the politics of the era was quite contentious. House Speaker Thomas Reed wrote, "These were not pleasant days. Men were not nice in their treatment of each other . . ." Populist leaders of the era such as William Jennings Bryan were likened to Robespierre, Danton, and others responsible for the terror of the French Revolution (this was before Hitler, of course). The 1896 Democratic platform was "made in Hell," and the candidate, William Jennings Bryan, was a "mouthing, slobbering demagogue whose patriotism is all in his jaw bone."[12] Brady argues that a major factor that contributed to the historic levels of roll call polarization in the McKinley congresses was the distinct nature of the parties' electoral coalitions. In the 1896 House elections, for example, 86 percent of the victorious Republicans came from industrial districts, whereas 60 percent of the victorious Democrats came from agricultural districts.[13] Thus, each party contained a heavy majority of members with common interests—interests that were in conflict with the dominant interest of the other party.

Much the same holds in the current era. Consider the party coalitions after the 1960 elections—a less polarized and more civil era—compared to those coalitions after the 2010 elections. The regional heterogeneity of each party was greater in 1960 than it is today. Democratic representatives came from all regions and dominated in the South. Republicans also came from all regions—except for the South. Today, the Democratic caucus has lost most

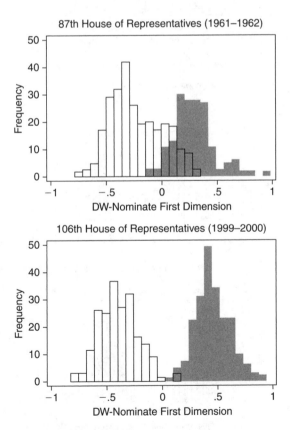

FIGURE 10.1A   Congress has Polarized since the 1960s

Source: Data provided by Keith Poole.

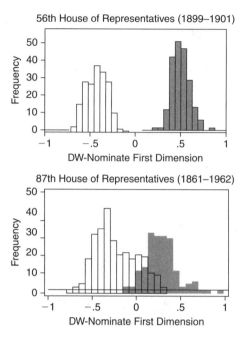

FIGURE 10.1B   Congress Depolarized Between 1900 and 1960

Source: Data provided by Keith Poole.

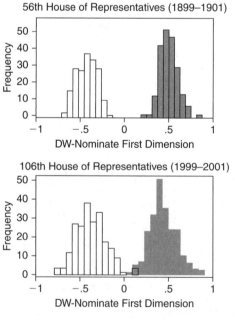

FIGURE 10.1C   Congress Looks about the Same Now as a Century Ago

Source: Data provided by Keith Poole.

of its southern wing. It is now largely a northeastern and western coastal party. In contrast, the Republican Party now dominates in the South and it has almost disappeared from New England. The preponderance of its membership comes from districts lying between the coastal Democratic states. Urban–suburban differences reinforce these regional bases of support. The Democratic Party today is a more urban party, whereas the Republican Party is far more suburban and rural. In particular, as Bruce Oppenheimer points out, many of the remaining southern Democratic districts are in the burgeoning metropolises of the Sunbelt, so they are more similar to northern districts than they were at mid-century.[14]

The natural consequence of parties that become more homogeneous with respect to some demographic or social characteristic is that political issues associated with such characteristics become more divisive. If the Democratic Party includes representatives from both urban and rural districts, and the same is true for the Republican Party, both parties feel pressure to moderate their stances on such issues. The pressure comes from their members who are associated with points of view that diverge from the party majority. Such members will threaten to defect on party proposals they find objectionable to their districts, and for their part, party leaders will fear sending such members down to defeat if the leadership persists in pushing proposals that harm those members' districts. But if Democrats are largely an urban party and Republicans a suburban and rural party, their members will have less knowledge of and less sympathy for the interests of the other party. Why should Republicans worry about the problems of the cities if the urban districts only elect Democrats? Homogeneity encourages both parties to advocate less balanced and more extreme programs that reflect the parties' preponderant interests.

Demographic differences are not the only source of political divisions, of course, nor are they the only reason politics today has become more divisive. Many of our state capitals have also become more polarized. In some cases it is possible to make a regional argument analogous to that just sketched for the U.S. Congress. California, for example, has split along a coastal–inland axis that pits an urban coastal Democratic Party against an agricultural-rural Republican Party.[15] But demographic divisions alone probably cannot explain the growing polarization in our smaller, more geographically homogeneous states.

One likely possibility is that parties have become more homogeneous on issues that are not geographically or demographically based by incorporating social movements that emerged at the mid-twentieth century and later. The Democrats incorporated the Civil Rights movement, the feminist movement, the environmental movement, and, more recently, the gay rights movement. Republicans incorporated the tax revolt, the evangelical resurgence, and, most recently, the Tea Party. Again, by throwing their lot entirely with one party or the other, the issue activists associated with such movements generate increased substantive polarization between the parties. Each party gradually comes to have less contact with, knowledge of, and sympathy for the constituencies of the other. If one party is heavily white, why should its representatives support policies that redistribute income or advantages from its voters to those who vote for the opposing party? If one party's adherents are heavily employed in the public sector or are recipients of government benefits, why should its representatives ever support policies that cut taxes and public spending?

Until the feminist movement, Republicans had traditionally been somewhat more supportive of an Equal Rights amendment. Until the mid-1970s, the environmental issue was up for grabs, leading Republican president Richard Nixon to support the Clean Air Act. Until the early 1990s, Republicans and Democrats were about equally supportive of and opposed to abortion. And until the 1992 election, the presidential vote division between regular churchgoers and seculars was small. The natural result of such party heterogeneity was much less of a partisan divide on such issues. But once advocates of a particular issue become exclusively associated with one party or the other, balance and moderation are the casualties. For several decades now, Republican elites have advocated a constitutional amendment to prohibit abortion altogether while Democratic elites have felt compelled to defend third trimester abortions for nonmedical reasons. The fact that 90 percent of the electorate falls somewhere in between gets overlooked in the partisan battle. Most recently, confused voters were offered a choice between global warming as either an imminent planetary threat or a gigantic liberal hoax.

Many argue that another factor contributing to contentious politics is associated with the aforementioned incorporation of social movements into the parties. These movements often revolved around moral issues, or issues that could easily be framed in moral terms—racial equality, women's rights, traditional family values, and religious beliefs. Moral issues, the argument goes, are much less easily compromised than economic arguments, especially when framed in terms of fundamental rights, as Shea explains in his chapter in this volume. There is certainly something to this argument, although the contending sides often underestimate the willingness of Americans to compromise moral issues—they have little problem in the case of abortion, for example.[16]

Such issues are not new to the modern era, however. In fact, the New Deal period was historically unusual in that economic and, later, foreign policy issues crowded out moral issues. From at least the time that Catholic immigrants began arriving on American shores to the Depression, Protestant America worried about drinking and violations of the Sabbath. Regulating the use of foreign languages (French and German long before Spanish) in the schools also is an old issue. But the parties of earlier periods were patronage-based and generally kept such issues off the public agenda because of their (now and then demonstrated) potential to fracture party coalitions and jeopardize control of valuable jobs and contracts.[17]

But civil service, public sector unionization, conflict of interest laws, and investigative media have restricted the use of material incentives to generate political activity. In consequence, the parties have enlisted the activists from the social movements to serve as party foot soldiers, rendering it impossible to keep their issues off the agenda. Thus, substantive disagreement between the parties is greater now than half a century ago not only because of greater party differences but also because of a greater number of issues to disagree about.

In sum, in the mid-twentieth century period when politics seemed less contentious than today, the American parties were considerably more heterogeneous. The result was party platforms that were less divergent and more balanced among various interests, allowing greater room for compromise. In the ensuing decades the parties sorted along various regional, demographic, and ideological lines. The result is parties that are more homogeneous internally and more distinct from each other.

TWO DIMENSIONS OF CONTENTION

Discussions of contentious politics often conflate two conceptually separate notions. The first is substantive disagreement: Agreeing on a course of action is generally more difficult the greater the differences are between the contending parties. The discussion in the preceding pages focuses primarily on this aspect of contention. But a second, more affective or emotional element is increasingly prominent in discussions of incivility: How much does one dislike the proposals of the other party—or, especially, how much does one dislike the *people* who advance them? When commentators decry the incivility apparent in contemporary politics, they usually are focused on this second, more emotional aspect of contention. The two aspects are logically distinct: It is perfectly possible for two people with highly divergent views to have a civil discussion of their differences. But one does not have to be a professional psychologist to see how the two dimensions often are correlated in practice. Consider Figure 10.1A once again.

In both panels of the figure, the Democrats are on the left and the Republicans are on the right. But the party delegations are further apart in the bottom panel than in the top. A centrist compromise will be further from nearly everybody in both parties in the bottom panel than in the top. If the parties are not only more divergent but also more homogeneous, as they are in the bottom panel, this reinforces the preceding implication. Thus, the party sorting that has made the parties more homogeneous and more distinct during the past half-century makes compromise less attractive than previously.

Reflecting the preceding logic, in an earlier work I argued that party sorting has raised the stakes of politics.[18] In an era of heterogeneous parties and low party cohesion, party control of Congress makes relatively less difference in what kinds of policies emerge than in an era with the opposite characteristics. Party control always matters, of course—a Democratic Congress would not have passed the Taft-Hartley labor legislation in 1947. And party control always matters for committee and subcommittee chairmanships, control of staff, offices, and other institutional benefits—but it matters relatively less for substantive outcomes when the parties are heterogeneous and fragmented.

Party control today obviously matters a great deal. Without a Democratic majority in the House the Democratic health care plan would have failed to pass in 2010. Without a Republican majority in the House, the debt ceiling extension would have passed easily in 2011. Thus, the stakes of politics generally rise with substantive disagreement, and by whatever psychological mechanism(s), so does emotional involvement. If I am forced to accept a compromise far from my preferred position, I will feel disappointed and frustrated. The more important the issue is to me, the greater my emotional reaction.

The increased homogeneity of the parties heightens the frequency and intensity of such feelings. If day after day representatives associate only with people who agree with them politically—colleagues, interest group activists, campaign donors and workers—they will slowly lose understanding of, sympathy for, and eventually tolerance of those who do not (if they ever had much of those qualities to begin with). They will gradually come to believe that their positions are so self-evidently correct that they will lose the capacity to critically evaluate their own positions and to recognize any validity in opposing positions. Opponents' arguments are to be dismissed or ignored entirely, not rebutted with logic or facts. And it becomes natural to question the motives of opponents. Your political opponents advocate particular policies because they are racists, or bought and paid for by Wall Street or the Koch Brothers. Or they hate America and consciously plan to undermine it and establish a socialist state. And as for the *hoi polloi* who are taken in by either side, they deserve no respect, only contempt. They are "bitter and cling to their gods and guns" and "anti-scientific primitives." Or they are "economic illiterates," "taxeaters" and parasites.

In sum, the evolution of American political parties from loose coalitions of disparate interests to groups of like-minded people is a major factor contributing to the contentious politics of today. Substantive differences between the parties are on average greater today, and as the political agenda expanded (the personal is the political), they have found more things to disagree about. And for familiar psychological reasons, substantive conflict generates emotional affect and personal animosity. Many political scientists of the 1950s looked at their parties and found them wanting. They wanted the parties to look more like they do today. But many of today's political scientists look at our parties and wonder whether it would be better for the country if they looked more like they did in the 1950s.

OTHER FACTORS CONTRIBUTING TO CONTENTIOUS POLITICS

The Media

In virtually any discussion of contentious politics the subject of the media eventually comes up. Over the course of the last half-century the notion of a neutral press has eroded greatly. It is now commonplace to attach ideological labels to specific media—Fox News and the *Wall Street Journal* are conservative. MSNBC and the *New York Times* are liberal. CNN and *USA Today* are somewhere in between. A generation ago the media themselves would have vehemently resisted such labeling; today they generally accept it.

In addition, the communications revolution has resulted in a proliferation of media. The broadcast era gave way to the narrowcast era, and the explosion of the Internet further magnifies the fragmentation. Americans no longer read or watch a few media outlets that have mass outlets; instead, they can pick and choose among myriad political publications, cable TV shows, and individual bloggers. It is safe to say that the research community has not yet reached a consensus on the effects of this media transformation. Some view it as a major factor in shaping contentious politics, while others believe that media influence is overstated. Several of the articles in this volume explore these issues.

Jamieson and Hardy argue that the "rise of partisan media menaces civil engaged argument." To the extent that partisans of the left or right restrict their news consumption to their own side (whether Keith Olbermann or Rush Limbaugh), they come to inhabit alternate realities where they do not share the same facts, let alone the same arguments and conclusions. "Partisan media also . . . invite moral outrage by engaging emotion, replace argument with ridicule and *ad hominem*, and often invite their audiences to see the political world as a Manichean place unburdened by complexity, ambiguity or common ground."

In her chapter, Diana Mutz argues that even if politics today is no more contentious and uncivil than in earlier eras, people *perceive* it as being so and a principal reason is television. Two centuries ago very few people could actually see the sneers of contempt on Jefferson's and Adams' faces or hear the anger in their voices when they attacked their opponent. Television enables the mass audience to personally experience the incivility they could only read about or hear about in the pre-television era. In addition, Mutz argues that the natural reaction of people to conflict is to "back-off" and put some space between themselves and the source of conflict. But television's use of close-in shots rubs the viewer's face in conflict, so to speak, and arouses them emotionally.

Of course, we should recognize that no one is forcing us to watch what the media provide. As I have written elsewhere:

> . . . the media cover what is newsworthy, and what is newsworthy is by definition what is uncommon or unrepresentative. Erikson's comment a generation ago is even more true today: "A considerable portion of what we call 'news' is devoted to reports about deviant behavior and its consequences . . ."[19] Conflict has news value as well, especially unusually severe or episodic conflict. Something in human nature makes us more likely to take note of disagreement and division, polarization, battles and war, than agreement and consensus, moderation, cooperation and peace. If we pass two people chatting on the street, we barely notice. If they are yelling at each other we pay them some attention as we pass. If they are rolling around on the sidewalk pummeling each other, many of us will stop and watch—but that does not mean that we would want to elect either of the combatants to Congress—providing that we had a more reasonable choice.

Thus, although the media may give us what we will watch, by way of entertainment, they are less likely to provide what citizens *need* than they did in an earlier era when prominent media figures considered it their duty to inform as well as to entertain and persuade.

Campaign Financing

In contemporary politics money is more important than in earlier eras. Money buys media time, polls, communications expertise, lawyers, and other expensive items that were less relevant or entirely absent when campaigns were conducted by state and local party organizations staffed by patronage workers. Sometimes money is given as a *quid pro quo*—in exchange for favorable policies, as with the financial industry, which appears to have both political parties in its pockets today. But for many contributors, the motivation is more ideological—an attempt to change the direction of the country or prevent it from changing. And in this case conflict is a positive.

People are more likely to contribute to a party if they view the opposition as a bunch of socialists intent on turning the United States into France, or if they see the opposition as a bunch of Bible-thumpers intent on turning the United States into a Christian theocracy. If potential contributors can be convinced that the opposition consists of monsters motivated by a desire to destroy America as we know it, they are more likely to contribute than if they see the opposition as fellow citizens who happen to have a different view of the role of government. In her chapter, Eilperin discusses the rising demands for congressional leaders to raise money and how that contributes to the enhanced partisanship in the Congress.

Moreover, as noted earlier in this chapter, heightened conflict encourages incivility. Republican Representative Joe Wilson of South Carolina shouted "You lie!" during a speech by President Obama in 2009. He raised nearly $4 million by the summer of 2010, compared to $360,000 at the comparable time in 2008.[20] Among other instances of name-calling, Democratic Representative Alan Grayson of Florida compared former Vice President Dick Cheney to a vampire and called Fed Chairman Ben Bernanke a "K Street whore."[21] Grayson also raised more than $3 million in outside contributions compared to about half a million at a comparable time in 2008. Apparently, incivility pays—literally.

SUMMARY

In this chapter, I have argued that the fundamental cause of today's climate of uncivil politics is the sorting of politically active Americans into parties that have grown much more homogeneous than they were in the mid-twentieth century. Particular interests (other than Wall Street) appear to receive protection from only one of the two parties. Particular values seem to be defended by only one of the two parties. And particular kinds of people seem to receive a sympathetic hearing by only one of the two parties.

The consequence is that the actions considered by government bodies are more likely to present stark choices today than in some earlier, less polarized, more civil eras. In consequence, elections matter more. And as the stakes rise, civility falls.

Endnotes

1. For wrap-ups of the uncivil nature of much of the discourse, see the articles by David Harsanyi and James Taranto. Accessed at: http://www.realclearpolitics.com/articles/2011/08/03/when_we_balance_the_budget_the_terrorists_have_won_110810-comments.html. http://online.wsj.com/article/SB10001424053111903520204576484303256286950.html.

2. http://www.mediaite.com/online/tea-party-billboard-shows-obama-alongside-hitler-and-lenin/.

3. http://en.wikipedia.org/wiki/Barack_Obama_%22Joker%22_poster.

4. http://www.nydailynews.com/news/politics/elizabeth-warren-massachusetts-senate-candidate-called-a-socialist-whore-tea-party-heckler-video-article-1.972213?localLinksEnabled=false.

5. Morris P. Fiorina, Samuel J. Abrams, and Jeremy C. Pope, *Culture War? The Myth of a Polarized America,* 3rd ed. (New York: Longman, 2011); Morris P. Fiorina and Samuel J. Abrams, *Disconnect: The Breakdown of Representation in American Politics* (Norman, OK: University of Oklahoma Press, 2009).

6. William S. White, *Citadel: The Story of the U.S. Senate* (New York: Harper, 1956). Cf. Nelson W. Polsby, "Goodbye to the Inner Club," in *Congressional Behavior,* Nelson W. Polsby, ed. (New York: Random House, 1971).

7. Donald R. Matthews, *U.S. Senators and their World* (Chapel Hill, NC: University of North Carolina Press, 1960).

8. Richard F. Fenno, *The Power of the Purse* (Boston: Little, Brown, 1966), ch. 4.

9. John F. Manley, *The Politics of Finance* (Boston, Little, Brown, 1970), ch. 3.

10. Francis E. Lee, *Beyond Ideology* (Chicago: University of Chicago Press, 2009).

11. David W. Rohde, *Parties and Leaders in the Post-Reform House* (Chicago: University of Chicago Press, 1991); Gary C. Cox, and Mathew D. McCubbins, *Legislative Leviathan* (Berkeley, University of California Press, 1993), ch. 6.

12. These quotations are all taken from David Brady, *Congressional Voting in a Partisan Era* (Lawrence, KS: University of Kansas Press), 1973, pp. 1–3.

13. *Ibid.* p. 102.

14. Bruce Oppenheimer, "Barack Obama, Bill Clinton, and the Democratic Congressional Majority," *Extensions,* Spring 2009.

15. Frederick Douzet, Thad Kousser, and Kenneth P. Miller, *The New Political Geography of California* (Berkeley Public Policy Press, University of California Press, 2008), passim, esp. ch. 1.

16. Fiorina, et al., 2011, ch. 5.

17. For a discussion see Joel H. Silbey and Samuel T. McSeveney, *Voters, Parties and Elections* (Lexington MA: Xerox College Publishing, 1972), Part 3.

18. Fiorina and Abrams, *Disconnect*: ch. 7.

19. Kai T. Erikson, *Wayward Puritans* (New York: Wiley, 1966), p. 12.

20. http://www.usatoday.com/news/washington/2010-07-01-Congress_N.htm.

21. http://www.cbsnews.com/8301-503544_162-5425045-503544.html.

11

Polarized by Design: The Modern-Day Congress

Juliet Eilperin

If there was any doubt as to how deeply polarized U.S. politics had become, one of the world's most prominent credit rating agencies summed up America's predicament neatly on August 4, 2011, when it took the government off its list of risk-free borrowers for the first time in history.

"The downgrade reflects our view that the effectiveness, stability, and predictability of American policymaking and political institutions have weakened at a time of ongoing fiscal and economic challenge," Standard & Poor's said in a statement, adding that it lacked confidence in the nation's ability to address its economic problems given "the gulf between the political parties."[1]

While S&P's downgrade did not devastate the U.S. economy—it has struggled recently for a range of much more profound reasons—the agency's statement underscored an uncomfortable truth. Republicans and Democrats are so far apart it is no longer clear whether they can address the most profound questions facing the nation.

Recent congressional voting records prove what voters understand intuitively: Partisanship is at an all-time high in Washington. *National Journal,* which has calculated political rankings since 1982, found that for only the second time since it began keeping track, every Senate Democrat compiled a more liberal voting record than every Senate Republican, and every Senate Republican boasted a more conservative voting record than every Senate Democrat. The only other time this happened in *National Journal's* record, keeping was in 1999.

In contrast to 1999, however, the House was even more polarized in 2010, making the 111th Congress the most partisan on record. Only five House Republicans in 2010 collected vote rankings that were more liberal than the House's most conservative Democrat—Rep. Gene Taylor (Miss.)—while just four Democrats obtained ratings that were more conservative than the chamber's most liberal Republican, Rep. Joseph Cao (La.).[2]

By contrast, three decades ago voting behavior and party affiliation in the Senate were much more loosely connected. In 1982, according to *National Journal*, 24 Republicans had voting records at least as liberal as the most conservative Senate Democrat and 36 Senate Democrats were at least as conservative as the chamber's most left-leaning Republican.[3]

The roots of the political divide facing the nation today lie in a movement launched more than 20 years ago, when a Republican congressman named Newt Gingrich began his quest to win control over the House of Representatives. In my 2006 book, *Fight Club Politics: How Partisanship has Poisoned the House of Representatives,* I argued that the tactics Gingrich and his deputies championed—including crafting lopsided congressional districts that packed in voters from a single party—largely explained why congressional politics had become so extreme.

Now, half a dozen years later, much of that argument still holds true. But now even broader political forces—some stemming from the changes that Gingrich and others put in motion, others arising from technological innovations and other factors—have produced a polarized electorate, not just a polarized political elite.

In 2006, I called the House of Representatives the "House of Unrepresentatives" because lawmakers held much more partisan views than those of their constituents.[4] That is still true, to a large extent. But Americans themselves have become more partisan, choosing to live among like-minded citizens and connecting to them online. These are some of the factors that have helped produce the Tea Party and MoveOn.org, powerful grassroots movements that influence who wins office and how they behave once they're in Washington.

Still, it is important to look at how "the gulf" Standard and Poor's decried came into being. A decade and a half before he sought the presidency, Newt Gingrich (R-GA) established a new model for governing the House of Representatives. The Republicans' victory in 1994 marked the culmination of a protracted battle over the House of Representatives, a prize that Democrats had held for 40 years before Gingrich's triumph.

The 435-member "people's House" occupies a unique place in the American political system: Because of the frequency of its election cycles, its members are meant to be closest to ordinary citizens and to mirror the politics and the prejudices of the U.S. public. The House is a diverse place, relatively speaking: When the GOP took control in 1995, the chamber boasted 48 women, 38 African Americans, 17 Latinos, and 7 Asian Americans and Pacific Islanders. While law ranked as the dominant profession in that 104th Congress (as it had for years before), there were 14 fewer lawyers than the year before. Moreover, the new body boasted 4 funeral directors, 3 dentists, 2 automobile assembly line workers, 2 veterinarians, a florist, a riverboat captain, a jewelry maker, and a taxi driver.[5]

House members represent smaller groups of voters than their Senate and presidential counterparts—roughly 709,760 people, depending on the state— and face reelection more frequently, every two years. The House, which operates on majority rule and without the same elaborate procedures as the Senate, often drives public debate by passing legislation that goes faster and farther than senators or the president might want. It is a place House Republicans set out to discredit and destroy, so they could rebuild it in their own image.

Creating a Political Echo Chamber

While Gingrich and his lieutenants revamped Congress from the inside, party operatives far away from the Capitol were reshaping the country's political landscape through redistricting.

The traditional decennial rite in which the country divvies up citizens into voting blocs and maps out new congressional seats in all 50 states is a wonkish one, with a handful of practitioners working largely behind closed doors to determine politicians' and constituents' fates. Redistricting may seem impenetrable to outsiders, but it explains how GOP leaders have successfully pursued policies that reflect their own beliefs, as well as those of their adherents, while leaving many other Americans by the wayside.

Anyone who wondered whether redistricting matters in our current political system got a clear answer on September 28, 2005, when a grand jury in Austin, Texas, indicted House Majority Leader Tom DeLay (R-TX) of criminally conspiring with two political associates to funnel illegal corporate donations into 2002 Texas state elections. The fund-raising gambit by DeLay and his allies helped their party take over the Texas House for the first time in 130 years, allowing the GOP to redraw Texas' congressional map a year later so it could solidify its once-thin majority in Washington.

DeLay denied the charges, telling reporters, "I have the facts, the law and the truth on my side," but he had to step aside as majority leader. The fallout from the unprecedented indictment, coupled with the scandal involving GOP lobbyist and DeLay confidant Jack Abramoff, tarnished the national GOP, ended the careers of several prominent lawmakers, and allowed Democrats to retake the House in 2006. On January 3, 2006, Abramoff pleaded guilty in federal court to fraud, tax evasion, and conspiracy to bribe public officials; four days later DeLay abandoned his bid to become majority leader again, and he ultimately resigned from the House in June 2006. Four-and-a-half years later, on January 10, 2011, DeLay was sentenced to three years in prison for conspiracy and money laundering.

The creation of politically safe, more ideologically tilted congressional seats through redistricting over the past two decades, moreover, has produced two major consequences that extend far beyond Texas. It has ensured that more politicians from both the extreme left and right have Washington sinecures, from which they face little chance of being ousted.

House Republicans are not the only ones responsible for this modern predicament. Their Democratic counterparts have balked at legislative compromise and have crafted election-proof districts across the nation as well. Both parties have used hardball tactics that have polarized Washington, with Democrats and Republicans alike punishing members who cross party lines and rewarding loyalists with generous campaign contributions.

From House Minority Leader Nancy Pelosi's (D-CA) private tongue lashings of Democrats who supported the GOP's 2003 Medicare prescription drug plan to then-House Minority Leader Richard A. Gephardt's (D-MO) use of face paint and a kilt to rally his troops as "Braveheart" before the 2000 election, Democrats have been waging a daily war in Washington against the GOP as unrelenting and nearly as virulent as that of their counterparts on the other side of the aisle.

Both sides openly acknowledge that politics in the House has become more about strategy than policy. When asked to describe the House Democrats' overall legislative strategy while in the minority, Pelosi spokesman Brendan Daly responded, "It's not about governing. We're focused on message."[6]

Demographic changes across the United States have exacerbated the divide between Republicans and Democrats inside the Beltway. Americans are increasingly choosing to live with like-minded neighbors, a kind of political segregation that gives lawmakers on the far left and far right a boost in the election calculus. In addition, fewer House members have opted to move their families to Washington in recent decades, a trend that limits the opportunities for lawmakers to get to know each other. Both of these factors have made it more difficult for House members to understand each other and their differing points of view.

Indeed, it is hard to exaggerate how much House Republicans and Democrats dislike each other these days. The much-discussed red state–blue state divide captures the duality, but not the animus, of this relationship. They speak about their opponents as if they hail from a distant land with strange customs, all of which are twisted. Republicans see members of the minority as a bunch of sore losers who assail them on procedural grounds because they lack a compelling vision of how to rule the country. Democrats view the GOP majority as a ruthless band that will do anything to maintain its power. When asked to describe each other in interviews for my book, House members used words like "control freak," "childish," "asinine," and "whiners." And as the feud continues, voters' view of Congress continues to plummet. It had just an 11 percent approval rating in a December 2011 Gallup poll, its lowest rating since Gallup began asking the question in 1974.[7]

Political observers have written and spoken at length about the symptoms of political polarization: the two parties' scorched-earth approach to judicial nominations, the partisan drive to impeach Bill Clinton, the Democrats' scorn toward President Bush. And the idea of a modern "culture war" has captured the media's attention, as reporters chronicle communities that provide a study in contrasts, with gun-toting religious conservatives on one side and Chardonnay-sipping atheist lefties on another. The irony is that while many U.S. voters are more complex than these stereotypes, sometimes their elected representatives are not.

But fewer analysts have looked at the problem's roots: how some of our nation's highest-ranking officials have fostered a divide through redistricting and internal congressional reforms that will last for years to come, regardless of popular sentiment. House members—aided by their state counterparts—have rigged the system to guarantee that they, and politicians who think like them, return to Washington year after year. And once they arrive, House leaders on both sides go to extraordinary lengths to reinforce the partisan divide, worsening an already tense situation.

Both the Republicans—and then the Democrats—undermined their genuine attempts to reform Congress as they sought to consolidate power. In doing so, they have undermined the institution's attentiveness to public sentiment by silencing moderates. House Democrats pioneered many of the repressive tactics now favored by GOP leaders, and they used some of those same approaches during the time they held power once again from 2007 until 2011.

New Hampshire Representative Charlie Bass, a moderate and a member of the Class of 1994 that helped deliver the majority to the GOP, mused a few years ago that his leadership was as deaf to popular opinion as the Democratic barons they felled a decade before. While today's Republicans may not be any more despotic than the heavy-handed Democratic chairmen of the 1970s and 1980s, they have failed to live up to their own promises of reform.

"The leadership ought to be prepared to lose from time to time," Bass said. "The opposition just doesn't exist. I think the public would become enthusiastic about issues in Congress if there was some surprise about how it would come out."[8]

A variety of factors—including more sophisticated political mapping techniques, House rules that have curtailed dissent, and more powerful party leaders—have fostered this national divide. Lawmakers have become less accountable to the public and more beholden to the party apparatus, which in turn has encouraged them to become more ideologically entrenched and less inclined to reflect voters' broad political interests and views.

From the 1950s to the 1970s, the two parties feuded often, but they shared a more similar position on taxes, spending, regulation, and use of armed force than today's Republicans and Democrats do. The parties were less ideologically based: a broad swath of the GOP accepted the welfare state, while many Democrats backed the military. The current congressional fight reflects a much larger policy conflict (as well as a blatant power grab by influential leaders and a skewed political map).

House Democratic leaders' heavy-handed tactics made headlines and infuriated even some of the most moderate GOP members. Wright managed to get through a 1987 budget bill, for example, by adjourning the House and then calling it back into session 20 minutes later on the grounds that it constituted a "new" legislative day. In a 1987 election dispute over what became known as the "Bloody Eighth," Democrats insisted on seating Democrat Frank McCloskey as the House member from Indiana's Eighth District although state officials had declared his GOP opponent, Richard McIntyre, the winner. O'Neill dressed down Gingrich on the House floor after the combative Republican delivered a fiery late-night speech, a highly unorthodox move, and refused a customary straight vote on President Reagan's 1981 budget. Instead, he split it into seven parts.

Most of these efforts backfired, and Gingrich, Richard K. Armey (R-TX), and other back-benchers embarked on an unprecedented campaign of their own to convince Americans that they needed to overthrow the established order. This cadre of younger Reaganites was not willing to accommodate senior Democrats and embraced the daunting task of winning back the majority. They launched a sustained attack, questioning House leaders' ethics, and focused on crafting an alternative policy agenda rather than on pursuing legislative compromises with the majority.

Republicans tapped into voters' unease by portraying the House as an evil institution: Representative Jim Nussle (R-IA) demonstrated his outrage on national television by appearing on the House floor with a paper bag over his head, declaring he was ashamed to be a member of the House. Shortly before the Republican takeover, Gingrich's political action committee, GOPAC, came up with a series of "contrast words" Republican candidates could use against their opponents. The phrase list included "decay, failure, shallow, traitors, pathetic, corrupt, incompetent, sick."[9]

A MORE CENTRALIZED, IDEOLOGICAL HOUSE

After shocking the Democrats, many political pundits, and even Republicans by winning control of the House in 1994, GOP revolutionaries enacted a series of brash changes aimed at making the chamber more accountable to the public. They had appealed to the public by vowing both to consider popular legislative initiatives that had been stymied in the past—such as the balanced budget amendment and term limits on lawmakers—and to make the House more accountable to the public. While several legislative planks of the GOP's "Contract with America" didn't make it into law in the end, Republicans enjoyed considerable success in changing the way the House did business. Some internal changes House GOP leaders made—such as launching the THOMAS website so that ordinary citizens could track legislation in real time—helped open up Congress' inner workings to the public.

But other changes aimed more at centralizing power than at cleaning up the House. Gingrich made it clear from the outset that committee chairs answered to the leadership and, by extension, to the entire Republican Conference. "Prior to us, power was centered in the chairmen and you had a relatively permissive leadership on the Democratic side that could only maneuver to the degree the chairmen would tolerate," Gingrich recalled. "We had exactly the opposite model: a very strong leadership that operated as a single team—a single team that had lots of tension inside obviously—but nonetheless operated as a single team. And then you had the chairmen who operated within the framework of that leadership."[10]

Former Representative Robert Walker (R-PA), Gingrich's best friend and a procedural expert who helped police the Democrats when the Republicans were in the minority, said he and his colleagues "believed the way you win votes is you hold all of your own party together, rather than reaching out for consensus."

House Republicans also changed the way incoming members learned about Congress. For years new members had attended a bipartisan orientation at Harvard University, as well as joint sessions in Washington. Gingrich sent the Class of 1994 to the conservative Heritage Foundation instead, and held a separate "Speaker's dinner" for his ground troops. For a few years in the late 1990s, members of the two parties spent a weekend in Hershey, Pennsylvania, in a retreat aimed at fostering greater civility on Capitol Hill. While the retreat at first attracted two hundred members in 1997, organizers had to abandon it a few years later because of a lack of interest. Some lawmakers made an effort to revive it for the 109th Congress, but subsequently canceled the program after the November 2004 election.

"The message is loud and clear for freshmen," said Sherrod Brown (D-OH), who served in the House during that period but has since won a seat in the Senate. "We'll do it on our own."[11]

Gingrich had set out to create a more modern, ideological, and centrally controlled House, and he succeeded.

THE PARTIES EXERT CONTROL

In the mid-1990s, House revolutionaries also pioneered another aspect of governing: fund raising. Top congressional leaders had doled out money to junior members for years, but Republicans took this to a new level with leadership political action committees (PACs). These campaign coffers, which have proliferated on Capitol Hill over the past two decades, allow lawmakers to attract larger donations than they could accept for their own campaigns, provided they in turn donate the money to other federal candidates. Any House member can accept up to $5,000 each calendar year from a given donor, for example, and then dole it out to other aspiring lawmakers in $5,000 increments per election. Ambitious Republicans saw leadership committees as the best way to unseat House Democrats, by steering campaign contributions to challengers and to junior lawmakers who could not independently attract the big donors' largesse.

Armey was the earliest practitioner of this approach. In 1986, the former economics professor gave $75,000 to House GOP candidates, making him the second most generous incumbent next to Bob Michel. Other Republicans followed suit: When Armey told his colleagues at the leadership table in 1994, "I'm going to pledge half a million dollars, and I'm sure Tom [DeLay] will want to match me," Gingrich was quick to one-up them all, vowing to steer $1 million to House GOP candidates.[12] Gingrich saw their "unending campaigning" as essential to maintaining the united backing of his conference, and this approach was important to DeLay's upset victory over Walker in the 1994 majority whip's race. DeLay had raised hundreds of thousands of dollars and traveled to countless districts for many members of the Class of 1994, while Walker had focused more on inside-the-Beltway tactics and policymaking. To this day Walker dislikes leadership PACs, saying they "make leadership elections less competitive on issues of leadership. . . . This leadership PAC thing has gotten out of bounds."[13]

But leadership PACs strengthened the Republican majority on several fronts. They enhanced leaders' standing among rank-and-file members who were grateful for the financial support they couldn't have commanded on their own. The committees made the most efficient use of the GOP's ties to business and other wealthy interests by directing money to key races. And it spurred competition among ambitious members, pouring funds into GOP campaign coffers that might otherwise have gone untapped.

New York Republican Bill Paxon, who chaired the National Republican Congressional Committee during the GOP's victorious 1994 campaign, attributed the party's shift in fund-raising tactics to an empty war chest rather than to a grand strategic vision.

"We did it because we were desperate," Paxon said. "We didn't have any money."[14]

DeLay took this fund-raising approach to a new level in 1999, in an effort to defend Republicans who had backed the impeachment of President Clinton. After analyzing the previous election, the whip and his aides decided they would be best off raising a substantial amount of money early on for these lawmakers, to intimidate potential Democratic challengers. Dubbing the venture Retain Our Majority Program, or ROMP, DeLay convinced both his whip team and outside lobbyists to muster more than $1.3 million for ten House Republicans, two of whom prosecuted President Clinton and eight of whom voted to impeach him. At the time, DeLay spokesman Michael Scalon described this unusual way of soliciting lobbyists as a simple matter of efficiency: "There's nothing new going on here. All of the representatives of the business community have a stake in reelecting a Republican majority and we are just expediting that process for them."[15]

ROMP was a success. DeLay held a celebratory lunch at the Capitol Hill Club in June 1999 for the ten targeted Republicans and their lobbyist backers, complete with an oversized check for $1.3 million that was displayed on cue by two of his female staffers. The lobbyist crowd even sounded out a version of a drum roll just before DeLay announced the program's grand fund-raising total.[16] And while two of the program's high-profile beneficiaries lost, the rest won reelection.

As one prominent GOP lobbyist who asked not to be identified observed, "ROMP sent a signal to the downtown [lobbying community] rank-and-file that you are accountable to the leadership for what you do in swing districts. It matters to Tom DeLay what you do in a swing district."[17]

Not to be outdone, Armey headed up a later round of ROMP, summoning several lobbyists to a meeting at the National Republican Congressional Committee to dole out fund-raising assignments. As his aides handed out a list of vulnerable House Republicans, Armey told his downtown allies they should call their clients and instruct them to give money to the 10 incumbents. As one participant in the meeting put it, "You have the majority leader walking across the street to tell a group of lobbyists, 'This is important to me.' When I call my clients for [Kentucky Republican] Anne Northup, I can now say I'm helping Armey hit his ROMP numbers. It's a totally different thing."[18]

Democratic leaders began copying Republicans' use of leadership PACs to gain influence over junior lawmakers and to solidify their party's financial footing. A month after the Republicans won the majority, Gephardt and his wife Jane had Gingrich and his then-wife, Marianne, over for dinner at Gephardt's Herndon, Virginia, home. (While the exact menu now eludes Gephardt, he thinks they ate chicken. "We're politicians, we go through chicken withdrawal," he explained.)[19]

Gephardt congratulated his Republican counterpart and asked how he had achieved such a stunning victory.

"Money," Gingrich replied.[20]

Gephardt took the lesson seriously, embarking on a frenetic fund-raising drive that amassed millions for his party from the high-tech, as well as the television, movie, and music industries. In 1999, the latter three industries alone gave House Democrats nearly $1 million, twice what they had given them in 1997 and 1998 combined.[21] Gingrich doled out tens of thousands of dollars from his own campaign war chest to his colleagues, and his successors imitated him. In the run-up to the 2000 election, Nancy Pelosi and Steny Hoyer (D-MD)—who were vying for the post of minority whip at the time—raised enormous sums for Democratic candidates. Hoyer raised about $1.5 million while Pelosi collected $3.9 million.[22] Now Pelosi and Hoyer sit atop the House Democrats' leadership ladder, the party's number one and number two, respectively.

ROMP—which has been renamed The Patriot Program—and its Democratic counterpart, Frontline, have now become institutions, a way of rewarding loyal lawmakers and of shunning others. When GOP leaders unveiled their ROMP list for 2005, they left out Representative Christopher Shays, an outspoken Connecticut moderate who barely won reelection the year before. (Shays eventually lost to a Democrat, but not in that election.) The Democrats publish their own Frontline roster, listing the lucky marginal members who have won the attention of party leaders.

Democrats are just as demanding as Republicans when it comes to asking their senior members to pony up campaign cash. In late June 2005, Pelosi and her top lieutenants informed their colleagues that if they did not pay their designated "dues for the 2006 election cycle" to the Democratic Congressional Campaign Committee (DCCC), they could no longer use the phones and other amenities at the DCCC's members' services center.

Writing in bold ink and underlining it for emphasis, the June 29 memo warned, "This policy will be strictly enforced! We hope that we will not have to deny service to any Member and strongly encourage you to pay your dues so that you can continue taking advantage of our services. The 2006 election is going to be tough and we need all of our members to play an active role in our effort to regain the majority."[23]

The leadership PAC frenzy has boosted both the lawmakers' campaign coffers and House leaders' sway over junior members, who are hesitant to anger their political patrons. Party bosses no longer determine which candidate can run for office in a district, but senior House leaders on either side of the aisle can decide whether a given lobbyist cuts a check for a little-known member, or whether these same lobbyists troop to a swing district just before an election to drive voter turnout.

SOCIAL TIES FRAY APART

At the same time party leaders were gaining influence over their members through fundraising, personal connections between lawmakers from across the aisle began to weaken. Thirty years ago, new members were more likely to move their families to D.C. after an election. They were eager to become part of the capital's social scene and wanted their spouses and children near to where they spent most of their week. Families often socialized with each other regardless of party, and these personal ties curbed members' tendency to demonize each other. If Wisconsin Democrat David Obey attacked Representative Willis Gradison (R-OH) on the House floor, his wife Jane would lambaste him at home, pointing out that they were likely to have dinner with the Gradisons later in the week.[24]

This sort of lifestyle disappeared in the late 1980s and early 1990s when GOP firebrands like Dick Armey declared themselves members of the "Tuesday to Thursday Club" and spent as little time as possible in Washington. They chose to sleep in their offices rather than waste money on a proper apartment, and they sharply questioned why their colleagues would relocate to the nation's capital. Just a few decades before this, the moniker "Tuesday to Thursday congressman" was an insult that implied the person in question was not a serious legislator. But Armey and Gingrich— and the leaders who have followed them—turned it into a badge of honor, warning new members to keep their families away from D.C.

Now, the majority of lawmakers live in their district and commute to D.C., rather than the other way around. While this keeps them in touch with their constituents, it makes it unlikely that they can forge the social connections that keep tempers and political rhetoric in check.

PICKING CONSTITUENTS TO SUIT THEMSELVES

The districts these members spend time in are more politically slanted than they were before. While politicians have always sought to craft legislative districts that favor one party over another, technological advances have made constituent shuffling more sophisticated. Back when California

Democrat Phillip Burton redid the state's congressional map in the 1980s—an egregious partisan gerrymander, which badly damaged the California GOP—he estimated a neighborhood's partisan leanings by the kind of cars on the street. (Saabs and Volvos meant wealthy Democrats were living on the block, Buicks indicated middle-class Republicans, and Chevys pointed to middle-class Democratic homes.)[25] Now mapmakers can get detailed information about an area's political makeup—down to the voting history of an individual block—and plug it into a computer, allowing them to carve up neighborhoods with precision. The new software ensures both parties can maximize their partisan advantage in a congressional district, provided they have enough political clout to shepherd a map into law.

The results of California's 2000 redistricting, for example, couldn't be starker. Not a single incumbent lost his or her election bid after the new map went into effect. Democratic Rep. Ellen Tauscher, who had managed to unseat a Republican incumbent in the previous decade and then had fought fiercely to preserve her seat—didn't even have a general election opponent in 2002. In 2004 the state offered just one competitive race—to fill the seat of retiring Democratic Representative Cal Dooley, a Central Valley moderate. The Republicans outspent the Democrats by nearly four to one in the race, but state Senator Jim Costa (D) still won handily, 54 to 46 percent. That same year not a single one of California's 153 federal or state legislative seats listed on the ballot changed party control.

The way California power brokers—as well as veteran politicians in Michigan, Pennsylvania, and elsewhere—reshaped the country's legislative map during this decade helps explain why Congress is so split today. Working to protect incumbents across the country, the men and women who drew the nation's current congressional districts made the House less accountable to the public and more divided as a body.

Both Republicans and Democrats share the blame for this phenomenon, although the GOP managed to extract greater political gain in the redistricting process in 2000 that has helped bolster its congressional majority for much of the past decade. While political gerrymandering is nothing new in the United States—Democrats used identical tactics when they had the opportunity in years past—the system has now spiraled out of control, with party operatives engaging in a never-ending game of tit-for-tat that has alienated voters as well as some of their elected representatives. This has not provided lawmakers with total immunity; control of Congress changed twice in the decade after redistricting in 2000. But it has protected many House members from voters' obvious unease with their performance.

Rep. David Dreier (R-CA), who helped draw the state's congressional map after the 2000 Census but did not oppose former Gov. Arnold Schwarzenegger's plan to subsequently depoliticize the process, said he and Democrats produced "a reasonable plan" that has enabled three Californians to rise to the top of three exclusive House committees. "For the people, for the voters, it has worked pretty darned well," he said.[26]

But several California lawmakers from both parties—such as Costa and William M. Thomas, who chaired the House Ways and Means Committee before retiring from Congress—say representatives shouldn't be afraid of a fair fight. Costa put it this way: "As a person who's passionate about representative democracy, I believe competitive seats make for balanced public policy."[27]

Thomas, who sparred with Burton over California redistricting in the 1980s, tried unsuccessfully for several years to place a redistricting reform initiative on the state's ballot. In 2004, even minor parties like the Greens and the Libertarians didn't field a candidate against him, let alone the Democrats.

"I had no one," Thomas said. "That's outrageous. . . . You have the creation of districts that are more selected by the candidate than the constituent."[28]

Michigan's legislative landscape over the past decade shows what happens when a party takes a partisan approach. Michigan remains one of the country's top battleground states, but Republicans controlled the entire process after the 2000 Census and took full advantage of their position. From the very beginning, the only question was how badly the Democrats would suffer.

Both parties have exploited redistricting to serve their interests over the course of Michigan's history. In one particularly charged incident in 1983, the Democrats ushered through a new districting plan for the state legislature in the middle of the night, even though one of the senators casting the decisive vote had just been recalled from office. (The courts later overturned the plan.) It was no surprise that when the Republicans saw their chance to take a congressional delegation tilted nine to seven in favor of Democrats and flip it the other way, they moved quickly.

The GOP governor at the time, John Engler, at first envisioned a delegation leaning eight to seven in favor of Republicans, since the state's shrinking population had cost Michigan's delegation a seat. This meant throwing several Democrats into districts with each other.

As in other states, Michigan Republican mapmakers used sophisticated software that could spit out dozens of possible plans in rapid succession. In the early 1990s, the state GOP's political director, Terry Marquardt, would have to wait as long as three hours for aides to load the proper computer program when he was drawing electoral maps. (He would ask party aides to install it when he was leaving his Olivet, Michigan, home in the morning; it still wouldn't be up and running when he arrived in Plymouth an hour and 45 minutes later.) By the time Marquardt drafted the state's congressional districts after the 2000 Census, it took him a matter of minutes to run the software.

Ten years of technological development made the process quicker and sharper. In the spring of 2001, Marquardt unfurled his final version of the congressional map in the governor's ceremonial office at the state capitol building and told Engler the plan would elect nine Republicans and six Democrats. He could tell by the expression on his face that the governor was surprised: "It was the classic Engler raise of the eyebrows when he likes something."[29]

The Michigan GOP wasted little time in shepherding through the new plan. The state House of Representatives held one hearing on the 167-page bill at 11:00 p.m. on July 10, 2001, and passed the measure at 2:35 the following morning.[30]

Democrats fought the GOP's map in court, arguing in part that the plan disenfranchised Michigan voters who gave Democrats 52 percent of the vote in the 2000 congressional elections compared with the GOP's 46 percent.[31]

Veteran Michigan Democratic Rep. John Dingell, who headed the legal effort, said, "We knew the deck was stacked but we knew it was the only game in town. We had to play."[32] The Democrats lost. While lawmakers later discovered the Republicans' hasty push for their plan had flaws, including that it failed to assign 4,578 voters to any of the state's 15 districts, the Republican Secretary of the Senate remedied the situation by drafting a new bill that she sent directly to the governor. Engler signed the bill at 4:54 p.m. on September 11, 2001, attracting little attention in the midst of the worst terrorist attack in U.S. history.[33]

One of the beneficiaries of the map was Michigan Republican Thaddeus McCotter, who won the following year in a House district he helped craft as chair of the state senate redistricting committee. He has served there ever since.

By shifting the real election to the primaries, lawmakers have had to shift to the left or right of average voters. This has even occurred in the Senate, where in 2010 two Republican senators and one Democrat lost their renomination bids, almost as many as in the past quarter-century combined.[34]

These three factors—strong-armed tactics by party leaders, a weakening of social ties among lawmakers, and slanted political maps—set the table for the kind of polarization we have observed in the past decade. But an additional pair of factors—social networking and a more ideological media landscape—intensified this trend, contributing to the political breakdown we are now witnessing.

THE RISE OF THE TEA PARTY

Some of these movements, such as MoveOn.org and the Tea Party, initially grew organically out of voters' frustration with the economy and political leaders. But they have become more orchestrated over time, leading to an assault on the sort of rational political discourse that underpins our democratic process.

Sometimes they take place on the national stage, like when Rep. Joe Wilson (R-SC) called out "You lie!" in the midst of President Obama's speech to a joint session of Congress in September 2009. Or, in yet another joint session speech Obama delivered two years later, when the President spoke about how he planned to deliver jobs—and Republicans chuckled. Not just when he said, "You should pass this jobs plan right away!"—which prompted Sens. Bob Corker (Tenn.) and Lindsey Graham (S.C.) to laugh. The line "this isn't political grandstanding," cracked up House Budget Committee Chairman Paul Ryan (Wis.).[35] A serious address about reviving the nation's economy became a comedy show.

But more often, this bitter fight is taking place in settings away from the national limelight in town hall meetings, an ancient American rite where lawmakers hold freewheeling discussions with their constituents.

In May 2009, Democratic Rep. Jim Himes called a town hall meeting in Fairfield, Connecticut, to discuss an economic strategy for his part of the state. Bob MacGuffie, a conservative activist angry over President Obama's stimulus plan, helped disrupt the meeting. The protest was so successful that MacGuffie drafted a document titled, "Rocking the Town Halls—Best Practices," which he distributed to like-minded voters. It became a blueprint for taking over congressional listening sessions.

"Spread out in the hall and try to be in the front half," the playbook reads. "The objective is to put the Rep on the defensive with your questions and follow up. The Rep should be made to feel that a majority, and if not, a significant portion of at least the audience, opposes the socialist agenda of Washington."

"You need to rock-the-boat early in the Rep's presentation," it adds. "Watch for an opportunity to yell out and challenge the Rep's statements early."[36]

The strategy worked beyond MacGuffie's expectations, as conservatives across the country upended Democratic lawmakers' town hall meetings in 2010 and helped usher in a new Republican majority in the House. But Democratic activists decided to follow suit, further eroding the quality of our political discourse. Mark Vallone, a resident of Epping, New Hampshire, decided to interrupt Frank C. Guinta during a session in August 2011, because he saw Tea Party adherents use it against the Democratic House member Guinta unseated the year before, Carol Shea-Porter.

"The next town hall, I'll be there," Vallone told *The Washington Post*.[37]

Now some Republican lawmakers are complaining they can't get a word in edgewise. Rep. Lou Barletta (R-PA) suspended his own meetings in the summer of 2011 after liberals affiliated with groups such as MoveOn. org interrupted him. When Justin Ruben, MoveOn.org's executive director, explains his organization's strategy, he sounds like MacGuffie: "What we say is, 'Get there early, bring signs and be visible, and ask tough questions.' "[38]

This sort of dialogue has deteriorated so badly that Rep. Rob Wittman (R-VA) was forced to defend himself during a town hall meeting in Yorktown, Virginia, against charges that he was "acting like a terrorist."

"I take umbrage with your assertion that I'm a terrorist," Wittman told his Democratic detractor. "I am not." [39]

With political exchanges like these, it's no wonder our legislative branch is sharply divided.

The conservative Republicans who are ascendant in Congress, such as House Republican Conference Chairman Mike Pence (IN), made it clear to voters just before the 2010 elections that they had little interest in forging compromises with a Democratic president.

"Look, I want to be very, very clear with people around the country. There's going to be no compromise on ending the era of runaway federal spending, borrowing, bailouts, takeovers, deficits and debts. There's going to be no compromise on repealing Obamacare lock, stock and barrel," Pence said in an interview on Fox News' "On the Record with Greta Van Susteren" on October 22, 2010. "There's going to be no compromise on supporting our troops or protecting the values of the American people in the way we spend the people's money. So, you know, let's be clear on this."[40]

Pence and his colleagues have delivered on that vow, rejecting bipartisan agreements on everything from spending to tax policy.

David Goldston spent years on Capitol Hill working for Sherwood Boehlert, a moderate Republican who pushed environmental measures even when it meant defying his own leadership. Boehlert retired from Congress in 2006, and Goldston now directs government affairs for the Natural Resources Defense Council, an environmental advocacy group. When it comes to the current brand of conservatives that are driving politics on Capitol Hill, Goldston said both voters and other elected officials have to recognize that compromising is not in the equation.

"We don't have a political culture where the media or the public know how to deal with people who mean what they say," he said. "It's like abolitionism. They're saying, 'We're done compromising. You have to decide which side you're on.'"[41]

Even Gingrich, who helped pioneer these techniques in the late 1980s and early 1990s, has come under assault as not being partisan enough during his 2012 presidential campaign. The new conservatives pilloried him for his decision to appear in a 2006 ad with Nancy Pelosi funded by Al Gore's advocacy group, the Alliance for Climate Protection. Gingrich told the radio host Paul Wescott in July 2011 that he regretted making the commercial, which called for national, bipartisan action on climate change: "Look, I was, I was trying to make the point we shouldn't be afraid to debate the Left, even on the environment, and that was obviously misconstrued, and that's one of the things I probably wouldn't do again."[42]

And that is where things stand. House Majority Whip Kevin McCarthy (R-CA) sees the nation in the midst of a major transition. Americans voted for more government in 2010, and when they disliked the consequences, they voted House Republicans into power.

"The argument will be about what the size and shape of what government should be," McCarthy said in an interview. "You have to have a debate. 2012 will be the deciding mark that actually moves us through all this."[43]

The answer couldn't come a moment too soon.

Endnotes

1. Binyamin Appelbaum and Eric Dash, "S.& P. Downgrades Debt Rating of U.S. for the First Time," *The New York Times*, August 5, 2011.
2. Ronald Brownstein, "Congress Hits New Peak in Polarization," *National Journal*, February 24, 2011.

3. Ibid.

4. I owe this phrase in part to Jenner & Block attorney Sam Hirsch, who wrote the law review article "The United States House of Unrepresentatives: What Went Wrong in the Latest Round of Congressional Redistricting," *Election Law Journal 2* (2), 2003.

5. Congressional Research Service Report 95-2000, "Membership of the 104th Congress: A Profile," January 25, 1995, 1–3. However, an *Austin American-Statesman* editorial, published shortly after the GOP won control, noted that if the 104th Congress accurately reflected the nation, it would have included 222 women, 52 African Americans, 39 Latinos, and 13 Asians. "A Lopsided Congress Needs Honest Views on Affirmative Action," *Austin American-Statesman*, March 26, 1995.

6. Brendan Daly, interview with author, March 10, 2005. Daly outlined a different vision of Pelosi's leadership after she won election as House speaker in January 2007.

7. Frank Newport, "Congress Ends 2011 With Record-Low 11% Approval Rating" Gallup website, December 19, 2011.

8. Charlie Bass, interview with author, November 23, 2004.

9. Martin Walker, "Republicans' Fiery Avenger; Newt Gingrich Takes Up His Powerful New Washington Role Determined to Dismantle the U.S. Welfare State," *Guardian* (London), December 5, 1994.

10. Gingrich interview.

11. Sherrod Brown, interview with author, February 9, 2005.

12. Armey interview.

13. Walker inetrview.

14. Bill Paxon, interview with author, March 30, 2005.

15. Jim VandeHei, "DeLay Banking on Lobbyists: Private Meeting Sets Cash Goals for Aiding 10 Members," *Roll Call*, May 10, 1999.

16. Juliet Eilperin, "House Whip Wields Fund-Raising Clout; Network of Lobbyists Helps DeLay Gather Millions for GOP Campaigns," *The Washington Post*, October 18, 1999.

17. GOP lobbyist who asked not to be identified, interview with author, January 20, 2005.

18. Ibid.

19. Richard A. Gephardt, interview with author, June 16, 2005.

20. Ibid.

21. Juliet Eilperin, "And the Winner Is . . . House Democrats; Spacey Heads a Cast of Fundraisers," *The Washington Post*, March 25, 2000.

22. Juliet Eilperin, "The Making of Madam Whip; Fear and Loathing—and Horse Trading—in the Race for the House's No. 2 Democrat," *The Washington Post Magazine*, January 6, 2002.

23. Memo to the House Democratic Caucus from the Democratic Leadership, June 29, 2005.

24. David Obey, interview with author, February 10, 2005.

25. John Jacobs, *A Rage for Justice: The Passion and Politics of Phillip Burton* (Berkeley: University of California Press, 1995), p. 431.

26. David Dreier, interview with author, July 11, 2005.

27. Jim Costa, interview with author, March 2, 2005.

28. William M. Thomas, interview with author, March 27, 2005.

29. Terry Marquardt, interview with author, March 4, 2005.

30. Sam Hirsch, "The United States House of Unrepresentatives: What Went Wrong in the Latest Round of Congressional Redistricting," *Election Law Journal 2* November 2, 2003: 206.

31. George Weeks, "Redrawn Districts Cost Dems; Republican Proposal Would Give State GOP a 9-6 Edge in Congress," *Detroit News,* June 15, 2001.

32. John D. Dingell, interview with author.

33. Hirsch, "The United States House of Unrepresentatives," 207.

34. Brownstein.

35. Dana Milbank, "President Irrelevant," *The Washington Post*, September 11, 2011.

36. "Rocking the Town Halls—Best Practices," courtesy of Bob MacGuffie.

37. David A. Fahrenthold, "American Town Halls More Contentious Than Ever, in Part by Design," *The Washington Post*, August 27, 2011.

38. Ibid.

39. Ibid.

40. Rep. Mike Pence (R-IN), Interview on "On the Record with Greta Van [CR_EN] Sustren," FOX News, October 22, 2010.

41. David Goldston, interview with author, July 18, 2011.

42. Wendy Koch, "Gingrich Regrets Climate Change Ad with Pelosi," *USA Today*, July 27, 2011.

43. Kevin McCarthy, interview with author, September 11, 2011.

12

The News Media and the Rise of Negativity in Presidential Campaigns: A New Hypothesis[1]

John G. Geer

"Ads are about news coverage these days."

Mark McKinnon, November 2009

As you have seen throughout this book, much of the blame for the rise of nasty, mean-spirited politics has been placed on the media. Talk radio, the 24-hour news cycle, over-heated blogs, and much else have changed the way we gather and process political information. But there may be yet another piece to the story, as you will soon read. John Geer suggests the news media now cover negative campaign advertisements so extensively that they have given candidates and their consultants extra incentive to produce them. By playing such close attention to these ads, the news media have given ads ever-greater importance—which, of course, increases their usage and leaves the public discouraged by the tone of electoral politics.

Negativity is part and parcel of American politics. A full year before the 2012 presidential election, President Obama faced an onslaught of negative ads.[2] The typical assumption is that negativity is a product of what I will call the Karl Rove mentality. Consultants urge more and more attack ads because the "dark arts"[3] help their candidates win elections. Surely the actions of consultants are part of the explanation for the rise of negativity. But the untold story is that the news media's behavior is encouraging more and more attack advertising. Journalists, I contend, began to pay substantial attention to advertising during the 1988 presidential campaign and have continued to do so. And most of this attention is dedicated to *negative* advertising. This shift in the coverage of campaigns has recast the incentives of consultants, altering the way they approach presidential elections in general and advertising in particular. Consultants now know that attacks can draw significant attention in the free media, which gives them more incentive to produce and air negative ads than 25 years ago.

This chapter, as a result, offers the unconventional argument that changes in the actions of the news media have helped to fuel the rise in attack politics. Because this argument is unorthodox, I will marshal as much evidence as possible. The most compelling pieces of evidence come from personal interviews I conducted with leading journalists and consultants. By shedding light on this important and recent development, I hope to advance our understanding of negativity, campaigns, and the news media. This better understanding offers timely lessons for those interested in assessing the tone of contemporary politics. I say "timely" because I believe the rate of negativity in American elections will continue to increase in the coming years. In other words, what President Obama faced in 2011 is only the tip of the iceberg.

BACKGROUND

By most accounts, the 2008 presidential campaign was the most negative in the modern era. Barack Obama and John McCain exchanged fire on many fronts. McCain cast doubt on Obama's readiness to serve as commander-in-chief. Obama tied the senator from Arizona to the unpopular policies of the Bush administration.[4] It was a robust exchange, to say the least. The 2012 campaign, as suggested above, is likely to be even more negative than the 2008 campaign. And this pattern is sure to continue for the foreseeable future. Consider the 2010 Supreme Court decision in *Citizens' United*. Under this new ruling, interest groups of all sorts should be able to raise sizable amounts of money, much of which can be spent on television advertising. One recent estimate suggested that spending in 2012 will be more than $3 billion, which would be nearly 50 percent more than in 2008.[5] If history is a guide, nearly all these third-party ads will be negative.[6]

While negative ads are now commonplace, it is important to remember that attacks are hardly new in American politics. Thomas Jefferson, for example, was attacked as being the "anti-Christ" in 1800.[7] Andrew Jackson was called a cannibal during the 1828 struggle for the White House.[8] In 1864, Abraham Lincoln was referred to as "a liar, buffoon, ignoramus, swindler, and butcher."[9] Harry Truman, during the 1948 presidential campaign, equated the Republicans and Thomas Dewey to Adolf Hitler and Nazi Germany.[10] The harsh tone of these claims goes well beyond Texas Governor Rick Perry's claim in the fall of 2011 that "Obama's socialist policies are bankrupting America. We must stop them now."[11]

Whether presidential campaigns in the nineteenth century were more or less negative than those in the twenty-first century is far from clear. Perhaps, as suggested by Susan Herbst in this book, incivility has always been a strategically used political resource. But what is clear is that over the last 50 years there has been a steady rise in negative advertising by presidential candidates (see Figure 12.1). In the 1970s, attacks constituted about 20 percent of the content of political ads aired on television. By the 1990s, they had grown to around 40 percent. Since the turn of the twenty-first century, negative appeals in presidential elections have averaged about 50 percent, with those in 2008 comprising more than 60 percent.

What has caused this near doubling of attack ads from the 1970s to the present day? One explanation is that with the polarization of the parties,[12] candidates now have more disagreement about policy than 30 years ago. These disagreements manifest themselves in the form of attack ads. There is good reason to believe that this explanation has some merit.

As Figure 12.2 shows, there is a strong statistical correlation (.88) between negativity and polarization.[13] But correlation does not mean causation. Perhaps the negativity is driving the polarization.[14] On the surface, that argument seems problematic. To begin with, there is limited evidence that ads influence the choices of voters[15] and even if it does, the duration of the effect is a matter of days.[16] It makes much more sense that a structural change in the country, such as polarization, would be the driving force behind negativity. In past research, I showed that at the presidential level the increased polarization of the parties seems to be driving the rate of negativity.[17] And even more compelling, personal attacks have *not* increased in frequency over the last 40 years and this recent jump in negativity has corresponded with increasing disagreements on policy—evidence that supports this hypothesis.

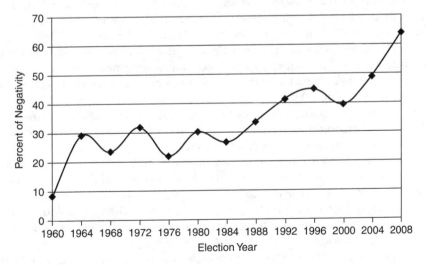

FIGURE 12.1 Share in Negativity in Presidential Campaigns

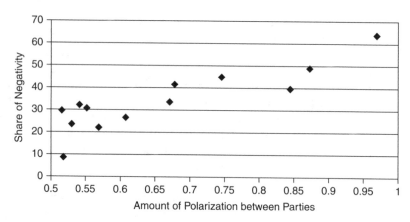

FIGURE 12.2 Polarization and Negativity

A second explanation for the rise of negativity is what I mentioned at the outset—what I term the "Karl Rove mentality." Attacks are increasing because consultants believe they are more effective than positive ads. While the scholarly literature does *not* indicate that attack ads work better than positive ads,[18] practitioners apparently do think that they work better and it is that perception that helps account for this increase. There is surely merit to this hypothesis, but it is unclear how much. Attacks have always been part of American politics, as mentioned earlier. Why would attacks be more effective in 2012 than in 1960? Or 1860? Do consultants know more about campaign tactics now than they did back then? Perhaps, but when we think about the political skills of people like Teddy Roosevelt, Abraham Lincoln, or James Madison, that claim becomes less compelling. These individuals were masters at their trade. Further, successful candidates have long had access to good advice, whether it was James Farley for Franklin Roosevelt, Mark Hanna for McKinley, or Alexander Hamilton for George Washington. Certainly, candidates from the past have gone on the attack, often fiercely, and with success. It is easy to say consultants have new and better techniques to practice the "dark arts," but every era has witnessed new ways, such as radio in the 1920s, to communicate with voters. And each of these technological changes has been put to good use by practitioners of the day. I do not want to dismiss completely this hypothesis, but I do want to urge caution before putting too much weight on it.

What I am even more interested in is offering a third hypothesis. My contention is that the news media also bear responsibility for this rise in negativity. The core idea is that the news media now cover negative ads so extensively that they have given candidates and their consultants extra incentive to produce them. Candidates want to get their message out, hoping to control the terms of the debate. They can air a positive ad and try to influence voters with that spot. But the news media will likely ignore it. Why cover an ad that says John McCain wants better educated children? Surely the senator wants educated children. Nothing is newsworthy in such a spot. A negative ad, however, can generate controversy and conflict, drawing attention from journalists. So, in 2008, when John McCain aired a spot claiming that Barack Obama favors "legislation to teach comprehensive sex education to kindergartners," that drew interest from the press.[19] It is such coverage by the news media that helps candidates get their message out to the public and allows them to shape the all important narrative of the campaign. Let's now consider the evidence that lends support to this new hypothesis.

THE NEWS MEDIA'S COVERAGE OF POLITICAL ADVERTISING

The best example of the news media's excessive attention to negative advertising comes from the 2004 presidential campaign. As a result of the attention paid to a set of controversial ads aired by Swift Boat Veterans for Truth (SBVT) against John Kerry, the term "swift boat" has become part of the American political vocabulary. These attacks became so well known that political commentators now refer to making nasty allegations during a campaign as being "swift boated." The facts are that few Americans actually saw the attacks aired on TV. SBVT made limited ad buys for these spots in three battleground states (Iowa, Wisconsin, and Ohio).[20] An estimated 1 million people saw these spots actually aired on TV,[21] which is not even one percent of the voting public. Americans learned about these ads *from* the news media's coverage of them. Journalists became enamored with these attack ads on Kerry, and gave them a huge amount of attention. Consider that according to a Lexis-Nexis search, the term "swift boat" received 40 percent *more* coverage from the news media during the presidential campaign than the term "Iraq War."[22] This comparison is quite alarming. We were in the middle of an increasingly unpopular war that was the single most important problem to the American public at the time.[23] Yet, the Swift Boat controversy drew more press attention than the Iraq War. It should come as no surprise that in September 2004, 80 percent of Americans had heard something about these advertisements.[24] The public awareness of these spots could not have come from the ads themselves. It had to arise from the attention paid to them by the press.

The Swift Boat case does not stand alone. Consider that only four years later the McCain campaign caught the attention of journalists with the now famous "celebrity" ad that compared then-Senator Obama with Paris Hilton and Britney Spears. A key part of the motivation for McCain's campaign to air this ad, according to Alex Castellanos (a Republican consultant), was "to start a debate in the news media about Obama's experience."[25] It is clear that the "Celebrity Ad" drew the interest of journalists, playing into their reporting of the campaign. As evidence of this attraction, a Lexis-Nexis search about the presidential campaign yielded 50 percent more news stories mentioning "Paris Hilton" than the "Iraq War."[26] The Iraq War was not as central an issue in 2008 as it was in 2004, but the comparison remains telling.

It is important, however, to move beyond these examples and see whether there has been a systematic shift in the behavior of the press. The Swift Boat case, as Adam Nagourney of the *New York Times* warns,[27] may be an outlier. So, have the news media *in general* started to cover advertising more than they did in the past?

Figure 12.3[28] provides a clear answer to this question. Starting in 1988, the news media began to pay a great deal more attention to political advertising during presidential elections. The subject drew some attention in the press prior to 1988, but the number of stories in the *New York Times* and the *Washington Post* jumped from 88 in 1984 to 197 in 1988. The amount of attention increased again in 2004—surely reflecting the Swift Boat ads.[29] The data above are from traditional newspapers. What about the other media? The network news shows (e.g., CBS Evening News) also indicate a big jump in coverage of negativity in 1988.[30] For newer forms of media, we cannot, of course, look back historically. But we can look at the type of coverage. The network news only plays a 3- to 5- second sound bite of a 30-second negative spot. But cable news often replays the *full* ad, in effect, giving the spot more free airtime. A recent study by Clinton and Geer finds that more than 90 percent of the full replays of television ads are done by Fox, MSNBC, or CNN.[31] Thus, we should expect some differences in the impact of this coverage to vary by the kind of media. But the overall attention to negativity by all forms of media, new or old, remains extensive and increasing.

These data about changes in the news media's coverage of ads at first glance seems compelling. But a skeptic might note that the press has always enjoyed conflict and ask why negative ads have drawn so little attention prior to 1988. Moreover, one might ask: "What about the Daisy Spot?" The so-called Daisy spot,[32] which Lyndon Johnson aired in 1964, is one of the most famous negative ads of all time. Even though it appeared more than 45 years ago, we still talk about it today. The conventional wisdom is that this ad, which was aired in the early days of television and a quarter of a

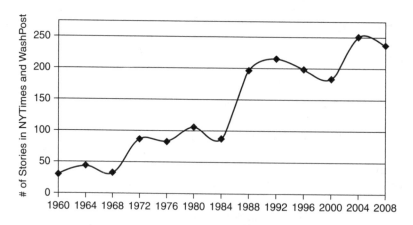

FIGURE 12.3   News Media Attention to Advertising, 1960–2008

century before the jump reported in Figure 12.3, generated a good deal of attention by the news media. Yet Figure 12.3 suggests that the spot drew little coverage—at least by comparison to coverage of advertising in more recent campaigns. Might these data be misleading? To answer this question, I collected additional evidence that provided a detailed look at the attention paid to the Daisy spot and compared it to the attention given to other controversial ads.[33]

Table 12.1 reports the number of stories in the *New York Times* and the *Washington Post* for seven well-known spots. Two things stand out in the table. First, the data confirm in dramatic fashion the amount of attention the news media paid to the Swift Boat controversy. It got more press coverage than all of these other spots *combined*.[34] Second, and more relevant to the question at hand, the Daisy spot received the *least* attention of the seven ads I examined. Admittedly, the difference between the attention paid to the Daisy spot and the Tank ad (or the Revolving Door Ad) is quite minor. But those two ads, while well known, are not nearly as famous as the Daisy spot. Further, the Willie Horton ad drew four times more attention than Daisy, and the Boston Harbor ad drew three times more attention. The Willie Horton ad remains controversial today, so that difference is not so surprising. Considering the press paid so much more attention to the "Boston Harbor" spot than the Daisy ad is not only a bit curious, but also underscores in dramatic terms the core claim I am making about this surge in coverage of negative ads.

These data actually suggest we may want to reconsider the idea that the Daisy spot drew so much attention from journalists in 1964. Perhaps the conventional wisdom that this ad received a lot of attention may speak more to current discussions about negativity than what actually unfolded in the Johnson–Goldwater campaign. That is, we think the Daisy spot is so controversial because it has become part of the current dialogue over attack

TABLE 12.1	What about the Daisy Spot?			
Name of Ad	Period of Coverage	# of Stories in *New York Times*	# of Stories in *Washington Post*	Total Stories
Daisy Spot	9/7 to 11/3/64	12	4	16
Willie Horton	9/21 to 11/8/88	28	34	62
Revolving Door	10/5 to 11/8/88	11	7	18
Boston Harbor	9/13 to 11/8/88	25	23	48
Tank Ad	10/17 to 11/8/88	8	12	20
Swift Boat	8/5 to 11/2/04	153	191	344
Celebrity Ad	7/31 to 11/3/08	23	38	61

advertising. The rise of negativity may have made this ad far more famous now than it was at the time.

The data in Figure 12.3 and Table 12.1 offer strong confirmation of what I call the "McKinnon Hypothesis," namely that "ads are about news coverage these days." It is not, however, just any kind of advertising that draws the interest of journalists; it is, as suggested earlier, *negative* advertising that is of most interest. Consider Table 12.1. There is no positive ad aired in the last 50 years that approaches the attention given to any of these ads. Even the famous "Morning Again in America" ads of Ronald Reagan drew little attention by the standards of the spots mentioned above.

Further evidence for my hypothesis can be found in the personal interviews I have conducted. As Dan Okrent, the first public editor of the *New York Times,* said when commenting about news coverage, "Negative is where the story is." Editors, Okrent argues, are not going to be interested in whether candidates favor world peace.[35] Surely the nominees do. What is newsworthy is something we do not know, something that is pointed or in dispute. Dan Balz, National Political Correspondent for the *Washington Post,* agrees, noting that journalists "love conflict." Balz goes on to point out that this love of conflict often leads journalists to "exaggerate how negative things are." Balz comments that we often "make a big deal out of small things."[36] David Chalian, ABC News political director, continues this theme, talking about the need among journalists for "controversy." And, as Chalian notes, "Negative ads get at that. They are the most base form of controversy being injected into the campaign."[37] Of course, the very fact that all the ads listed in Table 12.1 are negative certainly suggests that the attack ads are what have drawn interest.

Figure 12.4 strongly confirms the idea that negative ads draw the lion's share of attention from journalists. When taking a close look at the stories on

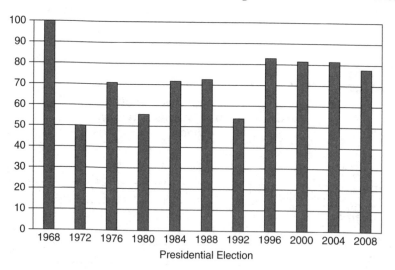

FIGURE 12.4 Percent of News Stories on Negative Ads

the nightly network news, about 75 percent are about negative ads.[38] In fact, since 2000, the share of attention paid to attacks is about 80 percent. The notable exception is 1992, which may reflect the interest by journalists in the Perot ads, which were almost all positive.[39] Journalists do indeed like conflict and have given attack ads substantially more air time than positive ads.

These data actually call for a modification to the McKinnon Hypothesis: "*Negative* ads are all about news coverage these days."

WHY DID THE NEWS MEDIA CHANGE?

Why did the news media start paying much more attention to political advertising during the 1988 presidential campaign?[40] Thomas Patterson has ably pointed out that journalists started shifting their coverage of news in the 1970s from description to interpretation of events.[41] By the 1990s, his data show that 80 percent of stories were "interpretive" compared to only 10 percent in 1960. Negative advertising provides a wonderful opportunity for journalists to interpret strategy and to assess the conflict between the candidates. So, there is a fit between the changes in the news media and negativity.

Second, it appears that Lee Atwater,[42] campaign manager for Vice President George H. W. Bush, was a central figure in the surge of attention. Joe Klein has made this point about Atwater, as did Ed Goeas, Dan Balz, and Adam Nagourney. When I asked journalists and consultants what happened in 1988 to produce this change, each of these individuals raised the name of the mercurial operative from South Carolina, *without* prompting on my part. My question was open ended, but Atwater was at the top of their list. Klein's account is perhaps most telling. Klein recalls observing focus groups organized by Atwater in Patterson, New Jersey, in June 1988. Atwater was showing these elite journalists the power of attacks on the soon-to-be Democratic nominee, Michael Dukakis. According to Klein, "We were all skeptical." The public does not care about "flag factories." Yet these attacks "moved the dials," he said. Klein contends this experience gave journalists a "new appreciation for the impact of the dark arts of consultants."[43]

During the Bush campaign, some of the most controversial and discussed negative ads were aired (recall Table 12.1), and as we know, Bush went on to win the 1988 election. A quick look at the campaign suggests that Dukakis was ahead in the summer and then once the attack ads began to fly from the Bush campaign, Bush took command. From this perspective, it seemed like Atwater was able to transform the race. But in retrospect we now know that Bush regained his lead in the Gallup poll *before* he aired any of his attack ads against Dukakis.[44] Bush's victory in 1988 was most likely due to a strong economy and the popularity of President Reagan.[45]

The perception that these attack ads were decisive lingered, fueling a sense of unhappiness among journalists concerning the 1988 campaign.

It was, however, this unhappiness that gave the press reason to continue its newfound interest in advertising. Most notable here is David Broder's call to action. Reflecting on the problems during the 1988 campaign, Broder made the following suggestion on January 14, 1990:

> [W]inning candidates in both parties force-fed a garbage diet of negative ads down the country's throat . . . . Candidates and political consultants have concluded that this is the way to win and are not about to kick the habit. We need to do something about this win-at-all-costs mentality that is undermining our political process. By "we," I mean, first of all, the political reporters like me, who cover the campaigns . . . . We should treat every ad as if it were a speech . . . . We routinely flyspeck those speeches, weighing the assertions against the evidence, setting the political charges against the context of the relevant information. We need to do this, just as routinely, with political ads . . . . And we ought not to be squeamish about saying in plain language when we catch a candidate lying, exaggerating or distorting the facts.[46]

Broder, in effect, was recommending that journalists focus on ads and treat them like speeches. Ads should be assessed, judged, and measured. It was clear that Broder was much more concerned about negative ads than positive ads. As the dean of political reporters, his call to arms carried weight. His colleagues now had even more reason to continue the so-called Ad Watches. By 1992, the major newspaper in every state had instituted some form of an ad watch.[47] Broder's intent was clearly good. But the effects of his recommendation are less clear, as we have seen above and will also see below.

ARE THE NEWS MEDIA (PARTIALLY) RESPONSIBLE FOR THE RISE OF NEGATIVITY?

The usual assumption is that the news media are simply reflecting what is happening in campaigns. They are covering negative ads because candidates and their consultants produce them. That is only part of the story. The news media's recent surge in attention to negativity has altered the incentives of candidates to produce and air negative ads. Ads today are about news coverage—they are "not about persuading voters," observes David Chalian.[48] Peter Fenn, a Democratic consultant, expands the point that "ads are for the media these days," contending that spots "are often video press releases designed to play into the 24-7 news coverage."[49] Sam Fiest of CNN concurs, noting the ads are often "video press releases."[50] Matt Erickson, another Democratic consultant, was even more pointed, noting that "negative ads at the presidential level have taken the function of press releases."[51] This connection between ads and press releases at the presidential level underscores one of the core arguments of this chapter.

Mark McKinnon has already made the point that presidential ads are no longer for voters, but for the news media. It seems to be a near consensus among the people I talked to. In fact, when I asked GOP consultant Alex Castellanos to name a few ads that were created in presidential campaigns for news coverage, he responded, "Well, about all of them." He mentioned the much discussed "wolves"[52] ad from 2004. The spot sought to generate discussion in the country about security and terrorism. "We wanted the media," contends Castellanos, "asking the question: Was Kerry able to protect the country?" These comments all underscore Chalian's observation that "consultants know they can drive news coverage with ads."

Given that candidates want to influence voters, the free media offers a powerful way to get their message out. For presidential elections, Chalian said, "The free media narrative is the single most important thing to control." But, as shown earlier, candidates must have a message that sparks controversy or otherwise it gets no coverage. The best way to do that is through attacks—that is, negative ads. In order for candidates to get their message out and to control this all-important narrative, the news media have unintentionally given candidates even more reason to create and to air attack ads. This argument recasts how we think about the rise of negativity, since the news media have increased the incentives to go negative.

What evidence do I have for this new hypothesis? I will not offer a smoking gun. Moreover, that there is negativity, and even more of it in 2008 than 2004, is *not* evidence that supports my argument. Negativity is part of nearly all campaigns. I am arguing, instead, that a shift in incentives led to more attacks than we would have seen under the pre-1988 system.

While this is a tricky hypothesis to test, there are some suggestive pieces of evidence. For example, if I am correct, candidates should be "fishing" with negative ads. That is, in 2008 we should have seen more negative ads produced, but not aired, than positive ads. The idea here is that candidates hope to get the news media to cover their ads without making any major investment in airing them on TV. Certainly, there were a number of "web" ads with that purpose. Are web-only ads more likely to be negative than positive? Of the 8 "web" ads listed on *livingroomcandidate.org* from the two presidential candidates in 2008, 75 percent were negative. That offers only a hint. More telling are the comments made during my interviews with consultants and journalists, who offer valuable confirmation of this idea. Peter Fenn observed that "campaigns are making ads that will not be aired." And these, he said, are usually "negative" or what he called "comeback" ads.[53] Stephanie Cutter, a high-ranking Democratic operative, argued that the Obama campaign was putting out a lot of negative ads with minimum media buys in the hope of shaping the narrative of the campaign. It was not until late October that they stopped doing it, when "the media finally caught on."[54]

During the 19 elite interviews I conducted during the fall of 2009,[55] I asked about the merits of this hypothesis that the news media have unintentionally given campaigns more reasons to produce and air negative ads. Nearly all of them (17 of 19) thought the idea was on target (90 percent). I use the phrase "on target" intentionally, since some of these experts gave more nuanced responses. Given that this idea is implicitly critical of the press and gives consultants a bit of a free pass, I had expected journalists to be more skeptical of the idea. But that was not the case. I interviewed 10 journalists and all of them agreed with the hypothesis. The only disagreement came from two of the consultants I interviewed.

Here are some of the specific reactions to this hypothesis. John Harris of *Politico* said, "I absolutely believe that." "That is probably correct," commented Dan Balz. Tom Fiedler, who had been editor at the *Miami Herald,* had some reservations, but was "willing to believe" that coverage of ads had altered the incentives of consultants.[56] Adam Nagourney added, "I think that is right." Mark McKinnon responded immediately, saying that it was "exactly right." Alex Castellanos simply said "yes." Nick Ayers "completely agrees."[57] Sam Fiest was a bit more cautious, but still supportive, observing "there is something to it." Finally, David Chalian noted: "Hard to argue it is not true." He then went on to say that the news media "have crafted a marketplace for negative ads." It is that observation that highlights the core claim of this chapter.

IMPLICATIONS AND THE FUTURE

My central purpose in this chapter is to suggest that we revise how we think about the causes of this rise in negativity. The news media are not just reflecting the goings on of campaigns. Instead, their coverage has altered the conduct of campaigns. They do more than cover the process; they shape it. That is, the increase in attacks in presidential campaigns is partly the result of the news media's extensive coverage of advertising, in general, and negative advertising, in particular. As Nick Ayers comments, journalists have "incentivized the process" for attack ads. Negative ads are now being run and produced not so much with an eye toward influencing voters directly, but with the hope of altering the news media's narrative in the campaign. It is that narrative, then, that can provide candidates a chance to win over voters and secure a victory in the election.

There has been a long-standing assumption, certainly in the academic world, that the purpose of ads is to influence voters. The idea was that candidates could control the message in these 30-second (or longer) spots and that these messages would shape the preferences of the public. This assumption needs some revision. It is clear that negative ads have a new audience: Journalists. But what about positive ads? Since most positive ads are not controversial and, hence, do not draw the attention of the public, it is likely that the main target of these spots remains voters. This means that an important asymmetry may have arisen between the goals of positive and negative ads that demands attention not only by journalists, but by scholars.[58] Political scientists, for example, have almost exclusively focused on sorting out the *direct* impact of ads on voters.. That focus needs to change.[59]

The news media are obviously undergoing lots of change with the rise of the Internet and the decline of local newspapers and the audience share of the big three television networks. Might the news media undergo additional change that would lessen the incentive for campaigns to go negative? While no one can be sure, the answer is likely no. In fact, the payoff from producing negative ads to drive press coverage is likely to *grow* in 2012. The reasons can be found in the 2008 election cycle. Previously, journalists and news directors wanted to see evidence of a substantial ad buy before the press would give a spot attention. Sam Feist of CNN made this point, as did Dan Balz. But this standard eased in 2008. As Balz points out, the blogs would discuss an ad that might just have been posted online, generating buzz about it. There was no way to ignore that buzz, contended Balz, and so the mainstream press ends up giving the spot coverage. Of course, with a need for 24-hour news, the press are willing accomplices, Balz admits. Feist continues, noting that many of the ads posted on the web were interesting and often funny. They would "go viral," and "we gave them coverage." So this shift means that it is easier for campaigns now to draw attention to their spots without having to expend money to air them. This will only encourage campaigns to produce more spots in the hope of shaping the coverage of the candidates. Most of these spots will likely be negative so as to capture interest and attention from journalists.

The extensive attention to negative ads may well have a potentially corrosive effect on the public. The attention to these attacks surely leaves citizens with a more pessimistic picture of American campaigns than if there were more balanced coverage of campaign ads. Perhaps, then, it should be no surprise that nearly 90 percent of the American public thought the 2008 presidential campaign was negative.[60] Yet as Figure 12.1 shows, nearly 40 percent of the McCain and Obama ads had positive messages. In 2004, although the share of positive ads was about 50 percent, still about 85 percent of the public talked about negative messages in the campaigns.[61] The bottom line is that this type of coverage could undermine the public's faith in our electoral process. Such effects cannot be good for the long-term health of the country.

But before we get too negative about the news media's coverage of negativity, it is worth restating that journalists are not intentionally giving excessive coverage to negative ads. What they are interested in is controversy, conflict, or cleverness. Negative ads are good at that. But positive ads can fit the bill at times. Consider Herman Cain's ad in 2011 in which Mark Block, his campaign manager, touted the leadership of the former CEO of Godfather's Pizza, ending the 60-second spot by puffing smoke from his cigarette.[62] This spot and its unusual ending drew substantial attention, getting more than 2 million hits on YouTube alone.[63] Sam Fiest of CNN stressed this point that positive ads can generate "controversy." Another example of a controversial positive ad arose in March 2004. Soon after Kerry clinched the Democratic nomination, the Bush campaign aired spots that showed the President as the hero of 9/11, with pictures of the Twin Towers falling. Many thought the use of this tragedy was unacceptable and injected politics into the terrible loss of life on that fateful day. But the Bush campaign wanted that reaction and used this positive ad to meet its goals. In a post-election discussion at Harvard University, Matthew Dowd, chief strategist for Bush-Cheney, '04, argued, "We benefited by the fact that so many people in the press corps thought this was such a huge controversy. There was actually a discussion. Some people got a little queasy and said, 'Are we doing the right thing?' We got $7 million to $8 million worth of free run on this. The fact that George Bush's highest point of his presidency is related to 9/11 and we got ads with 9/11 in it, and everyone is talking about it—we could not have asked for better."[64]

The changes described in this chapter are, of course, part of larger changes that have been unfolding in the news media over the last two decades. I am only focusing on one very small piece of the pie. But it is, nonetheless, an important piece. There has been a tendency just to assume that the many attack ads we see on television (and the Internet) reflect the practice of what Joe Klein aptly called the "dark arts." Negative ads are a fundamental part of campaigns and have been so since the first elections in this country. But it is not at all clear that negativity is on the rise, because suddenly politicians and their aides think negative ads work better. I am sure when Harry Truman attacked Thomas Dewey in 1948, it was on a belief it would secure votes. We can quibble over whether consultants are more enamored with attack politics than in the past. Those quibbles certainly should not lead us to forget that polarization (recall Figure 12.2) is likely a key part of the story. And even more importantly, that discussion misses the central objective of this chapter: The news media themselves need to be part of this conversation over the rise of attack politics that has unfolded over the last 20 years. It is perhaps for these reasons that Alex Castellanos claimed that the "news media are the most negative force in American politics." I do want to go as far as Castellanos, but it is important to shine a bright light on this recent and potentially troubling development. And by so doing, we can forge a more complete understanding of attack politics in the twenty-first century.

Endnotes

1. I would like to thank the Shorenstein Center at Harvard University for the chance to spend the fall of 2009 in residence. It was a great experience, providing me both the chance to conduct many of the interviews reported here and to have time away from teaching to develop some of the ideas contained in these pages. I also want to thank Vanderbilt University for support that made this project possible. Finally, I would like to express appreciation to Marc Hetherington who collected some of the data on polarization presented here.
2. http://www.nytimes.com/2011/11/27/us/politics/television-attack-ads-aim-at-obama-early-and-often.html?_r=1.
3. Joe Klein of *Time* magazine used this term to describe the rise of attack politics in an interview I conducted with him on October 14, 2009.
4. I am not making a partisan statement here. By 2008, the public was disenchanted with the Bush Administration. The economy was in a near state of

collapse, the Iraq War was viewed by the public as a mistake, Hurricane Katrina remained a black mark against the administration, and the deficit was soaring out of control. President Bush's popularity was certainly at historic lows.

5. http://www.nytimes.com/2011/11/27/us/politics/television-attack-ads-aim-at-obama-early-and-often.html?_r=1.

6. Deborah Brooks and Michael Muvro (forthcoming), "Assessing Accountability in a Post-*Citizens United* Era: The Effects of Attack Ad Sponsorship by Unknown Independent Groups," *American Politics Research*.

7. http://www.theamericanrevolution.org/ipeople/tjeff.asp.

8. John Geer, *In Defense of Negativity* (Chicago: University of Chicago Press, 2006), p. 9

9. Ibid., p. 67.

10. Zachary Karabell, *The Last Campaign* (New York: Vintage, 2001).

11. http://politicalticker.blogs.cnn.com/2011/11/18/perry-stands-by-ad-calls-obama-a-socialist/.

12. See Morris Fiorina Samuel J. Abrams and Jeremy C. Pope, *Culture Wars*, 3rd edition (New York: Longman, 2010); Marc J. Hetherington, "Putting Polarization in Perspective," *British Journal of Political Science* 39, 2009: 413–448; Marc J. Hetherington and Jonathan Weiler, *Authoritarianism and Polarization in America* (Cambridge: Cambridge University Press, 2009); Nolan McCarty, Keith Poole and Howard Rosenthal, *Polarized America* (Cambridge: MIT Press for helpful assessments of polarization in American politics, 2006).

13. These data are Geer's negativity scores (see Figure 12.1). The polarization data were kindly provided to me by Marc Hetherington.

14. Stephen Ansolabehere and Shanto Iyengar, *Going Negative* (New York: Free Press, 1995).

15. Richard R. Lau, Lee Sigelman, Caroline Heldman, and Paul Babbitt, "The Effects of Negative Political Advertisements: A Meta-Analytic Review," *American Political Science Review 93*, 1999, :851–875; Richard R. Lau, Lee Sigelman, and Ivy Brown Rovner, "The Effects of Negative Political Campaigns: A Meta-Analytic Reassessment," *Journal of Politics 69*, 2007: 1176–1209.

16. Alan S. Gerber, James G. Gimpel, Donald P. Green, and Daron R. Shaw "How Large and Long-Lasting are the Persuasive Effects of Televised Campaign Ads?," *American Political Science Review* 105, 2011: 135–150.

17. Ibid.

18. Richard R. Lau, Lee Sigelman, Caroline Heldman, and Paul Babbitt, "The Effects of Negative Political Advertisements: A Meta-Analytic Review," *American Political Science Review 93*, 1999: 851–875. Richard R. Lau, Lee Sigelman, and Ivy Brown Rovner, "The Effects of Negative Political Campaigns: A Meta-Analytic Reassessment," *Journal of Politics, 69*, 2007: 1176–1209.

19. http://www.cbsnews.com/blogs/2008/09/09/politics/horserace/entry4433099.shtml.

20. http://www.gwu.edu/~smpa/faculty/documents/Swift_Boat_Article_FALR_000.pdf.

21. http://www.publicopinionpros.norc.org/features/2005/aug/borick.asp.

22. This percentage arises from a Lexis-Nexis search that I ran from July 1, 2004 to November 1, 2004 using the key words tied to the presidential campaign and "Iraq War" or "Swift Boat." I searched under "US newspapers and wires."

23. See Gallup Poll in October 11 to 14, where the Iraq War was cited by the public as the "most important problem" facing the nation. Data provided by the Roper Center.

24. CBS/New York Times Poll, September 12–16, 2004, data provided by the Roper Center.

25. Interview with Alex Castellanos on November 11, 2009.

26. This Lexis-Nexis search was done the same as the one concerning "Swift Boat."

27. Interview with Nagourney on November 10, 2009.

28. The data in this graph comes from a Lexis-Nexis search for articles in the *New York Times* and *Washington Post* on political advertising during the presidential campaign, covering the period of July 1 to November 1 for each election from 1960 to 2008.

29. This pattern of news coverage is further confirmed by a detailed content analysis of all stories aired on the nightly network news from 1968 to 2008. I have done a complete content analysis of the coverage of presidential advertising in the nightly news for the 3 major networks, using the Vanderbilt Televisions News Archives. Those data from 1968 to 2008 have a .86 correlation with the data in Figure 12.3.

30. Geer, *In Defense of Negativity*, p. 115.

31. See Clinton and Geer, "The News Media's Changing Role in Understanding Advertising," (2011) manuscript at the Center for the Study of Democratic Institutions at Vanderbilt University.

32. The "Daisy spot" is the current name given to this commercial. It was not the term used to describe the ad in 1964.

33. I asked informed observers to list the most famous ads from presidential campaigns (Geer, 2006). The top choices at the time (2003) were: Daisy, "Willie Horton," the "Tank ads," the "revolving door ad," and the "Boston Harbor ad." These spots, except for Daisy, all arose from the 1988 campaign. To update the list, I added "Swift Boat" from 2004 and the "celebrity" ad from 2008.

34. The reason for the amazing amount of attention is open to debate. Dan Okrent has offered the best hypothesis so far. He contended that the issue with Swift Boat was whether Kerry had lied or the ad had lied. This was not part of the previous ads.

35. Interview with Okrent on October 5, 2009.

36. Interview with Balz on October 28, 2009.

37. Interview with Chalian on December 2, 2009

38. Do not read too much into the percentages in 1968 (100%) and 1972 (50%). The network news had only 2 stories each year on political advertising.

39. Over 90% of Perot's ads were positive. This figure comes from my data of political advertising that is available on my website.

40. See also Geer (2006) for a more detailed discussion of 1988.

41. Thomas Patterson, *Out of Order* (New York: Knopf, 1993).

42. I want to acknowledge the invaluable insight of Bill Mitchell, a former reporter for the *Detriot Free Press*. He first alerted me to Atwater's potential role in reshaping coverage of advertising, which led me to approach my interviews with other journalists and consultants in a different fashion.

43. This material is all drawn from my interview with Klein on October 14, 2009.

44. See Geer (2006), ch. 6.

45. See Lynn Vavreck, *The Message Matters* (Princeton: Princeton University Press, 2009).

46. January 14, 1990, *Washington Post*, p. B1.

47. It is worth noting that ad watches did exist prior to Broder's call. Tom Fiedler, editor at the *Miami Herald*, had been employing them well before 1990. See also Kim Kahn and Patrick Kenney, *The Spectacle of US Senate Campaigns* (Princeton: Princeton University Press, 1999).

48. Interview with Chalian on December 2, 2009.

49. Interview with Fenn on November 11, 2009.

50. Interview with Fiest on November 17, 2009.

51. Interview with Erickson on December 8, 2009.

52. http://www.youtube.com/watch?v=MU4t9O_yFsY.

53. A "comeback" was a response to an attack ad, which could either be negative or positive.

54. Comments made by Cutter at Harvard University on September 17, 2009.

55. Joe Klein (*Time* magazine), John Harris (*The Politico*), Kathleen Parker (syndicated columnist), Dan Okrent (*Time* magazine and former public editor for the *New York Times*), Stephanie Cutter (former communications director for the Kerry campaign), Dan Balz (*Washington Post*), Amy Gershkoff (Partner for Changing Targets Media), Ed Goeas (President and C.E.O. of The Tarrance Group), Vin Weber (Republican strategist and former member of the House of Representatives), Tom Fiedler (former editor of the *Miami Herald*), Mark McKinnon (Chief Media Strategist for the Bush and McCain presidential campaigns), Adam Nagourney (the *New York Times*), Peter Fenn (President of Fenn Communications Group), Alex Castellanos (Republican consultant and CNN commentator), Sam Fiest (CNN's Political Director), David Chalian (ABC News political director), Robin Sprouls (Washington bureau chief for ABC News), Nick Ayers (Executive Director, Republican Governors Association), and Matt Erickson (consultant for Lafuens, Kully & Klose).

56. Interview with Fiedler on November 2, 2009.

57. Interview with Ayers on December 7, 2009.

58. This argument only applies for presidential election. Statewide (or more local) races have a different dynamic. Local media tend to cover topics such as crime, sports, and local interest. They do not give local elections the kind of attention that the national press pays to presidential campaigns. As a result, ads do provide the kind of link between politicians and voters we typically assume. Alex Castellanos made this observation to me during our interview. Nick Ayers strongly seconded Castellanos' observation.

59. John Geer, Richard Lau, and Lynn Vavreck (2011) "Advertising in an Era of Choice," manuscript Center for the Study of Democratic Institutions at Vanderbilt University.

60. Conducted by Gallup Organization, October 23–October 26, 2008 and based on 1,010 telephone interviews. Sample: National adult.

61. Cable News Network, *USA Today*. Methodology: Conducted by Gallup Organization, October 22–October 24, 2004 and based on 1,538 telephone interviews.

62. http://www.youtube.com/watch?v=qhm-22Q0PuM.

63. I did this count on YouTube on November 25, 2011.

64. *Campaign for President* (New York: Roman Littlefield, 2009), p. 109. This book arises from a conference sponsored at the Institute for Politics at the Harvard Kennedy School for Government.

13

Incivility in American Politics: Where It Comes from and What We Can Do About It

William A. Galston

This chapter explores many of the forces that have likely contributed to the decline in civility in politics. Along with the usual suspects, William Galston pays close attention to economic and cultural changes. He also explores the steps that might be taken to better ensure that fewer partisan citizens are adequately represented in Congress and in state legislatures. Galston has been instrumental in the creation of a new organization, called "No Labels," and this chapter outlines how this organization could play an important role in changing the tone of American politics.

THE CURRENT SITUATION

"You lie." When Rep. Joe Wilson (R-SC) flung those two words at Barack Obama as the president addressed a Joint Meeting of Congress in September 2009, he crystallized a growing concern about the degradation of American political discourse. The near-fatal shooting of Rep. Gabrielle Giffords in a rampage that left six people dead intensified these fears, as had the murder of Kansas late-term abortion doctor George Tiller while he was serving as an usher for a Sunday morning service at his Wichita church. Dr. Tiller, labeled "Tiller the Baby Killer" by Rep. Robert Dornan on the floor of the House of Representatives, had been discussed in unflattering terms nearly 30 times on Fox News' *The O'Reilly Factor* between 2005 and his death in May of 2009. According to Washington State University's Cornell Clayton, transcripts of Glenn

Beck's televised show revealed that President Obama and Democrats were compared to Hitler or the Nazis nearly 350 times before Beck parted ways with Fox.[1]

Harsh accusations have hardly been the exclusive purview of a single party. When the invasion of Iraq failed to turn up evidence of weapons of mass destruction, opponents of the war unveiled a slogan: "Bush lied, people died"—in effect, charging him with direct, knowing responsibility for the deaths of thousands of Americans and even more Iraqis. The possibility that a president of the United States who had access to such rich sources of intelligence might have made an honest mistake was dismissed as risibly naive.

As skeptics often observe, incivility in American politics is nothing new. The election of 1800 was famously vituperative on both sides. During the 1828 campaign, Andrew Jackson's enemies accused him of committing multiple murders and living in sin with his wife (presumably before they were married), while John Quincy Adams was said to have procured American virgins for the Russian czar. In 1856, abolitionist Senator Charles Sumner delivered a speech describing one of his pro-slavery colleagues as a "noisome, squat, and nameless animal . . . not a proper model for an American senator," to which South Carolina Representative Preston Brooks responded by beating Sumner senseless with a cane on the floor of the Senate.[2] Such examples could be multiplied many times over. Could it be that incivility is a constant in our politics and that only myopia makes us think that it is worse today?

A more plausible hypothesis is that political discourse moves in cycles, rising to peaks of unrestraint and then subsiding toward civility. When Americans talk about the degeneration of public talk, then, they probably are comparing it to some other portion of their lives, at least as they can remember it.

Beyond question, most Americans do believe that our relationships with our fellow citizens are deteriorating and that political discourse is in decline. In August of 2010, Rasmussen Reports found that 69 percent of Americans think their countrymen are becoming "more rude and less civilized."[3] A more comprehensive 2010 survey from Weber Shandwick confirmed that finding and added valuable detail: 65 percent regard the level of civility in the country today as a "major" problem, and 72 percent believe it has gotten worse in recent years. They identified government and politics as the least civil arena in all of American society, and many reported that the tone and temper of our politics was leading them to tune it out altogether.[4]

These are more than transient sentiments. When Weber Shandwick conducted a follow-up survey in 2011,[5] 65 percent of Americans continued to view incivility as a major problem, and 74 percent expect the 2012 election to be even worse than the 2010 midterms. Finer-grained questions revealed the following intriguing specifics.

	Civil (%)	Uncivil (%)
President Obama	67	28
CNN	55	32
MSNBC	44	37
Fox News	36	51
Democrats in Congress	34	56
Republicans in Congress	29	60
Tea Party Supporters	26	60
Political Campaigns	17	80

Americans are far from giving up hope, however. Only 33 percent accept the world-weary view that incivility is a routine part of the political process. A solid majority believes that things don't have to be the way they are, which only deepens their discontent with current conditions. Fully 90 percent say that the way a candidate "treats and deals with people he or she disagrees with" will be at least a somewhat important consideration in determining their vote. (Ascertaining whether this self-report reflects the actual influences on their choices is no easy matter, however.)

THE NATURE OF CIVILITY

The Nobel Prize-winning molecular biologist Joshua Lederberg once re-marked that "All of civility depends on being able to contain the rage of individuals."[6] This comment points us in the right direction: Civility is the successful outcome of efforts to contain a wide range of impulses that can undermine the quality, or destroy the possibility, of social life. There are two sources of containment: external—the incentives created by the system of rules within which individuals act; and internal—individuals' acceptance of norms that place limits on socially acceptable expressions of antipathy. The classic American example of the external strategy is Madisonian constitution-alism—the artful arrangement of countervailing powers so that "ambition . . . [is] made to counteract ambition" and the multiplicity of diverse interests pre-vents the tyrannical concentration of power.[7] At a more granular level, rules of decorum in the House and Senate are designed to regulate how members address and characterize one another, and they provide graded sanctions for violators.

The less well known but equally classic American example of the in-ternal strategy is found in George Washington's *Rules of Civility*, a minutely detailed list of 110 maxims whereby individuals can avoid words and acts that give needless offense.[8] The first of these rules reads: "Every action done in Company ought to be with some sign of respect to those that are pres-ent." The essence of incivility, Washington believed, is the overt expression of disrespect. That is not to say that we might not *feel* disrespect for at least some of our interlocutors. The point of civility is not inner saintliness, but rather habitual self-control. Civility, then, is at odds with the ethic of spontaneity and cult of authenticity.

In this vein, consider Washington's 23rd rule: "When you see a crime punished, you may be inwardly pleased; but always show pity to the suffering offender." While it is morally and viscerally satisfying when wrongdoers get their just desserts, civility demands that we restrain ourselves from outwardly expressing pleasure at the pain of others. By showing what Washington calls pity, we are recognizing that even wrongdoers retain their standing as fellow human beings. In one of the 2011 debates among the Republican candidates for their party's presidential nomination, a cheer went up from the crowd at the mention of the 234 executions over which Texas Gov. Rick Perry had presided. From Washington's standpoint, even if each and every one of these executions were justified, nevertheless the cheer violated the norm of civility and represented one more step in the coarsening of our public life.

For our purposes, one element of civility is especially pertinent—namely, the traits of character and habits of conduct that contribute to the sustained practice of democratic politics. At the most basic level, civility in politics requires the restraint of violence. Politics may be inherently conflictual, but it substitutes verbal competition for outright force whenever possible. That is why episodes such as the caning of Sen. Sumner constitute such a horrifying breach of basic political norms—and why events such as the Gabrielle Giffords shooting and the Oklahoma City bombing give rise to concerns about the relation between uncivil speech and violent action.

As these examples show, the simple substitution of words for violence does not suffice to produce civil politics; the tone and temper of those words is decisive. Civil discourse expresses respect for one's adversaries despite differences of principle and policy, and it proceeds on the assumption that all parties to ongoing controversies are members of the same community who are united in wishing it well. The assumption of civility is that we all intend the common good even if we disagree about the policies that will best promote it. That is why accusations about motives for action can be so damaging.

For example, when Republicans blocked President Obama's $447 billion jobs bill in the fall of 2011, some Democrats charged that Republicans were deliberately sabotaging the economy in order to diminish Obama's reelection prospects, whatever the costs in added misery for the American people. Perhaps some were; there's no way of knowing. But civility required the Democrats to engage their adversaries in the arena of public argument. Republicans characterized the president's proposal as a warmed over version of the 2009 stimulus, which they regarded as demonstrably ineffective. The civil retort is argument and evidence designed to persuade the people that the initial stimulus had warded off catastrophe and that a second tranche would spur recovery.

SOURCES OF INCIVILITY

Partisan Polarization

Past episodes of extreme incivility in public life have coincided with deep divisions about the future of the country. In 1800, the struggle was between those who saw the Federalists as quasi-monarchists and those who saw the Democratic Republicans as the entering wedge for social upheaval along the lines of the French Revolution. In the late 1850s, more and more Americans on both sides of the slavery issue were coming to agree with Abraham Lincoln's argument about a house divided. The 1890s featured a clash between populist agrarian forces fighting a rear-guard action and the proponents of the rising corporate-industrial economy.

Today, the polarization between the two major political parties is the most pronounced it has been since the 1890s. In the Senate, the most conservative Democrat is a bit to the left of the most liberal Republican, leaving no ideological overlap whatever, and things are nearly as stark in the House. This situation is the culmination of a decades-long process during which the parties have sorted themselves out. Most liberals and many moderates have exited from the Republican Party, leaving a homogeneously conservative base. The Democratic Party, though more ideologically diverse, is more liberal and less moderate or conservative than it was a generation ago.

These divisions have increased the distance between the members of the two parties in Congress, who are less likely to socialize across party lines, let alone form cross-party friendships of the sorts that existed as recently as the 1980s. The congressional calendar has exacerbated these trends: Most members fly home every weekend and encounter each other only in committee meetings and on the House and Senate floors during a truncated three-day work week. It is much easier to be uncivil to people with whom you have no personal relationships.

The polarization of the parties has coincided with the disappearance of common frames of reference. From the Eisenhower administration through the late 1970s, some version of Keynesian theory was the *lingua franca* of economic discourse. Richard Nixon memorably declared that we're all Keynesians now, but less than a decade later, the rise of the supply-side movement shattered that consensus. Today, one party says that when marginal tax rates are cut, revenues rise, while the other says just the reverse. Fiscal policy discussions are no longer the cool fitting of means to ends; they are more nearly a clash of world-views. Early in the intra-party competition for the 2012 Republican presidential nomination, all the candidates were asked whether they would accept a deficit reduction package that included ten dollars of spending cuts for every one dollar of tax increases. Not one said yes. Similar breaches between the parties have developed in areas from economic regulation to public investment.

In foreign policy, Vietnam shattered the Cold War anti-communist consensus that had dominated the immediate post–war period. After a confused decade of internal strife in both parties, doves dominated the Democratic Party while hawks clustered in the victorious Reaganite portion of the Republican Party. For a full generation, Democrats labored under a public perception that they were "weak on defense," a charge that moved many of them to support what turned out to be a flawed invasion of Iraq. While the bitter controversy that dominated George W. Bush's second term pivoted around the failure to find weapons of mass destruction, it drew from a well of divisiveness tracing back more than three decades.

In the area of society and culture, finally, the parties' tacit agreement to keep a wide range of issues off the public agenda shattered against the rocks of mass social movements and Supreme Court decisions. Civil rights, feminism, abortion, homosexuality, the role of religion in politics, immigration, even environmentalism—wherever one looked, it seemed, loud contestation erupted. And here again, the parties chose sides. When *Roe v. Wade* was decided in 1973, each party contained substantial "pro-life" and "pro-choice" wings, a division reflected in the 1976 platforms of both parties. By 1984, all traces of ambivalence had disappeared: The Democrats had become officially pro-choice and the Republicans pro-life, and for each party the issue had become a litmus test for aspiring candidates.[9]

I tell this story to make a simple point: Civility is easiest to attain when participants in public discussion agree both on the principal aims of policy and on a theory of how the world works. In recent decades, consensus in both these areas has weakened. Democrats and Republicans differ on the sources of economic growth and also on the value of growth relative to other goals such as fairness. What many liberals see as liberation from unjustified constraints, conservatives regard as license. What President Obama sees as smart twenty-first century multilateralism, Republicans characterize as "apology tours." Disagreements of this sort, which have come more and more to the fore in our politics, make it harder to retain civility in public discourse. We should not be surprised when civility erodes.

Polarization also creates incentives to ratchet up political rhetoric, especially during intra-party contests. If hard-core activists cluster around the left and right tails of the ideological bell curve, candidates who effectively articulate the distilled essence of each party's defining beliefs will tend to be nominated. We know that more and more elections—not just in gerrymandered districts, but also in counties and states with invariant boundaries—are taking place in jurisdictions dominated by one party or the other. In these circumstances, winning the majority party's nomination is equivalent to winning the general election, and the smaller, more activist-dominated primary electorate controls the overall result. In 2010, Sen. Robert Bennett (R-UT) had a solid conservative record, but evidently not solid enough to satisfy the conservative/Tea Party base of the Utah Republican Party, which blocked his quest for renomination in favor of a younger, more ardent conservative. Republicans everywhere took note, and Utah's remaining senior senator, Orrin Hatch, swiftly tacked away from anything that could be represented as cooperation, let alone compromise, with Democrats.

There are other concomitants of polarization that exert pressure on civil discourse as well. For one, the stakes are higher. Because both sides believe that the contested issues go to the core of the country's identity and prospects, the intensity of concern about the outcome is high, and so is the vehemence with which the parties express their views. When issues are framed, not as questions of more and less, but rather of right and wrong, even good and evil, it becomes harder to maintain and express respect for one's interlocutors. It is all too easy to slide from the premise that your adversary's view is morally mistaken to the conclusion that your adversary is morally flawed.

Three other features of polarization are noteworthy. First, party polarization in the context of a constitutional system of checks and balances tends to increase gridlock on contested issues. Everyday experience suggests that when we perceive others as thwarting our attainment of aims, we become intensely frustrated and often yield to explosive outbursts. Road rage is the classic example, and perhaps we are seeing its analogue in our public life.

Second, an expanding body of evidence suggests that when individuals find themselves in homogeneous groups, their views tend to intensify and become more extreme, while heterogeneous groups give individuals incentives toward moderation and at least make verbal bows to differing views. This proposition applies not only to face-to-face groups but also to the virtual communities that develop around Internet sites, talk radio, and televised political commentary. People have sorted themselves out, not only geographically, but also in their patterns of media consumption. Broadcasting, whose mass market encouraged center-seeking stories and the presentation of multiple points of view, is giving way to "narrowcasting." The proliferation of outlets for expression encourages the development of niche markets for particular points of view. When conservatives watch Fox News, they become more fixed in their view, and the same is true for liberals who watch MSNBC. Neither works very hard to restrain incivility.[10]

And finally, polarization tends to create a Team A/Team B mindset that often leads to conflict for reasons other than the content of the contest. Outbursts of extreme incivility and even violence are all too common among fans of competing teams. There seems to be something in human nature or the deep structure of society that makes our species find satisfaction in sharp distinctions between members and non-members of their respective communities. (In a psychodynamic vein, one might conjecture that membership in homogeneous groups provides a basis for socially approved and gratifying aggression against non-members.)

The Economy: Inequality Amidst Hard Times

I have dwelled on partisan polarization as a source of incivility, in part because it represents a long-cycle trend whose consequences have played out over decades. Another such trend is the growing inequality of income and wealth. A Congressional Budget Office report released in October 2011 documents what casual observation suggests: Since the late 1970s, the top one-fifth of earners have done much better than the rest, and the top 1 percent have sailed off into the financial stratosphere. During the past three decades, the after-tax income of households in the top 1 percent has nearly tripled, and their share of the national total has more than doubled. Meanwhile, households in the middle have gained less than 40 percent, an almost imperceptible 1 percent per year. [11]

Inequality has a number of effects that tend to unravel the fabric of civility. The first is increasing social distance between the most fortunate and the rest, making it harder for the wealthy to empathize with, or even to understand, the plight of those who have less than they do. To rationalize their privileges, the well-off must convince themselves that they deserve what they have, which all too often leads them to conclude that the less privileged don't deserve what they don't have. It is easier to talk about inadequate skills and a deficient work ethic than the tectonic shifts that divide us economically and render entire industries redundant in the global market. Too often, the discourse of the successful strikes others as smug and even callous.

On the flip side, of course, are the sentiments these trends generate among those who are less successful, including anger, victimization, and a sense of injustice. Throughout American history, populists of both left and right have railed against concentrations of wealth and power, and mainstream politicians have often felt impelled to go along with them. On the eve of the 1936 election, the most successful president of the twentieth century had this to say about his first term:

> "We had to struggle with the old enemies of peace—business and financial monopoly, speculation, reckless banking . . . Never before in all our history have these forces been so united against one candidate as they stand today. They are unanimous in their hate for me—and I welcome their hatred. I should like to have it said of my first Administration that in it the forces of selfishness and lust for power met their match. I should like to have it said of my second Administration that in it these forces met their master." [12]

By FDR's standards, President Obama's occasional reference to "fat cats" is pretty weak tea. But it draws from the same well of public sentiment—"They got bailed out, we got sold out" is a leading slogan of the Occupy Wall Street movement—and, as Obama learned to his surprise, creates a reciprocal sense of grievance and victimization among the fortunate few.

Hard times exacerbate the sting of inequality. The persistent unemployment and underemployment that have pervaded the United States since 2008 have generated strong feelings, including anxiety, anger, frustration, and fear—and fiscal retrenchment only makes things worse. A central finding of behavioral economics is that individuals respond more negatively to loss than they do positively to gain. A system perceived as taking away things that people once took for granted is bound to be volatile—witness rural Americans in the 1890s and industrial workers during the 1930s. The starkest recent example is Greece, where unsustainable spending and debt accumulation gave way to harsh austerity. The result was heightened social strife and threats of street violence.

Diversity

The increasing diversity of the U.S. population is a third key source of diminished civility. The most obvious sign of this is the rancorous debate over immigration reform. But the consequences of diversity are subtle and pervasive.

Robert Putnam's recent work has highlighted these short- and mid-term effects. Increased diversity leads to "out-group distrust and in-group solidarity." Simply put: The more we are brought into physical contact with those unlike us, the more we stick together with our "own kind" and the less we trust the "other." Diversity is the parent of mistrust. And it is correlated with a wide array of other measures of social capital and civil engagement. In conditions of greater diversity, citizens demonstrate:

- Lower confidence in local government, local leaders, and local media
- A lower sense of political efficacy—that is, diminished confidence in their own ability to influence events
- Less expectation that others will voluntarily cooperate to solve collective problems
- Lower frequency of registering to vote
- More interest in and knowledge about politics and more participation in protest marches and social reform groups.

Amazingly, these correlations seem to apply to all groups within a diverse society, though not with equal force.[13]

In the long run, Putnam argues, diversity can strengthen a society—especially one with the United States' remarkable capacity for absorption and assimilation. But when a society is in the process of diversifying, the consequences are bound to weaken the kinds of bonds that nurture civility across lines of ethnic, religious, and political difference. We have seen this process at work in the decades before the Civil War, when waves of Catholic immigration introduced new stresses; during the four decades from the 1880s to the 1920s, in which the gates were flung open to the immigrants who would work in burgeoning mines and factories; and again since the mid-1960s, when 40 years of immigration restrictions gave way to waves of immigrants from countries and continents not previously prominent in the U.S. population.

Some have argued that we need at least a "pause" in our open-door policy to allow the forces of absorption to do their slow work. It is certainly true that during the pause from 1924 to 1965, many social tensions associated with immigration diminished while levels of social trust rose. If Putnam is right, the historically high level of political consensus during the 1950s and early 1960s is partly attributable to these developments. But today, the suggestion that we should restrict immigration is itself a source of controversy. And even if we were to implement such a policy tomorrow, it would take a long time to make a difference.

WHAT IS TO BE DONE?

My proposed explanation for rising incivility in public life would seem to be a counsel of despair. If, as I suggest, this trend is rooted in structural developments that are anything but transient, then prospects for ameliorating it anytime soon appear bleak. Besides, some have argued, incivility has its uses. It signals intensity of feeling and commitment, which is relevant to decision-making in a constitutional democracy. And it is a weapon to which those excluded from power and privilege often resort in order to shake up the complacent consensus of those who are satisfied with the status quo. The author Gregory Rodriguez suggests that democracy itself is part of the problem: Individualism, populism, and the striving for upward mobility discourage broadly accepted codes of conduct.[14] Diversity of culture and class generates different understandings of how individuals should speak to one another, in both public and more intimate situations.

However this may be, the American people today are not satisfied with the way public officials comport themselves. One response to their discontent would be: "Before you point your finger in blame, take a look in the mirror. Most of these officials occupy their offices because you sent them there or because you elected the leaders who chose them. If you don't like the way they behave, replace them with new ones who learned in kindergarten how to play nicely with others."

But this retort isn't quite fair. Our elected officials are not simply a microcosm of the American people because the institutions and procedures by which they are selected reflect public opinion imperfectly at best. While the evidence suggests that people are more polarized than they were a generation ago,[15] it shows unequivocally that the parties—especially in Washington DC—are more polarized than the people. Individuals and groups in the left and right tails of the ideological bell curve are well represented in today's national politics; this is not true for many moderates and independents, who shift their allegiance from election to election in search of an ever-receding point of equipoise.

There are steps we could take to give these less partisan voters more adequate representation. They include:

- taking the congressional redistricting process out of the hands of elected officials and entrusting it to non-partisan boards, as several states have already done
- allowing independents to participate fully in primary elections, as California is the latest to do
- adopting procedures such as instant runoff voting, which gives individuals in multi-candidate races incentives to build bridges to other

candidates and constituencies rather than to mobilize an intense faction of supporters

- experimenting with mandatory voting, which has significantly increased participation by fewer partisan voters in other advanced democracies such as Australia.[16]

Citizens' groups who favor less polarization and more civility are also pushing for changes in congressional rules and procedures that could create more cooperation across party lines. One such measure would require a 60 percent majority to elect the Speaker of the House, which would usually force the majority party to reach out to the minority. There is nothing to stop such groups from organizing to put their votes and their money behind primary candidates who place civility and cooperation across party lines, ahead of scorched-earth rhetoric and partisan solidarity.[17]

This is more than a speculative possibility. In 2010, a small band of Democrats, Republicans, and independents who were troubled by the polarization and incivility of our politics came together to form a new organization, "No Labels." Their core goal was to move the push for a politics of problem-solving from occasional pieces in op-ed pages to a sustained grassroots movement in communities around the country. No Labels was formally launched on December 13, 2010, with a full-day conference in New York that drew one thousand citizens (who paid their own way) from all 50 states. The conference, which received massive media coverage, featured current and former elected officials, nationally known print and TV journalists, policy experts, and civic activists.

No Labels, which runs on shoestring financing with a bare-bones Washington headquarters, has helped identify cross-party leadership teams in every state and congressional district, many of whom have taken the initiative to organize their own local groups. These activists spent much of 2011 seeking (with some success) to influence the ongoing debate over the debt ceiling crisis and the country's fiscal future—not by taking a specific position on the substance, but by pushing for a serious discussion leading to bipartisan agreements. One of their slogans, "Everyone at the table, everything on the table," crystallized the process they wanted and soon became part of the everyday discussion. When it appeared that the House of Representatives might take a four-week recess at the height of the debt ceiling standoff, No Labels activists deployed a catchy demand, "Stay on the floor until you fix the ceiling," and President Obama added his voice a few days later. Not long after, Speaker of the House John Boehner canceled the scheduled recess—a small victory for the fledgling organization, to be sure, but one that suggested the possibility of larger accomplishments down the road.

On December 13, 2011 (the one-year anniversary of its launch), No Labels convened a bipartisan group of current and former elected officials to unveil a legislative reform agenda, "Making Congress Work." Some of the proposed reforms—for example, requiring all completed presidential nominations to receive up-or-down votes within 90 days—were designed to break through the gridlock that often grips the Congress. Others—aligning the House and Senate schedules around five-day work weeks—were intended to set aside more time for committee work and for consideration of legislation on the floors of the House and Senate. Still others sought to promote a greater measure of civility and deliberation—for example, by instituting an American version of the British House of Commons "Question Period" and by organizing meetings that bring together the caucuses of both parties. Citizens in the No Labels movement have decided to spend 2012 pushing for these process reforms, many of which could be adopted through simple rule changes in January 2013 when the 113th Congress convenes.[18]

CONCLUSION

George Bernard Shaw once remarked, "Democracy is a device that ensures we shall be governed no better than we deserve"—wittily but accurately leaving open the possibility that we could be governed even worse than that. If our current political arrangements faithfully mirrored the sentiments and conduct of the people they purport to represent, the American people would have no democratic cause for complaint. But in key respects, our politics does not meet that standard. Most Americans cannot understand why the problem-solving cooperation they see in their local communities is so conspicuously absent in Washington and in an increasing number of state capitals as well.

Although our system is not fully representative of the people, it is highly responsive to them. Clear demands forcefully articulated do make a difference when a critical mass of citizens comes together to articulate them. We are not on the verge of a new Era of Good Feeling. But if the tens of millions of Americans turned off by the hyper-partisanship and incivility of today's politics gave effective voice to their displeasure, there is little doubt that candidates and elected officials would get the message.

Endnotes

1. Cornell, Clayton "Understanding the 'Civility Crisis'," *Washington State Magazine*, Winter 2010. Accessed from wsm.wsu.edu.
2. Larry, Clark "Civility and Politics in Campaigns," *Washington State Magazine*, Winter 2010. Accessed from wsm.wsu.edu.
3. Cited in Gregory Rodriguez, "Our Civility Deficit," *Los Angeles Times*, April 11, 2011.
4. Available at webershandwick.com.
5. Available at webershandwick.com.
6. Cited in Alex Kearns, "Civility in America?" Accessed from likethedew.com.
7. James Madison, *The Federalist Papers*, no. 51.
8. Available at gwpapers.virginia.edu/documents/civility.

9. For the details of this revealing evolution, see William A. Galston, "Incomplete Victory: The Rise of the New Democrats," in Peter Berkowitz, ed., *Varieties of Progressivism in America* (Stanford: Hoover Institution Press, 2004), pp. 67–69.

10. A good summary of the argument and evidence is found in Cass Sunstein, *Going to Extremes: How Like Minds United and Divide* (New York: Oxford, 2009).

11. Congressional Budget Office, "Trends in the Distribution of Household Income between 1979 and 1997," Washington, DC, October 2011.

12. Franklin D. Roosevelt, speech at Madison Square Garden, New York City, October 31, 1936.

13. For the full argument and evidence, see Robert D. Putnam, *"E Pluribus Unum*: Diversity and Community in the Twenty-first Century," The 2006 Johan Skytte Prize Lecture, *Scandinavian Political Studies* 30 (2), 2007: 137–174.

14. Rodriguez, op. cit.

15. For the most convincing argument along these lines, see Alan I. Abramowitz, *The Disappearing Center: Engaged Citizens, Polarization, and American Democracy* (New Haven, CT: Yale, 2010).

16. For detailed discussion of these and other options, see Pietro S. Nivola and William A. Galston, "Toward Depolarization," in Pietro Nivola and David W. Brady, eds., *Red and Blue Nation? Volume Two: Consequences and Correction of America's Polarized Politics* (Washington, DC: Brookings, 2008).

17. Nothing in our formal institutions, that is, But Diana Mutz raises the troubling possibility that the psychology of political activism may force us to choose between broad-based participation and a more civil, deliberative brand of politics. See Diana Mutz, *Hearing the Other Side: Deliberative versus Participatory Democracy* (New York: Cambridge, 2006).

18. For much more on all of this, see nolabels.org. Full disclosure: The author of this chapter was one of the organizations' co-founders.

14

The Consequences of Uncivil Discourse for the Political Process

L. Sandy Maisel[1]

Sandy Maisel addresses the most difficult question that arises in any discussion of civility in politics: Does it matter? The attention the subject receives indicates that most people believe that incivility matters, and there is no shortage of clear assertions that it is important. But there is little by way of serious research on the veracity of such claims. Taking a broad historical view, the author points out a number of specific negative consequences for the political process that he believes can be traced to heightened incivility.

Congressman Alan West (R-FL) passed the incivility duck test when he described fellow Florida Congresswoman Debbie Wasserman Schultz (D) as "the most vile, unprofessional and despicable member of the House of Representatives." That read like incivility, sounded like incivility, and was universally interpreted to be uncivil; thus it probably was.

But West, an African-American Tea Party Republican, is often thought to be somewhat out of the mainstream, at least in terms of his rhetoric. And his attack on "the gentlewoman from Florida" was personal more than partisan. She had questioned his policy position as not representing his constituents in a floor speech while he was not present. Angered, he responded.

The problem, for those concerned with civility, was not so much the attack but the institutional response. There was none. While decorum on the House floor and expressions of respect for one's colleagues were once enforced by the House's presiding officers and elder statesmen, there was no response to West's tirade. Well, not quite. Actually there was a response. Democrats used the attack as a fundraising tool virtually immediately—and their followers responded generously.

When Congressman Joe Wilson (R-NC) interrupted President Obama during his health care speech to Congress in September of 2009 by shouting, "You lie!", a hush came over the House chamber and the Speaker gaveled for order. Wilson soon apologized for his outburst, but there were no consequences. Well, again, not quite. Both Wilson and his 2010 opponent used the outburst to raise funds, bringing in more than a million dollars to what had looked like a non-competitive race.

In his first week in office, Maine's Republican Tea Party-backed Governor Paul LePage, who during his campaign claimed he would tell President Obama to "go to hell," responded to a reporter's question concerning his decision not to attend the NAACP's annual Martin Luther King Day breakfast by saying that if they did not like it, "Tell 'em to kiss my butt!" His supporters praised his forthright honesty. Certainly, he suffered no reprisals that disturbed him at all.

We can easily multiply these examples with other recent incidents in which politicians, in attacking or even just responding to those with whom they disagree, step over well-recognized lines of civility—with few or no negative consequences to those engaged in uncivil public discourse. We also know that many—including many in the public arena—decry these incidents of incivility as detrimental to our governing process.

In 2005, Congresswoman Shelley Moore Caputo (R-WV) and her House colleague Emanuel Cleaver II (D-MO), the chair of the Congressional Black Caucus, formed the Congressional Civility Caucus. The response from their colleagues was disappointing, but Caputo and Cleaver carried on, holding civil and informed debates on the floor of the House to demonstrate that it was possible to disagree vehemently on policy without degrading the institution. Claiming that "true leaders guide with compassion and by example," the leaders of the Civility Caucus tried to reinvigorate the group in the days following the tragic shooting of Congresswoman Gabrielle Giffords (D-AZ) in Tucson in January 2011. Again, however, few followed their lead—and the debates in the 112th Congress over passing a budget and later raising the debt limit fell to new levels of incivility.

In the dog days of summer 2011, the United States government came within one day of failing to raise the debt ceiling, and, as a consequence of a demonstrated inability to govern rationally, lost its AAA rating from Standard and Poor's for the first time since those ratings were established. The nation watched in disgust as both houses failed to reach a compromise until the last hour. The disconnect between Washington and the rest of the nation seemed apparent to everyone living beyond the Beltway. What were these people thinking? Didn't they realize that the good of the nation was more important than party loyalty or ideological purity? Only the political comics seemed to enjoy the situation. The crisis fed right into Jon Stewart, Steven Colbert, Andy Borowitz, and others; raw meat for their nightly fare. Perhaps the line that epitomized the reaction of a sweltering nation to the machinations of their legislators was: "It's not the heat. It's the stupidity!"

A *New York Times* poll taken shortly after the crisis was averted captured the opinion of the nation. A record 82 percent did not approve of the job the Congress was doing. Fully four in five voters. The President's approval rating was higher, but still less than 50 percent. The Republicans' performance was evaluated as poorer than the Democrats', but the Democrats could take little solace as more than two-thirds of those polled disapproved of their actions.

It is easy to make the leap from observing Congress at work and from listening to or reading about the lack of civility that has characterized recent campaigns and congressional debates to concluding that this lack of civility has led to the decline in citizen approval of and trust in our institutions of government. But that logical step requires further exploration.

This chapter will examine the impact of the decline in civility on institutions generally and on political parties and the electoral process more specifically by addressing two related questions. Others in this volume have examined whether incivility is worse now than it has been at other times in our history. I will accept as a starting point that something is different in our current era of politics and will try to address the consequences of whatever it is that is different.

First, I will look at a very basic question: Why do we think incivility *per se* is necessarily bad? What are the values expressed in requiring civil debate? And, on the other side, are some American values threatened by requiring conformity to a certain standard of civility? In addressing these questions, it will be necessary to define the term "civility" as it should be applied to public discourse.

Second, I will turn to the question of whether we can point to direct negative consequences because of the lack of civility. We know that public faith in our institutions has reached all-time low levels, at least since modern polling has begun. However, has this decline been caused by the lack of civility? Or by the lack of results? If one views the lack of faith in public officials as a consequence of their inability to solve the nation's problems, has the decline in civility caused that decline in performance? How do we know? Are the consequences of uncivil discourse so nefarious that they require an institutional response, or are we in an era when uncivil discourse reflects the problems of our nation and the solutions proposed to address them divide our population?

DEFINING INCIVILITY

Eight Republican presidential candidates gathered in Ames, Iowa, on the eve of the quadrennial Iowa straw poll, one of the first tests of candidate strength to which the media pay (exaggerated) attention. The *New York Times* story on the debate led with the summary that "a withering critique of President Obama's handling of the economy was overshadowed by a burst of incivility among the Republican presidential candidates."[2] The key example of uncivil behavior was former Minnesota Governor Tim Pawlenty's attack on his fellow Minnesotan, Congresswoman Michele Bachmann, assailing her weak legislative record and standing "directly at her side and accus[ing] her of 'making false statements' and having 'a record of misstatements.'"[3] Bachmann shot back with the cruelest insult of all, claiming that Pawlenty's record was "a lot . . . like Barack Obama, if you ask me."[4] The *Times'* characterization of the debate was typical of that found in papers from coast to coast, of that found on the television networks and in the blogosphere, and even in the *Saudi Gazette.*[5]

Pawlenty did attack Bachmann—and it would not be hard to find factual evidence to back his claims. Bachmann did counter—and on some policies, like cap-and-trade, Pawlenty did agree with the President. Why were these "attacks" deemed uncivil? Because the candidates were standing next to each other? Because they did not couch their criticism in nuanced language? Because they said forthrightly what others have said behind their backs for some time?

Incivility implies a rudeness or impoliteness that violates some agreed upon standard of society. The problem for the current discussion is to agree upon what that standard is. In politics, where two or more individuals are competing for the support of the electorate based in part at least on the fact that they disagree fundamentally on policy, on the direction the country could take, on how to respond to pressing national problems, the question becomes how you can convince the voters that your view is correct—and your opponent's is wrong. Are critics saying that it is uncivil to make those claims in a straightforward and direct manner? To claim directly that your opponent is tooting his own horn when there is no horn there to toot? If one candidate stretches the truth or makes false claims, is that person acting uncivilly, or is the opponent, who calls the candidate to task for these falsehoods, to be judged uncivil?

Perhaps we can agree on answers to these questions if we are concerned with a legislative record or statements that are verifiable in factual terms. Robust public debate requires that the truth reach the public; how a candidate insists on the truth—when facts have been distorted—seems less relevant than that the truth be told.

But that statement only begins the debate on incivility; it settles nothing. In the same Iowa debate, Byron York, a conservative columnist for the *Washington Examiner*, asked Bachmann what she meant when she vowed to be "submissive" to her husband. The audience jeered at the question and clearly showed that they felt York had stepped over a line of rudeness, that he had injected a tone of incivility into the debate. Bachmann parried the implied attack, saying that "submissive" in her relationship with her husband meant "showing respect." No one pressed her on whether that was really what her religious tenets meant.

Bill Keller, former executive editor of the *New York Times,* disagrees with those who feel that questions like York's are uncivil and that Bachmann need not have been pushed further. He thinks all candidates should be asked pointed questions about how their religious beliefs will affect their governing. Keller, who has sent a questionnaire to each Republican candidate asking about the role of faith in their lives, feels that such questions are warranted, perhaps most particularly because:

> We have an unusually large number of candidates, including putative front-runners, who belong to churches that are mysterious or suspect to many Americans. Mitt Romney and Jon Huntsman are Mormons, a faith that many conservative Christians have been taught is a "cult" and that many others think is just weird. (Huntsman says he is not "overly religious.") Rick Perry, Michele Bachmann and Rick Santorum are all affiliated with fervid subsets of evangelical Christianity, which has raised concerns about their respect for the separation of church and state, not to mention the separation of fact and fiction.[6]

However, Keller himself acknowledges that it might well be a small step from asking candidates questions about their faith to bigotry or paranoia about the role that faith will play in governing. Is it possible to raise these questions in a civil manner? Remember that during the 2008 presidential election, both Barack Obama and John McCain were forced to repudiate preachers who either were close to them personally or had endorsed them—in each case men who had ideas far from the mainstream. If candidates appeal to the electorate at least in part based on their religious beliefs—and how those beliefs distinguish them from their opponents and put them in the same camp as those to whom they are appealing—as Bachmann, Texas Governor Rick Perry, and former Pennsylvania Senator Rick Santorum all have done—is it uncivil to question them on those beliefs?

In terms of civility, how can one navigate the steps from policy to the relationship between faith and policy, to the relationship between other aspects of a candidate's personal life and the policies he or she will pursue if elected? Does it overstep an agreed upon line if a reporter or another candidate questions former Speaker of the House Newt Gingrich about previous marital infidelity? To ask any candidate if there were any circumstances in which he or she would support a child who had been raped and decided to terminate the pregnancy that resulted from that forcible attack? If one feels that abortion is against God's law and that no candidate who supports a woman's right to choose should be elected—for that reason alone—how far can a candidate go in expressing those views, how graphic can a candidate's ad be before it is deemed uncivil? What was it about the words of Congressman West, Congressman Wilson, or Governor LePage, cited earlier, that made them uncivil? The substance of the remarks or the words themselves? Or the person who was addressed? Or the forum or manner in which they were spoken?

As a social scientist, I am uncomfortable with the duck theory of defining a concept—if it swims like a duck, waddles like a duck, and quacks like a duck, it is probably a duck. However, for years, a definition like that has sufficed for the United States Supreme Court. In the famous First Amendment case, *Jacobellis v. Ohio*, 378 U.S. 184 (1964), in a concurring opinion, Justice Potter Stewart said of hard-core pornography, "I shall not today attempt further to define the kinds of material I understand to be embraced within that shorthand description; and perhaps I could never succeed in intelligibly doing so. But I know it when I see it, . . ." (at 197). Perhaps today we must be satisfied with that kind of definition of incivility. Some acts are not civil; others, while perhaps objectionable to some, are. Incivility, however defined, has always played a role in American politics, as my colleagues argue elsewhere in this volume, but certainly something is different today. Before searching for direct negative consequences on incivility, we will first ask whether political discourse that lacks civility is anathema to American democracy.

DOES INCREASED CIVILITY VIOLATE BASIC AMERICAN VALUES?

How does this question of civility or incivility intersect with traditional American values? Why are we so concerned? I do not think that the answers are clear—but the philosophical bases of American society that define whether civility is central to our values can be outlined.[7]

On one level, the great American experiment in democratic governing is bringing together a diverse people into a common whole. "We the people" of the United States form this union. To do so, we implicitly accept Rousseau's concept of the social contract. In order to pursue the common good, we accept that some of our individual desires must be restricted, and among those restrictions is the necessity to adhere to widely held conventions on social interactions. Thus, civic republicanism implies that those participating as citizens in this nation, which had been granted powers (but restricted powers) in order to pursue the common good, do so in a civil manner.

Political philosopher Cheshire Calhoun makes the argument that civility has a moral importance that far exceeds social conformity for the sake of acceptable discourse.

> Civility involves conformity to socially established rules of respect, tolerance, and considerateness. I do not, however, take the social conformism built into civility to be a reason for discounting civility's moral importance. On the contrary, . . . this conformity is critical to civility's moral function. The function of civility . . . is to *communicate* basic moral attitudes of respect, tolerance, and considerateness. We can successfully communicate these basic moral attitudes to others only by following socially conventional rules for the expression of respect, tolerance, and considerateness. . . . [C]ivility's tie to social rules sometimes occasions a conflict between what it would be uncivil to do and what, from a critical moral point of view, is morally correct.[8]

[A number of other political theorists have argued, in various ways, that civil society was a necessary precondition for effective democracy. |Robert Putnam and a number of others[9] —almost all recalling de Tocqueville's fascination with the associational aspects of early American life—see social organizations as necessary to teach the traits needed and to build the social capital required for an effective democracy.]In *Political Liberalism,* Rawls (1996) reaches the conclusion that our shared conception of justice is not really a merging of the ideas of groups with very different principles but rather an agreement to disagree on those principles and to do so civilly, only within certain agreed-upon boundaries:

> In particular, [Rawls argues] we are civil exactly when we limit the reasons we use to argue for political decisions only to those that are contained in the overlapping consensus on specifically political principles, and do not go beyond those by employing sectarian reasons from our own specific comprehensive doctrine. Public reason is then the proper idiom that fellow citizens are to limit themselves to when arguing with one another about political matters.[10]

Rawls' writing has led, directly or indirectly, to a body of work on the importance of "deliberative democracy," that is, arriving at public policy through the process of rational—and by implication, civil—debate.[11] While scholars discussing deliberative democracy differ in a number of significant ways, what they have in common is an insistence on what Habermas frequently refers to as the "unforced force of the better argument." And that better argument, according to these thinkers, involves civil discourse.

But the importance of community discussion in arriving at a sense of the common good is not the only value that has been seen as fundamental to democracy in the United States. Another aspect of the great American experiment deals with the Lockean guarantees of individual liberty. The compromise that led to the ratification of the Constitution included a guarantee that the Bill of Rights would be added at the earliest possible moment. Those rights were guarantees that the government the people had agreed to join would not restrict their basic individual liberties—that its power to constrain individuals' actions was limited.

Classic libertarians, of course, are suspicious of norms of behavior that require individuals to act in ways they would not choose otherwise. Are individuals so restricted by not giving up the basic rights they sought to have guaranteed by entering into the social contract, by agreeing to be part of the union? In the current context, must we all speak according to accepted norms?

The extent to which toleration of abhorrent behavior is required in the United States has recurred throughout our history. Should the state restrict those whose religious beliefs set them apart? Should individuals be free to advocate evil practices? To oppose the most basic policies of our nation? In a sense, the debate over civility is asking whether individuals have a right to engage in uncivil political discourse or whether the communitarian values of our nation should restrict that type of behavior.

I am not certain that anyone argues in favor of "uncivil" speech, any more than women's rights advocates do not argue in favor of abortion but rather in opposition to restrictions on one's right to an abortion. The challenge to a doctrinaire insistence on civil political discourse is philosophically an argument for individual rights. It is presented in two ways.

|The first holds that the insistence on civility when individuals are debating important matters on which they disagree in fundamental ways is unrealistic. People feel passionately about political questions, they care if they win or lose, and they will resort to whatever tactics and strategies are necessary to win. To contend that this is inappropriate is the argument of academics behind ivy-covered walls, not the reasoning of street-savvy politicians.

The second rationale notes that the insistence on civility in political discourse further marginalizes those already at the margins of society. Civil discourse is the discourse learned through and practiced by the establishment. It is the discourse of Wall Street and perhaps Main Street, but it is not the discourse of the poor, the underclasses of American society, the Black and Hispanic, the immigrant and the powerless; it is not the discourse of Occupy Wall Street. It violates the basic tenets of our society to stipulate that political debate must be carried out with an upper class voice.|

In *Rude Democracy*, Susan Herbst takes these arguments to their logical extreme. She maintains that civility and incivility in today's political discourse should be seen not as virtues or vices but as strategies used to reach a desired end.[12] Her chapter on Sarah Palin[13] demonstrates how Palin uses civil and uncivil discourse, often at the same appearances, in order to make her political point to the different publics listening to her speeches. In a subsequent chapter,[14] she discusses how Barack Obama uses civility as a strategy to define himself to the American public.

My conclusion is that civility does have a place in the value structure of American democracy, but it is not an unchallenged place; civil discourse might be preferred, but it is not a fundamental necessity for American democracy to flourish. The debate over raising the debt ceiling in the summer of 2011 demonstrated clearly that governing is done best when ruled by the "unforced force of the better argument." But that is not the same as saying that those who will not or cannot present their case in a civil way can or should be silenced. If something is different about the nature of political discourse in our contemporary debates, and there are clearly negative consequences for our democracy, we are right to be concerned about the extent of incivility, regardless of the arguments for or against discourse of that type. But first, it is necessary to show what those negative consequences are. It is not enough to say that we do not prefer certain kind of actions by individuals. We must show that those actions are thwarting attainment of the common good.

ARE THERE DISCERNIBLE NEGATIVE CONSEQUENCES OF UNCIVIL DISCOURSE?

Because those of us writing (and reading) this book believe in civility as a virtue, it is so tempting simply to respond, "Of course there are consequences." But that will not suffice. I believe, however, that there are at least two specific consequences that impact the political process in predictable and negative ways.

DIFFICULTY IN RECRUITING CANDIDATES FOR PUBLIC OFFICE   First, I am concerned about political recruitment. Who enters the political arena? Are people deterred because political debate is often uncivil? While concrete data are not available, inferences from anecdotes are clear.

During the run up to the 2012 presidential election, a number of potentially strong Republican candidates resisted party leaders' entreaties to run for "personal" reasons. In some cases those personal reasons were clearly more political than personal. But in others, the balance was not clear. Indiana Governor Mitch Daniels, as one example, was worried about discussion of the period of time in his life when he and his wife separated—and then reconciled. She was very leery of his entering the race. And, despite the fact that he would have been an instantaneous frontrunner, he decided against running.

Mississippi Governor Haley Barbour, another potentially strong contender for the nomination, decided against a run, again at the urging of his family, but in part at least because of how experts felt his career in Southern politics would have played on the national stage. Would he have to defend the language he used in campaigns in Mississippi? Was what was acceptable in Mississippi beyond the national pale?

Recruiters for the four congressional committees charged with finding the best candidates willing to run as their parties' nominees for the House and Senate always claim that they have recruited the best candidates. But those who follow recruitment efforts point over and over to potential candidates who resist pleas that they run because they are not willing to put up with the kinds of personal attacks—not policy, but personal—that they would have to face if they ran for office. The question often turns not on what would be said about a candidate, but rather whether the candidate's family will be held up for public scrutiny. If a son or daughter has been guilty of some minor indiscretion, should the parent's political ambition place that on a public stage? The answer seems clearly to be that it should not, but examples abound of when it has. And candidates and their families understand that potential.

How often do rival campaigns actually use the children of candidates? How often do potential candidates decide against a campaign because of such concerns? We do not know, but recruiters talk about enough examples that this is a matter of concern. Whereas once parents were excited if their children were involved in public life, whereas once serving in elective office was considered among the highest callings, today parents proclaim that they would not want their children to be public figures, and polls show that elected officials are no longer among the most respected people in society. In fact, one recent poll revealed that politicians were the least respected among an array of professions rated, falling just below car salesmen; nurses, doctors, and teachers topped the list.

It is clear that a decline in civility in politics is not the only reason that potential candidates decide not to run.[15] Potential candidates cite the competitive disadvantages that stack the deck against challengers to incumbents, district lines drawn to favor one party or the other, difficulty in raising money or a distaste for having to do so, their conclusion that more "good" can be accomplished in other arenas than in public life, and a host of other reasons.

But among those reasons is that they do not want to be considered "one of those politicians," that the tone of political discourse and, as a result, the way politicians are viewed by the public makes running for office unattractive. To some extent, this is not a new phenomenon. In the early twentieth century, in *The American Commonwealth*, James Bryce wrote, "It may however be alleged that I have omitted one significant ground for the distaste of 'the best people' for public life, viz. the bad company they would have to keep, the general vulgarity of tone in politics, the exposure to invective or ribaldry by hostile speakers and a reckless press."[16]

But if the reasons related to incivility were bad a century ago, they are clearly worse today. Enough has changed about how campaigns are run, how political communication is disseminated, and how our government institutions function in recent decades—certainly in the area of civility of discourse—that many of "the best and the brightest"—those committed to doing their part to improve the lives of those around them—no longer view public service, and certainly not elective office, as a means to that end.

INABILITY TO GOVERN   The second area in which the negative impact of the decline in civility is apparent relates directly to one of the reasons that potential candidates give for not seeking elective office—that more can be done in other arenas. The frustration expressed by Tea Party activists on the right and by the Wall Street Occupiers on the left—frustrations often expressed in ways deemed to be uncivil—centers on the lack of results. The gridlock in Washington and in many state capitals is caused in part by partisan one-upmanship often expressed in ways that do not show respect for those with differing views.

In a *New York* magazine profile of House Majority Leader Erik Cantor (R-VA), Jason Zengerle quoted Cantor: "'I try to be deferential,' Cantor said in his buttery Southern accent. 'I mean, I'm a lawyer, I was raised in the sort of schooling, if you will, of deference to someone on the bench—and—certainly to the president.'" But Zengerle also concluded:

> No one in Washington has done more to disrupt Obama's first term—and threaten his chance at a second—than Cantor. The two men have clashed from the start. . . . Some veteran GOP lawmakers find Cantor's

coddling of the freshmen irritating. . . . But Cantor has realized that, in Washington these days, being liked is not a substantial advantage. Much better to be deemed so unreasonable that your opponents ultimately feel no choice but to bend to your will.[17]

And if your will is to prevent legislation from passing, to prevent the President's agenda from moving forward, to work the system to your political advantage, lack of civility works. The polling data that show that the public lack of respect for and general disapproval of the Congress is not a deterrent to the kind of actions we have seen in Washington—because the kinds of actions we have seen in Washington recently seem to work for political purposes. According to an NBC News-*Wall Street Journal* poll conducted in the fall of 2011, more than four out of five voters felt that the decisions made by Congress on the debt ceiling were made for partisan political advantage.

Four decades ago, Richard Fenno noted that Americans seem to dislike the Congress, but still admire their own members of Congress. Fenno's famous paradox explained this phenomenon by noting that members of Congress ran for the Congress by running against the institution. The institution is flawed, they argued, but I am not one of those bad people. I am the good guy who does wonderful things for your district. Given the number of those in the majority party who lost in 2006 (Republicans) and in 2010 (Democrats), one can surely question whether the electoral strategy noted by Fenno can still work today. In fact, in the same poll noted above, a majority of the respondents claimed that they would vote to throw the entire Congress—including their own representative—out, if they had the chance. While no one expects that to happen, incumbent advantage seems to be diminished by the fact that all politicians are tarred by the behavior of those who seem only concerned about political advantage.

And no one talks about the common good. I would argue that the lack of civility and the increased partisanship that we have seen in recent decision-making and campaigning is detrimental to the body politic, that we as a nation are worse off because partisanship, not concern for the public good, motivates congressional (and in many cases state legislative) decisions, but politicians engaged in such actions will not respond to such claims until the disgust that the public expresses at the polls is reflected in the voting booth. We are left to wonder how far off that day is.

HAS THE DECLINE IN CIVILITY HURT THE POLITICAL PROCESS?

Is it possible to draw a conclusion on the impact of the decline in civility on the political process that will satisfy a social scientist's desire for a verifiable conclusion? I don't think so. But that does not mean that a conclusion cannot be reached.

The question must, of necessity, revolve around how one defines success in the political process. The finding of the NBC News-*Wall Street Journal* poll that a shocking 54 percent of the respondents would vote to replace the entire Congress if they had an opportunity to do so, noted above, is cause for concern. While the support for individual congressmen has not yet fallen to a level that would cause vast numbers to change the tone of political discourse, the level of public dissatisfaction, expressed in polls, in street demonstrations, in public meetings, and elsewhere has risen to an alarming level. A polity is not healthy if a majority of the people want to replace all of those in office. It is a short step from there to dissatisfaction with the system of government as a whole—and the lack of civility in public discourse clearly contributes to this evident decline in such support.

What is it about the lack of civility in the current political scene that distinguishes today's politics from those of other eras? Certainly anyone reading the campaign literature or the personal letters from the Adams–Jefferson campaign would characterize those as uncivil.[18] The tone of congressional debate in the decades preceding the Civil War reached a critical level of incivility, in fact at one critical juncture to the point of physical violence, when Senator Preston Brooks caned Senator Charles Sumner on the Senate floor, after Sumner had insulted Brooks' cousin. Civility in political life during the McCarthy era set new standards for base behavior.[19] Why is today's situation so different?

The easy answer is the 24-7 news cycle, the unfiltered nature of much of the news that reaches the public over the Internet, and the resulting increase in public awareness of how politicians view each other, at least publicly. The highly partisan cable news outlets, radio talk shows, blogs, and Internet sites serve as a huge echo chamber. Whereas once an attack on a candidate, an exaggerated claim, or a personal insult might have been seen by a small audience and perhaps repeated on the "inside the Beltway" rumor mill, today repetition after repetition means that we as a public see and hear much more of the incivility in politics than was the case before. And because of that, politicians are much more likely to use these tactics purposely.

I can imagine no better example of that than Governor Rick Perry's attack on Governor Mitt Romney during the GOP candidates' October 2011 debate in Las Vegas: "And, Mitt, you lose all of your standing, from my perspective, because you hired illegals in your home and you knew about it for a year." Perry's lashing out at Romney was a complete non sequitor in the context of the debate. But his strategic goal in that debate was to attack Romney in this manner on immigration and to gain on Romney politically, and he took the first opportunity he had, even if his response had nothing to do with the question asked. After 24 hours, a Google search on "Perry attacks Romney on illegal immigrants" resulted in more than 200,000 hits. Clearly, how incivility is spread among the public and how it is used as a tactic by candidates contributes to its impact.

But I think that there are deeper, systemic answers. In earlier eras, those governing the nation lived in one city and spent all of their time there. Let's look briefly at the three periods of intense incivility I have noted above. In the early years following our nation's birth, while the country's leaders disagreed vehemently on the critical issues of the day—full funding of the nation's debt and assumption of the state debts, our relations with Great Britain and with France, the scope of the federal government—they also had been allies in the greatest struggle of their time, the fight for independence. Their dislike was often personal, and each knew the personal foibles of the other. But they also knew that each was a patriot, and that although they had different views of the nation's future, those views were not so fundamental that they had forgotten what bound them together. Adams and Jefferson might have disagreed with each other, and they were rivals on every level, but they respected each other and lived together and worked together among a small group of men forging the nation's future. One view of the direction the nation would take would prevail, but the losing side was not willing to sacrifice the nation for its political purposes.

During the run-up to the Civil War, one could not make that claim. The incivility in the political process at that time reflected a far deeper divide in the nation. In point of fact, those on the "losing side" in that great debate felt strongly enough about their position that they were willing to secede from the nation; they were brought back to the union only by force. Reconstruction was a period in which those who had seceded—the leaders who were not able to reach a compromise and favored dissolution of the union over conceding defeat in the political process—were not permitted to participate. That era was a time of governmental failure, not just failure to find a solution to the slavery issue, but failure to convince those in the South that the union was worth preserving. The Civil War was the tangible recognition that the political process had failed.

By the post–World War II period, when Senator Joseph McCarthy (R-WI) burst on the Washington scene, service in government had become a full-time occupation.[20] Republicans and Democrats lived together in Washington; so too did their families. While partisan differences abounded and rhetoric was often quite heated, at the end of the day legislators from both parties retreated to their homes in Washington and the nearby suburbs where their wives and children were often interacting with the wives and children of those with whom they had been debating vigorously on Capitol Hill. The result was a strident, but cordial, partisanship. Policy differences were profound, but personal animosity was muted.

Enter McCarthy—with a blatant disdain for the truth and total disregard for the personal lives he was ruining. He frightened the nation; he frightened Washington—not only Democrats, but also members of his own Republican party. His claims, though based only tangentially in fact, were cause for alarm. And for a time, the nation was cowed. But then sanity returned—symbolized by two moments. First, Maine Senator Margaret Chase Smith, a conservative Republican whose record on the nation's defense was beyond question, took the Senate floor on June 1, 1950, and in her famous Declaration of Conscience said that she had had enough: "Freedom of speech is not what it used to be in America. It has been so abused by some that it is not exercised by others." She would no longer be cowed.

Second, Joseph Welch, a Boston Brahmin lawyer from the most traditional of all Boston firms, Hale and Dorr, stood up to McCarthy during the Army-McCarthy hearings. As Senator McCarthy vituperatively attacked Fred Fisher, a young lawyer in Welch's firm, because of Fisher's membership in the Lawyers Guild (which McCarthy described as the legal bulwark of the Communist Party) during and shortly after law school, Welch had had enough. "At long last, Senator McCarthy," Welch pleaded, "have you no decency?" And Welch refused to go on. At the end, McCarthy was left ranting to an empty chair, as everyone left the room.

There are lessons from these examples and contrasts with today's context. The politicians of the Federalist period were united in a cause—and that unity overrode their differences, at least to the point that they could progress with the business of the nation. During the Civil War period, the division was so deep and so fundamental that the political process failed and the nation was torn apart. During the McCarthy era, while the concern over a threat from the Soviet Communists was real, our nation's leaders also understood that they were in a common enterprise and that the common experience they shared in governing required adherence to some rules. Among those rules were to treat others involved in the enterprise—those who agreed with you and those who did not—with respect and civility, and to have ultimate reliance on truth to win the day. When McCarthy threatened to tear apart the basic fabric of the nation, calmer heads prevailed.

And today? While we may have difficulty identifying exactly what aspects of the tenor of political discourse we find uncivil and worrisome, two stand out. The first is the lack of regard for other individuals in the process. Too often, the strategy is to demonize those with whom you disagree, with the ultimate goal of political victory. In an interview with the *National Journal* in October 2010, Kentucky Senator Mitch McConnell, the Republican leader in the Senate, compared the GOP's situation in 2010 with that in 1996. "The single most important thing we want to achieve is for President Obama to be a one-term president." In 1996, McConnell felt that the Republicans had erred in cooperating with President Clinton on welfare and other policies; the result was a second Clinton term. According to McConnell's analysis, his party's goal should be to avoid that mistake. So the Republicans should work against the Democrats and deride all of their proposals. Possible policy agreements are less important than political gain.

Why do politicians feel that victory is so essential? We hear talk of a polarized political scene, with the evidence being that Democrats and Republicans are far apart, do not negotiate, do not compromise. Evidence is seen in votes; commentators note, for instance, how often the Republicans in Congress vote unanimously against proposals submitted by President Obama. But what is less noted is the reason for this polarization. In a time when citizens despair about the future of our nation, when some see the United States in a decline in our global standing, when the economy is stagnating at a level with unacceptably high unemployment and many fearing for their own and their children's economic futures, the Democrats and

Republicans differ on the most fundamental issue—the role that the federal government should play in countering these trends. It is not merely that they disagree, but rather that they think if their opponents prevail, everything that we hold dear will be destroyed. In that context, incivility is a small cost if the gain is winning the ultimate battle. It is unclear that the public sees the stakes as that high. They merely want politicians to find solutions to the pressing problems. But political leaders—and remember that political leaders are ideologically more extreme than are their followers—do. The reason that they do not "respectfully disagree" is that they do not, in fact, respect the views of their opponents; they see them as dangerous.

And these views are exacerbated because those in government do not really know their opponents. When the legislative work week is over, they leave Washington and return to their political homes to discuss the situation with those whose views mirror their own. It is far easier to demonize those whom you do not know than it is to do so with your children's friends' fathers or mothers. And because far fewer Washington politicians now stay in Washington more than three days a week and even fewer families move to Washington, fewer politicians know each other out of the context of Capitol Hill. The rhetoric of campaigns leads to characterizing political opponents as enemies; and life in Washington does little to change that image. There are no Margaret Chase Smiths standing up to those who degrade the political process; those who might do so fear personal attacks, even within their own party, at home.

This lack of personal regard for fellow elected officials is compounded by a lack of regard for the truth. Politicians say what they want to say and need to say—about themselves and about those running against them—in order to be reelected. Television networks on the right and on the left repeat these falsehoods, giving credibility to them, because they have discovered that outlandish claims lead to bigger audiences and higher revenues. The same is true of radio talk show hosts. Polling data show that most citizens gather news from outlets with whose position they agree. Conservatives listen to Fox News and right-wing radio; liberals prefer MSNBC and talk show hosts on the left. Competition for viewers drives coverage and opinion. And, too often, efforts to rein in untruthful claims are lost in the cacophony of partisan repetition.

Earlier I raised Fenno's paradox and questioned whether its explanatory power will remain as strong as it has in the past. I believe that a new local-national dynamic regarding how incivility is viewed by the public may be at work. In my view, there is no question that the general public is fed up with the tone of political debate, that most of us, including most mainline political commentators, believe that the extent to which our political discourse has become uncivil is troubling. But recall the examples I raised at the beginning of this chapter. The supporters of Congressmen West and Wilson and of Governor LePage loved their attacks. If candidates can appeal to extreme elements to win primary elections—and many general election constituencies lean heavily to one party or the other—we may, in fact, be witnessing a corollary of Fenno's paradox, that we as a nation are fed up with uncivil discourse and the extent to which it prevents public officials from focusing on solving problems and from seeking the common good, but we love our own heroes when they behave in such a manner, demonizing those who do not agree with their preferred solutions.

In the 112th Congress, Republican House Speaker John Boehner of Ohio attempted to compromise with President Obama on issues regarding the budget and the debt ceiling. But the Tea Party members of Boehner's conference would not allow him to compromise in their names; they felt he was selling out their principles—and said so in very clear terms. Truth be told, Democrats in the House felt the same way about President Obama (for the opposite reasons), and they were only slightly more restrained in their criticisms.[21] The result was a raucous policy deadlock, insults thrown across the partisan aisle, and general recognition that the policy process had failed. But those who "stood on their principles" and caused the deadlock drew support from their true believer followers—on the left and right.

Those are the senses in which uncivil political discourse is hurting the political process. It is important to separate those aspects of political discourse—including the language or tactics used and even attacks on aspects of candidates' personal lives that *do* impact on their ability to govern, which are legitimate—from those that undermine the system. I do not think that the level of discourse in our politics needs to be restrained and colorless. I feel strongly that candidates and officeholders should vigorously debate the pressing issues of the day on which there is legitimate disagreement. But the polity loses and even is threatened when personal disregard for fellow politicians overcomes a basic sense of communitarian values and when regard for accurate portrayal of the truth is lost in an effort to press a partisan or personal advantage.

Endnotes

1. The author would like to thank G. Calvin Mackenzie, Joseph Reisert, and Walter Stone for commenting on earlier versions of this chapter. He would also like to thank Russ Wilson, who served as his research assistant.
2. Jeff Zeleny and Ashley Parker, "8 From G.O.P. Trade Attacks at Iowa Debate," *New York Times,* August 11, 2011.
3. Ibid.
4. Ibid.
5. "Incivility Marks Republican Presidential debate in Iowa," *Saudi Gazette,* August 13, 2011.
6. Bill Keller, "Asking Candidates Tougher Questions about Faith," *New York Times Magazine,* August 28, 2011.
7. This section draws heavily on the argument raised in a grant proposal submitted by the Center for Civil Discourse at the McCormack Graduate School of Policy and Global Studies at the University of Massachusetts, Boston, to the National Endowment for the Humanities to fund a National Forum on Civility in American Democracy. I would like to thank Dean Stephen P. Crosby for

including me on the advisory board for that project and granting me access to the document.

8. Calhoun Cheshire, "The Virtue of Civility," *Philosophy and Public Affairs,* *29*(3), 2005: 251–275.

9. Benjamin Barber, "Deliberation, Democracy, and Power," *Kettering Review* *17*(1), Fall 1999; Etzioni Amitai, *Public Policy in a New Key* (New Brunswick, NJ: Transaction Publishers, 1993); Robert D. Putnam, *Bowling Alone: The Collapse and Revival of American Community* (New York: Simon and Schuster, 2001).

10. John Rawls, *Political Liberalism* (New York: Columbia University Press, 1996); Center for Civil Discourse, Proposal for a National Forum on Civility in American Democracy, submitted to the National Endowment for the Humanities by the McCormack Graduate School of Policy and Global Studies at the University of Massachusetts, Boston, 2011.

11. Amy Gutmann and Dennis Thompson, *Democracy and Disagreement* (Cambridge, MA: Harvard University Press, 1996); Amy Gutmann, and Dennis Thompson, *Why Deliberative Democracy?* (Princeton, NJ: Princeton University Press, 2004); Habermas Jurgen, *Between Facts and Norms: Contributions to a Discourse Theory of Law and Democracy.* (Cambridge, MA: Polity Press, 1996); James S. Fishkin, *When the People Speak: Deliberative Democracy and Public Consultation* (New York: Oxford University Press, 2009); Cass R. Sunstein, *Going to Extremes: How Like Minds Unite and Divide* (New York: Oxford University Press, 2009).

12. Susan Herbst, *Rude Democracy* (Philadelphia: Temple University Press, 2011).

13. Ibid.

14. Ibid.

15. Cherie D. Maestas, Sarah A. Fulton, L. Sandy Maisel, and Walter J. Stone, "When to Risk It? Institutions, Ambitions, and the Decision to Run for the U.S. House." *American Political Science Review 100*(2), 2006: 195–208; L. Sandy Maisel, Cherie D. Maestas, and Walter J. Stone, "The Impact of Redistricting on Candidate Emergence." In Thomas E. Mann and Bruce E. Cain, eds., *Party Lines: Competition, Partisanship, and Congressional Redistricting* (Washington, DC: Brookings Institution Press, 2005); Walter J. Stone and L. Sandy Maisel, "The Not-So-Simple Calculus of Winning: Potential U.S. House Candidates' Nomination and General Election Chances." *Journal of Politics 65*(4), 2003: 951–977.

16. James Bryce, *The American Commonwealth,* Vol. II (New York: Macmillan, 1919).

17. Jason Zengerle, "Éric Cantor's America." *New York,* October 2, 2011.

18. Matthew Q. Dawson, *Partisanship and the Birth of America's Second Party, 1796-1800: Stop the Wheels of Government* (Westport, CT: Greenwood Press, 2000).

19. Richard H. Rovere, *Senator Joe McCarthy* (Berkeley and Los Angeles, CA: University of California Press, 1959). (reprint 1996)

20. Nelson W. Polsby, "The Institutionalization of the U.S. House of Representatives." *American Political Science Review 62*(1), 1970; 144–168.

21. Walter J. Stone and L. Sandy Maisel, "Boehner's Dilemma." In Mark D. Brewer and L. Sandy Maisel, eds. *The Parties Respond,* 5th edition (Lanham, MD: Rowman & Littlefield, in press).